AF323795

Liz Larner

Liz Larner

Russell Ferguson

The Museum of Contemporary Art, Los Angeles

This publication accompanies the exhibition *Liz Larner*
organized by Russell Ferguson
and presented at The Museum of Contemporary Art, Los Angeles
2 December 2001—10 March 2002.

Liz Larner is made possible in part by the generous support
of Susan Bay-Nimoy and Leonard Nimoy
and The Katherine S. Marmor Endowment for Emerging Artists.

Library of Congress Cataloging-in-Publication Data
will be found at the end of this book.

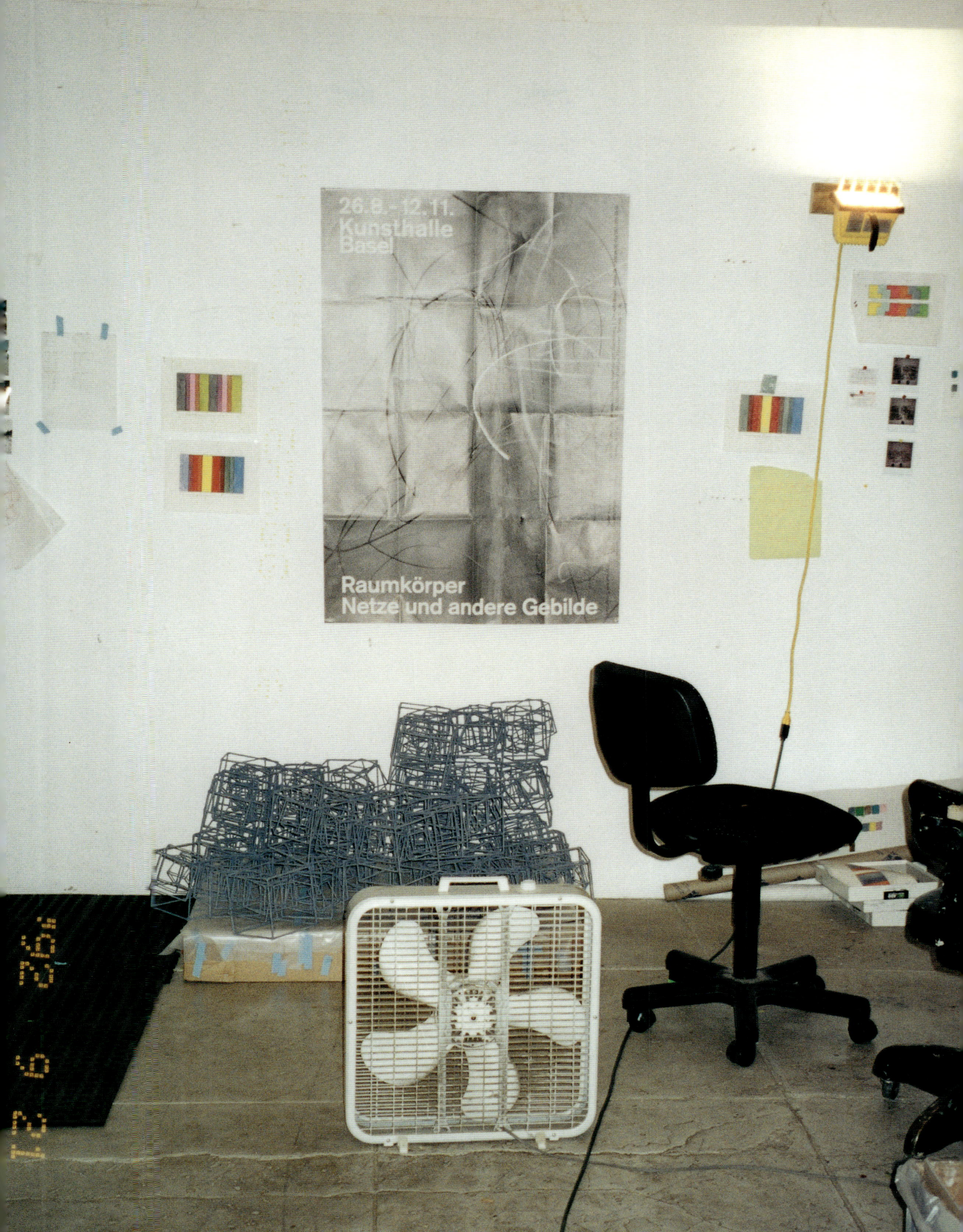

26.8. – 12.11.
Kunsthalle
Basel
Raumkörper
Netze und andere Gebilde

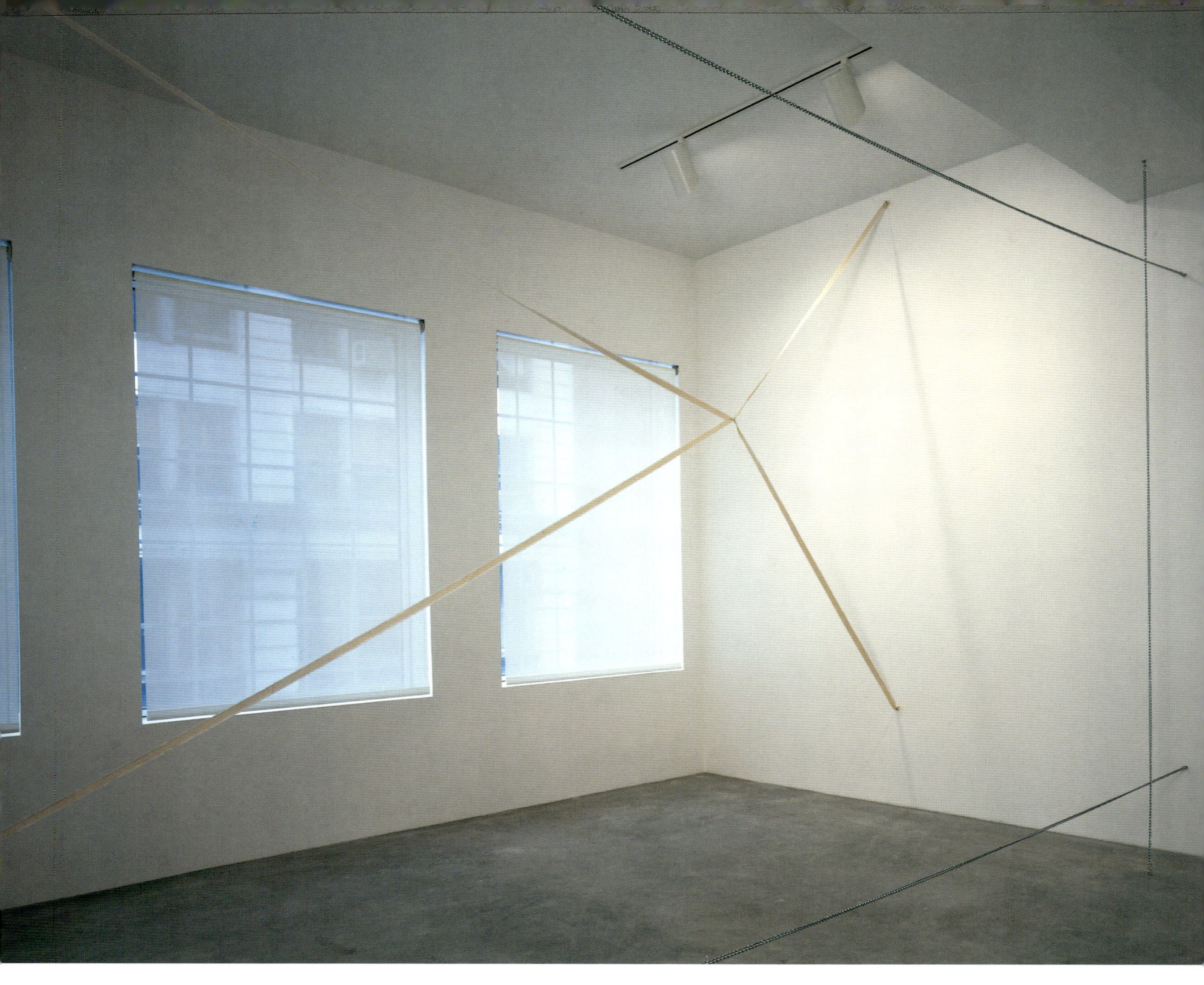

The Kiss, 1989

Liz Larner is easily one of the most important sculptors to emerge from Los Angeles in the past fifteen years. She rigorously interrogates the foundations of sculpture—volume, mass, materiality, even color—and returns with something that feels entirely new. Her works often seem suspended in between order and chaos, a testament to her deft manipulation of space. With an impressive exhibition history that includes solo exhibitions at the Kunsthalle Basel and the MAK—Austrian Museum of Applied Arts in Vienna, she has made a unique place for herself within contemporary sculpture. MOCA is proud to have been part of that process. In 1992 she was included in the seminal exhibition "Helter Skelter: L.A. Art in the 1990s," where her work *Forced Perspective (reversed, reflected, extended)* (1992) radically transformed the exhibition space and etched itself indelibly in the minds of many viewers.

As this exhibition and publication attest, Larner's work is clearly due for a more comprehensive examination. Russell Ferguson initiated the project during his tenure here at MOCA as associate curator and has since assumed the post of deputy director and chief curator at the UCLA Hammer Museum. Russell has written an insightful essay on Larner that is certain to remain a vital resource on her work for years to come. Thanks also go to MOCA Assistant Curator Michael Darling, who aided in the exhibition's organization and planning at all levels.

This exhibition represents an extension of MOCA's commitment to presenting work by today's most important artists. Such a commitment would be impossible without financial assistance from our generous sponsors. We are grateful to Susan Bay-Nimoy and Leonard Nimoy and The Katherine S. Marmor Endowment for Emerging Artists for their support of this exhibition and catalogue. In addition, I would like to express my profound gratitude to our Board of Trustees for their steadfast support.

Finally, I would like to thank Liz Larner for her creativity and dedication to this exhibition.
Jeremy Strick

No exhibition can be realized without the collaborative effort of a large number of people. I would like to take this opportunity to thank those most involved in presenting this mid-career survey exhibition of Liz Larner's work. First, I would like to thank Liz Larner, whose enthusiasm, pragmatism, and commitment have made the organization of this exhibition a pleasure from beginning to end. The early financial commitment by Susan Bay-Nimoy and Leonard Nimoy was crucial to the success of this project and I am deeply grateful for their faith in the significance of this exhibition.

MOCA Director Jeremy Strick has been supportive from the beginning, recognizing the importance of Liz's work to the community of artists working in Los Angeles and abroad. Jeremy also fully encouraged my continuing to work on the exhibition even after I left MOCA to assume the position of chief curator at the UCLA Hammer Museum, and Hammer Director Ann Philbin has generously supported my fulfillment of this responsibility. MOCA Chief Curator Paul Schimmel has also been a great backer of this project. Since including Liz in his landmark 1992 exhibition "Helter Skelter: L.A. Art in the 1990s" at MOCA, he has remained committed to her work.

We are extremely grateful to the lenders who have made this exhibition possible. Our deepest thanks go to Alan Dinsfriend; the Fogg Art Museum at Harvard University; Galerie Jennifer Flay, Paris; Kirby Gookin and Robin Kahn; Michael and Susan Hort; Dakis Joannou; Regen Projects, Los Angeles; Lawrence A. Rickels; Edward and Deedie Rose; Chara Schreyer; Rebecca and Alexander Stewart; Norah and Norman Stone; 303 Gallery, New York; the Whitney Museum of American Art; Sally Willcox and Daniel Ross; and three anonymous private collectors. Additional help in locating certain key works was provided by Thea Westreich Art Advisory Services. In addition to lending work, Liz's galleries have also been extremely helpful in gathering information and providing photography. I would like to thank Shaun Caley and Lisa Overduin at Regen Projects in Los Angeles, and Lisa Spellman and Mari Spirito at 303 Gallery in New York for being so generous with their time and energy.

Tim Jackson, Liz's primary assistant, has been endlessly helpful, and we are very grateful for his knowledge and experience. Thanks also go to others who have assisted Liz with her work: James Abbot, Andy Alexander, Matthew Betcher, Eric Blumberg, Samuel Casebolt, Samara Caughey, Andrea Claire, Roger Dickies, Lecia Dole-Recio, Taft Green, Lisa Gwilliam, Evan Holloway, Takeshi Kagami, Dan Knapp, Jason Meadows, Page Norris, Michele O'Marah, Jason Pilarsky, Dean Sameshima, Mary Stevens, Torbjörn Vejvi, and Chip Weaver.

This exquisite publication could not have come into being without the able oversight of MOCA Senior Editor Lisa Mark with her talented team of Jane Hyun and Elizabeth Hamilton, working in close collaboration with the great designer Lorraine Wild. I am indebted to Lisa, Jane, and Elizabeth for their careful reading and thoughtful editorial advice, and to Lorraine for her always sensitive response to the work. Thanks also to photographer Brian Forrest for his professionalism.

Though the beautiful installation in the MOCA galleries is not surprising given the nature of Liz's work, it is also the result of the diligent efforts of MOCA's exhibition team. Exhibitions Production Manager Brian Gray, Chief Exhibition Technician Jang Park, Exhibitions Production Coordinator Zazu Faure, Media Arts Technical Manager David Bradshaw, Media Arts Technician Tina Bastajian, Exhibition Technicians Shinichi Kitahara, Barry Grady, Valerie West, Jason Storrs, Monica Gonzalez, and a great crew of part-time installers all lent their expertise. The complexities of loans and shipping have been smoothly directed by Chief Registrar Robert Hollister and Assistant Registrar Amy Carlile, ensuring that all the objects arrived in a safe and timely manner. Educational offerings associated with the exhibition have been spearheaded by Acting Co-Directors of Education Caroline Blackburn and Suzanne Isken, while the tasks of fundraising have been handled by Director of Development Paul Johnson and his team of Denise Therieau and Kristen Kenyon. The promotion of the exhibition in the media has been taken up with energy by Media Relations Manager Katherine Lee, with Jennie Prebor and Heidi Simonian.

The input of my MOCA colleagues in the curatorial department is something I always seek out and value. Senior Curator Ann Goldstein, Curator Connie Butler, Curator of Architecture and Design Brooke Hodge, Associate Curator Alma Ruiz, and Manager of Exhibitions and Curatorial Affairs Stacia Payne, in addition to Beth Rosenblum, Julia Langlotz, Rebecca Morse, and Virginia Edwards, can always be counted on for their advice and support. Of all the MOCA staff, Assistant Curator Michael Darling has been the most intimately involved in every aspect of the process, and his management of the day-to-day details of the project has assured its smooth march toward completion. His many insightful comments on the first draft of my essay are much appreciated. Once again, I am happy to express my deepest gratitude to Michael for his unstinting commitment to the exhibition.

One of the most important sculptures in the exhibition, *2 as 3 and Some Too* (1997–98) was a gift to MOCA in memory of Stuart Regen. Liz joins me in recognizing Stuart's importance as a key supporter of her work. Also on her behalf we extend our thanks to Lita Albuquerque, Kitty Beamish, Eric Bonwit, Tom Chasteen, Jane Dickson, Kate Forst, Jeremy Gilbert-Rolfe, Boty Goodwin, Madeleine Hoffman, Judy Kameon, Mike Kelley, Debbie King, Sharon Larner, Virginia Larner, Catherine Liu, Ramsey Naito, Linda Norden, Peter Pakesch, Bridget Pavich, Patti Podesta, Ken Price, Martin Prinzhorn, Tim Power, Stephen Prina, Charles Ray, Jack Renner, Nancy Rosen, Pauline Stella Sanchez, Keith Sawa, Shug, Beth Thompson, Susanne Weaver, Lauren Zuckerman, and, for his consistent support and inspiration, John Baldessari.

Russell Ferguson

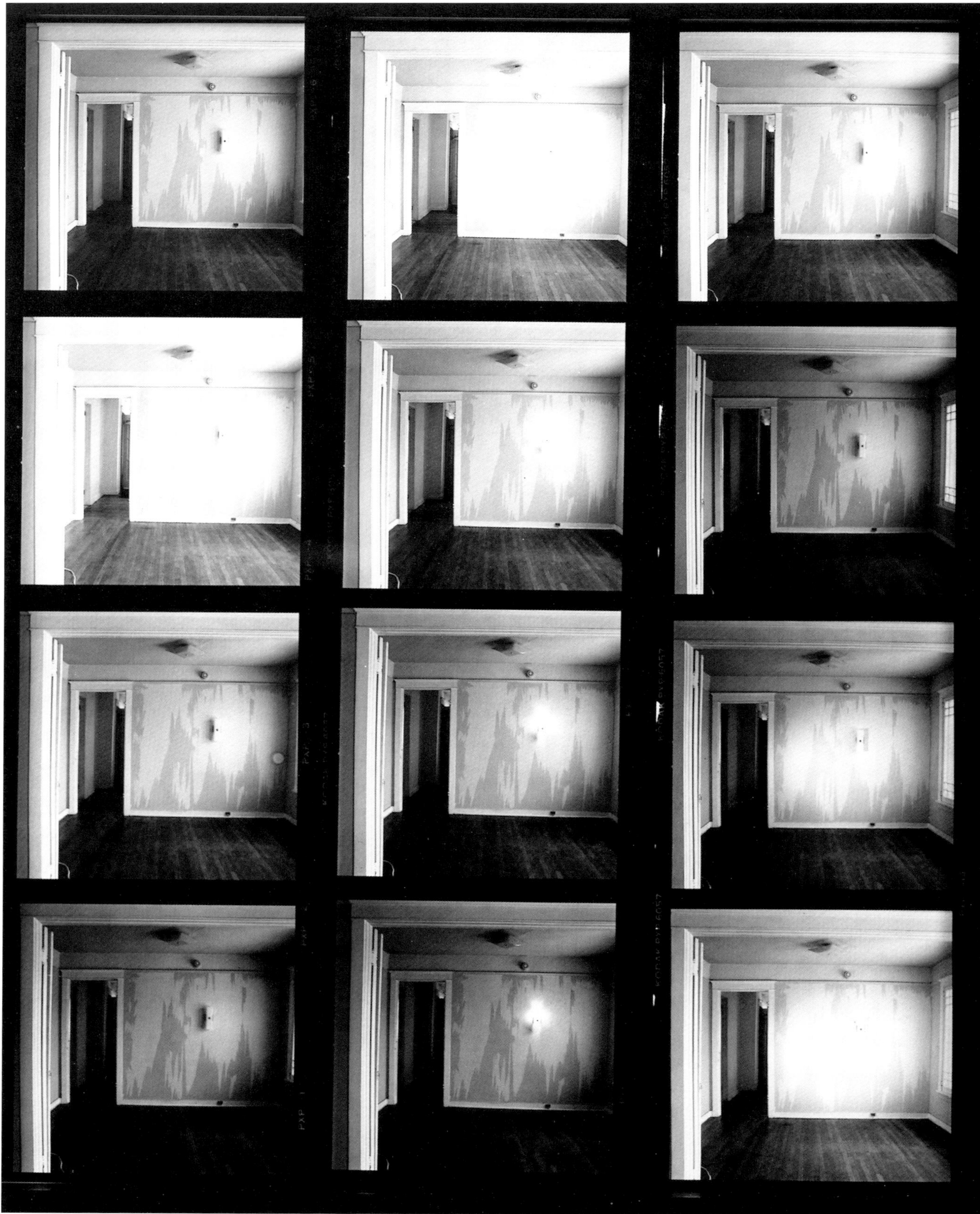

Untitled, 1985

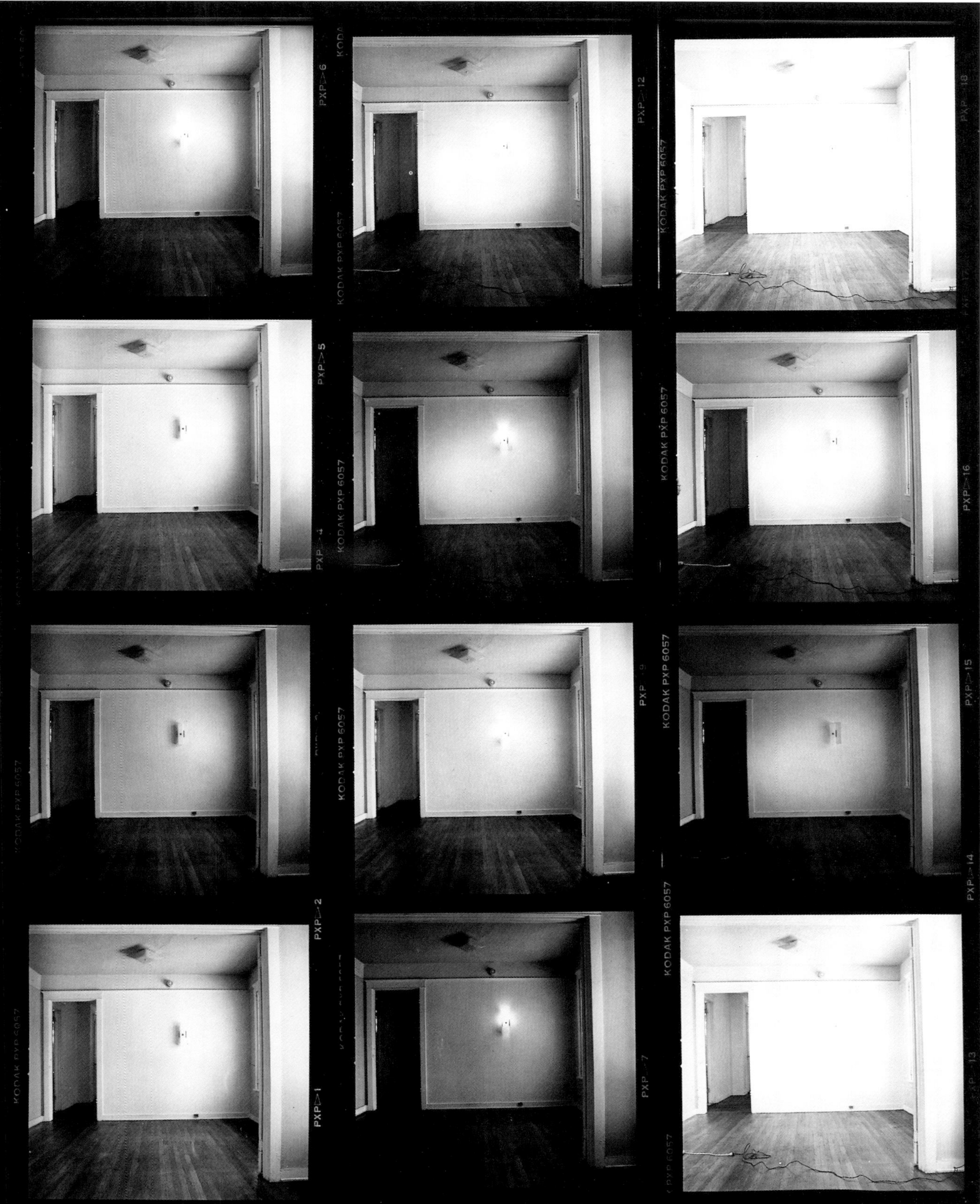

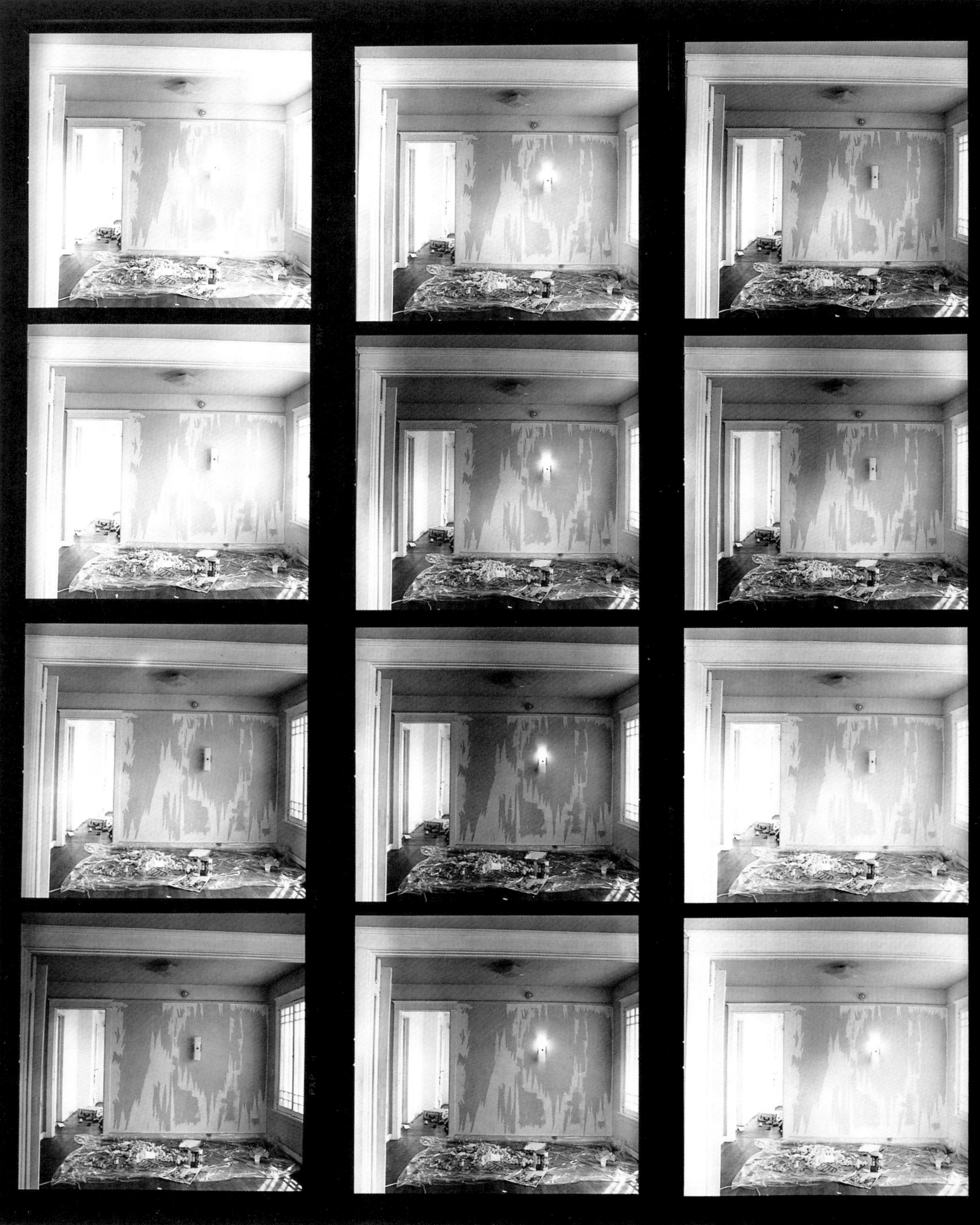

Russell Ferguson

A photo grid from 1985 shows an almost empty room, where Liz Larner has been experimenting with paint and walls in an attempt to articulate the otherwise generic space. Before long, however, space itself was not enough for her. The temptations of sculpture became increasingly hard to resist. "What we call 'real space'" she says now, "isn't really physical until something is in it."[1]

But what will be in it? From the very beginning, Larner has questioned many widely held assumptions about the attributes of sculpture. "There is a whole tradition where volume and density and mass are almost the same thing: that if something is big then we need to sense how heavy it is and how dense it is, and how massive it is. I wanted to try to take some of these things and change the relationships."[2] Volume, density, and mass are, of course, things that viewers customarily use to make their initial judgments about *what* an object might be and precisely *where* it is situated, both in a space generally and in terms of their own relationship to it. Larner's objects, however, cut against viewers' expectations. Her sculpture is often hard to read at first glance. Unexpected color and unconventional material destabilize our sense of volume. Mirrors often contribute to the fragmentation of spatial coherence. In *Between Loves Me and Not* (1992), the mirrors themselves are irregular. They are strewn on the floor, thus forcing

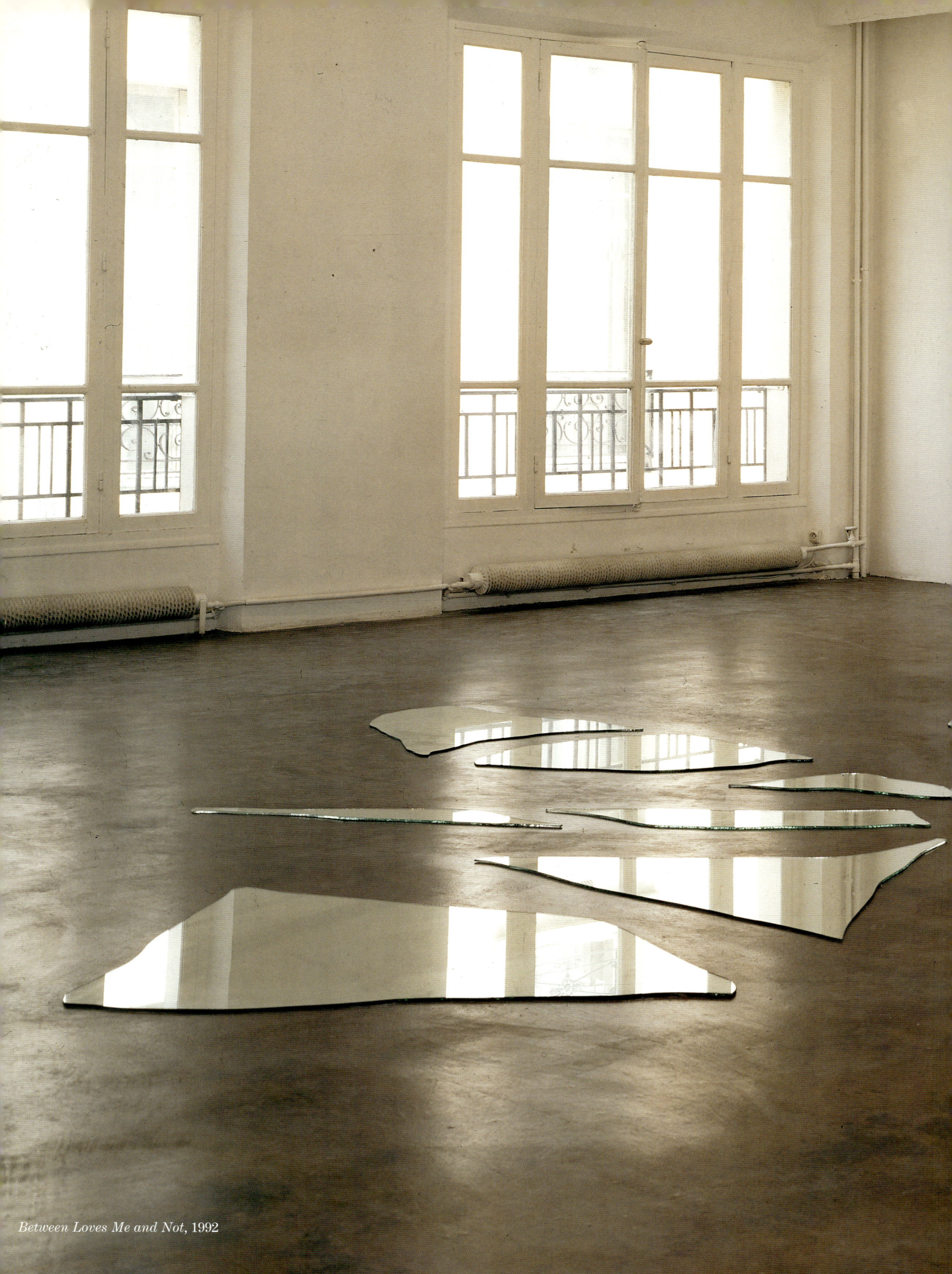

Between Loves Me and Not, 1992

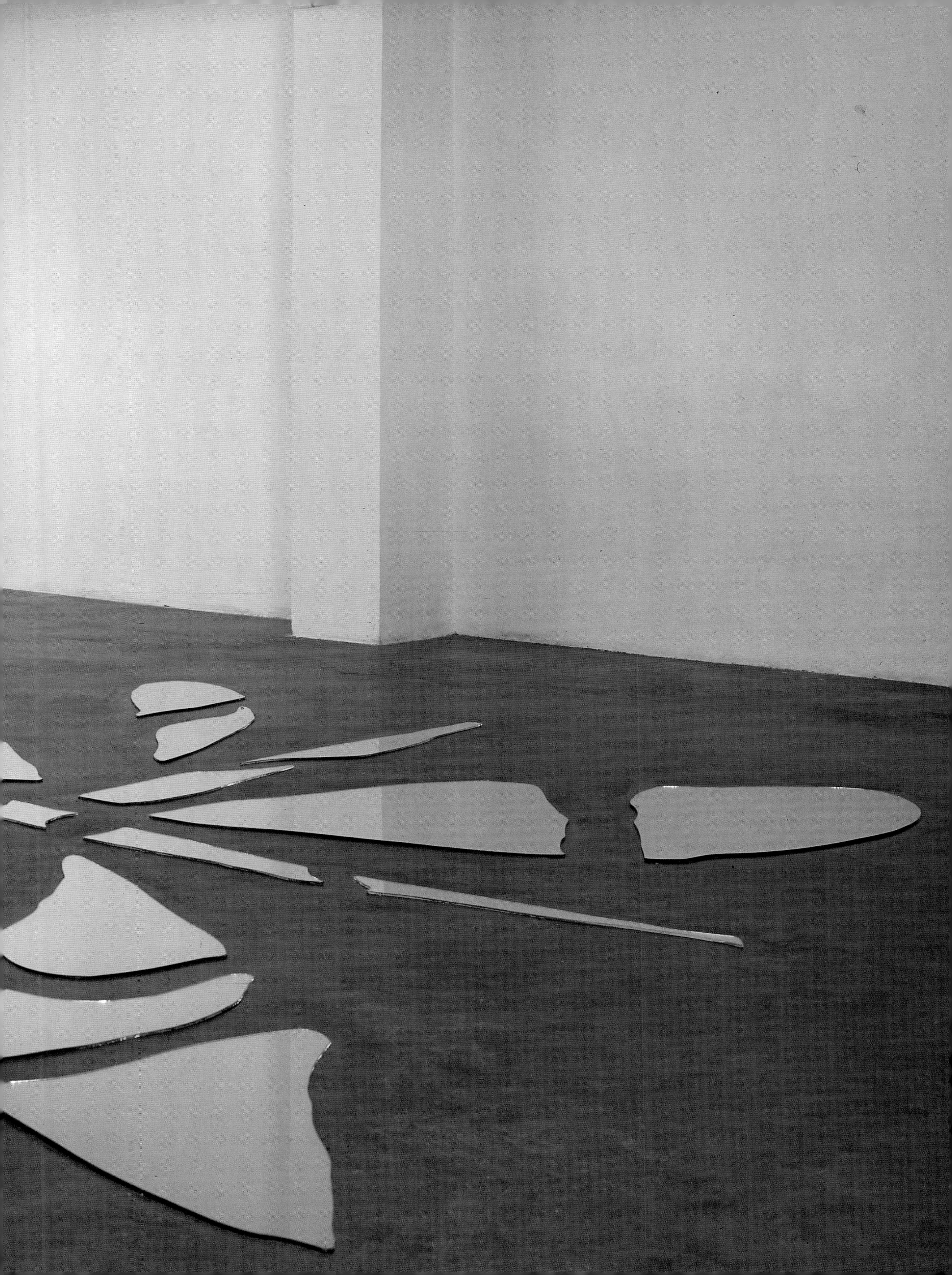

the viewer's gaze back up into the space at an angle that is unexpected, disorienting, and fragmented. Her work occupies significant amounts of space, but almost always without resorting to the density or solidity that are conventionally associated with a dominant volumetric presence.

Larner is not the first sculptor to have sought volume without mass. Certain artists of the 1960s were engaged in comparable explorations. Robert Morris's felt pieces were self-evidently soft, and suspension torqued them to reveal gaps and fissures that countered any residual sense of solidity. Even Richard Serra, an artist often considered the quintessential sculptor of mass and weight, in his early work explored the potential in their rejection. In works such as *Tearing Lead from 1:00 to 1:47* (1968), Serra experimented with metal deprived of rigidity and any vestige of verticality, yet capable of asserting an unequivocal spatial presence. For Serra, the process of making and the duration of his activity became more constitutive of this work than any conventional sculptural qualities.

By the end of the 1960s, a new generation of ambitious artists began to explore the possibilities of working directly with space, yet without identifiable objects of any kind. Mel Bochner's Measurement series dealt directly with specific interior spaces, and he rejected the introduction of three-dimensional objects. In an interview from 1969 he says, "The *Measurement: Room* [1969], where I mark the measurements of a room directly on the walls, like a three-dimensional blueprint, encompasses a concept of volume, without becoming a sculpture…. I feel that the basic question in my work…is how do you experience yourself in the world, which is to say, how do you inhabit an idea of the world?"[3]

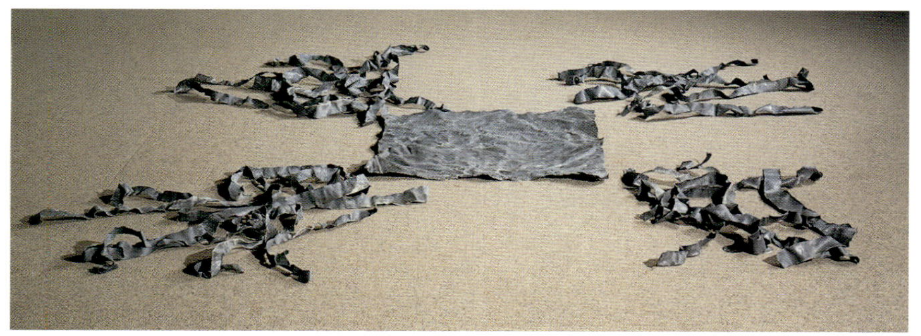

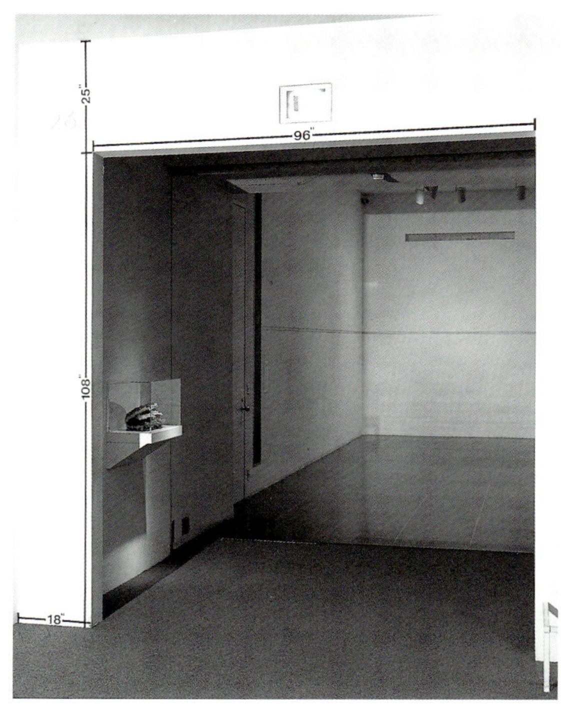

Richard Serra, *Tearing Lead from 1:00 to 1:47*, 1968

Mel Bochner, *Measurement: Room*, 1969

A more phenomenological approach to the experience of space itself can be found among the Californian artists of the "light and space" movement who succeeded in demonstrating the potential malleability of a given space without the aid of sculptural objects per se. The environments created by artists such as James Turrell and Robert Irwin seemed to conjure up the presence traditionally associated with sculpture, although the object itself was displaced into an apparatus intended to remain essentially invisible. The idea of creating a volumetric space that is simultaneously resistant to the terms of sculpture is the same kind of fundamental re-thinking of convention that has driven Larner's work, even if she has come to locate her own re-thinking in the context of physically present objects.

Donald Judd explained the widespread movement away from painting by ambitious artists of his generation in terms of a disinclination to follow paths that had already been thoroughly explored by artists of the previous generation. Painting in particular seemed to them to have reached a dead end, with no compelling new questions to answer. For Judd, the idea of sculpture itself also seemed spent, and thus he chose to refer to the objects that he and his peers were making simply as "three-dimensional work." However, Judd was at pains not to downplay the work of his predecessors even as he dissociated himself from them: "The disinterest in painting and sculpture is a disinterest in doing it again, not in it as it is being done by those who developed the last advanced versions." At the same time, "If the earlier work is first-rate it is complete."[4] If conventional forms were in fact complete—if they no longer offered new challenges—then it was necessary to move on into other fields.

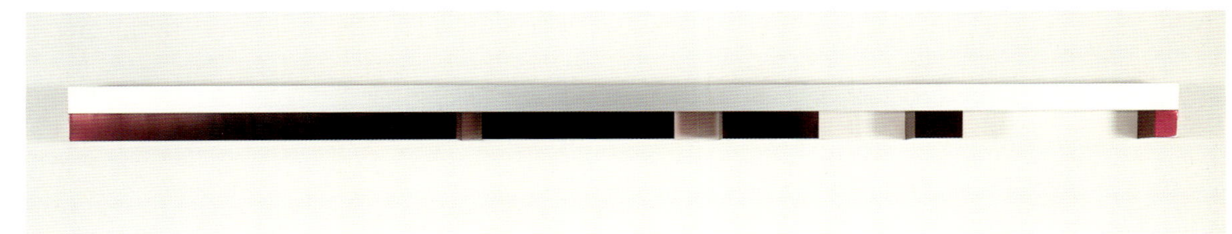

Donald Judd, *Wall Progression*, 1971

It did not take long for Judd's "specific objects" to be recognized as sculpture, albeit paradigm-changing sculpture, and other artists were quick to push further beyond the object. Lawrence Weiner's text and instruction pieces (which do not necessarily need to be executed), such as *ONE QUART EXTERIOR GREEN INDUSTRIAL ENAMEL THROWN ON A BRICK WALL* (1968), suggested a different way of negotiating space. In a series of works from 1969, Robert Barry released inert (and invisible) gases into the atmosphere. The "viewer" of these works was aware that on some level the space around him or her had changed, even without registering any visible sign. His *Marcuse Piece* (1970–71) consisted of a text written on the wall: "Some places to which we can come, and for a while, 'be free to think about what we are going to do.' (Marcuse)," making it clear that if the gallery space were to be occupied, it would be by the thought processes of the audience, and that Barry anticipated political consequences from such a response. Fluxus artists such as Yoko Ono had also increasingly placed the onus of the work on the viewer by means of various "instruction" pieces.

As practices such as those indicated above won authority, there seemed less and less room for sculpture that occupied space in a more conventional sense. Although Serra, Judd, and others of their generation were able to continue effectively working within the new vocabularies they had been instrumental in developing, the rapid and exhilarating series of paradigm shifts that marked art in the late 1960s ended by making sculpture seem as played out for younger artists as painting had seemed to be for their predecessors in the early 1960s. Even today, much sculpture by younger artists is hedged with an almost apologetic irony.

Liz Larner's work, however, is quite different in tone. She certainly employs ambiguity, but not irony. Her work is sincere. As Martin Prinzhorn has put it, her "position is taken in a way that does not allow for an ironic distance or fast movements on the surface. Instead it is a position of serious poetry, a poetry that is totally compatible with critical analysis. She also does not try to deal didactically with form, the form does not fall out of the analysis, the analysis is generated by the sculpture."[5]

No more than Judd is Larner interested in "doing it again." It is quite clear to her, however, that there are sculptural questions that remain unanswered; it is these problems that motivate her. Each piece she makes is a response to a new set of questions, perhaps raised by a previous work but not fully answered by it. And her questions are always driven by a visceral sense of the physicality of the object in space, not simply the space itself: "When you're with something, I think it's more than just visual…. There's almost a bodily tracking system, like the way you can tell how far away something is. Maybe it's like heat or sound." There is a fundamentally tactile quality to Larner's sculpture that seems almost to invite physical contact from viewers.

Yet Larner became a sculptor in a milieu that in many ways militated against the making of objects. Her education at the California Institute of the Arts (CalArts), from which she graduated in 1985, derived from the conceptual approaches of Michael Asher, John Baldessari, and Douglas Huebler. It was Huebler who said that "The world is full of objects, more or less interesting; I do not wish to add any more,"[6] and his attitude in many ways summed up the ethos of CalArts during Larner's years there.

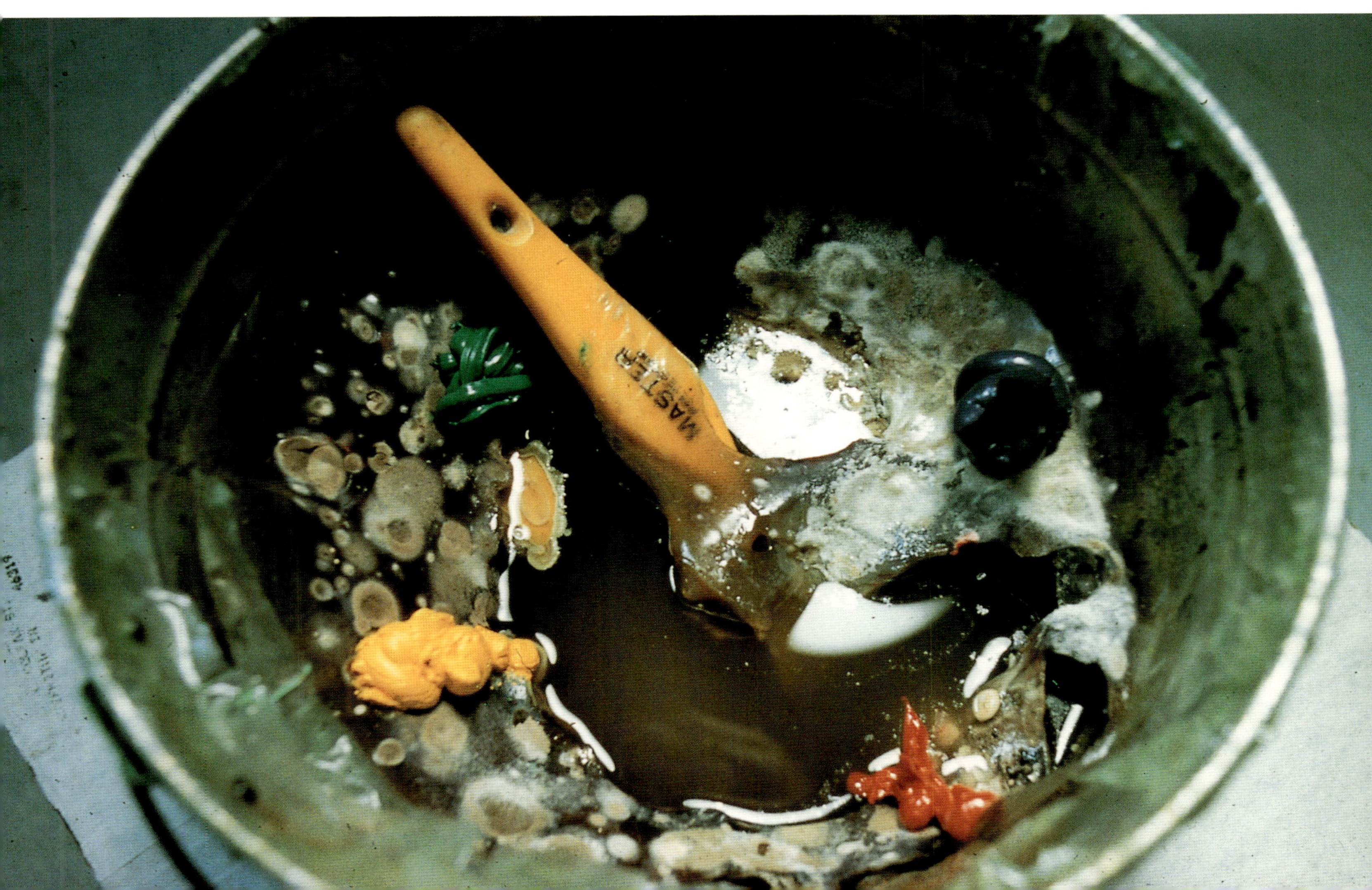

Among a number of CalArts students in the mid-1980s, there was an aversion to the bombast of mainstream contemporary art, emblematized by the triumphant return of big, assertive paintings. Though nominally a student of photography, Larner was influenced by artists working with issues of appropriation, including Richard Prince, Barbara Kruger, and Sherrie Levine. Alongside that tendency ran a simultaneous reaction against the perceived idealism of purely conceptual work. That in turn generated an attraction to the making of unique, unappropriated objects, even if the results were distinctly anti-heroic and anti-monumental.

Having absorbed all of these sometimes-contradictory influences, Larner finally began to make sculpture: unique objects that directly addressed real space. Her work takes on some of the most basic issues of sculpture, including the relationship between volume and mass, the place of the spectator, and the question of geometric form. Most fundamental of all to Larner is how her work will occupy three-dimensional space. The asking and re-asking of such elemental questions is perhaps the true legacy of her conceptually based education at CalArts. "I think that's what I'm trying to do in my work," Larner says, "the attempt at a definition or a re-definition. You know how words expand their own meanings, or mean different things at different times? That's a very fluid thing that happens in language, and I think it happens in art forms as well."

Alongside this willingness to stretch boundaries and question received definitions, Larner also brought with her from CalArts a certain residual suspicion of object-making. Many of her early works reveal an artist tempted by formal issues, yet at the same time determined to question each sculptural convention. In 1987, Larner and two other artists, Cindy Bernard and

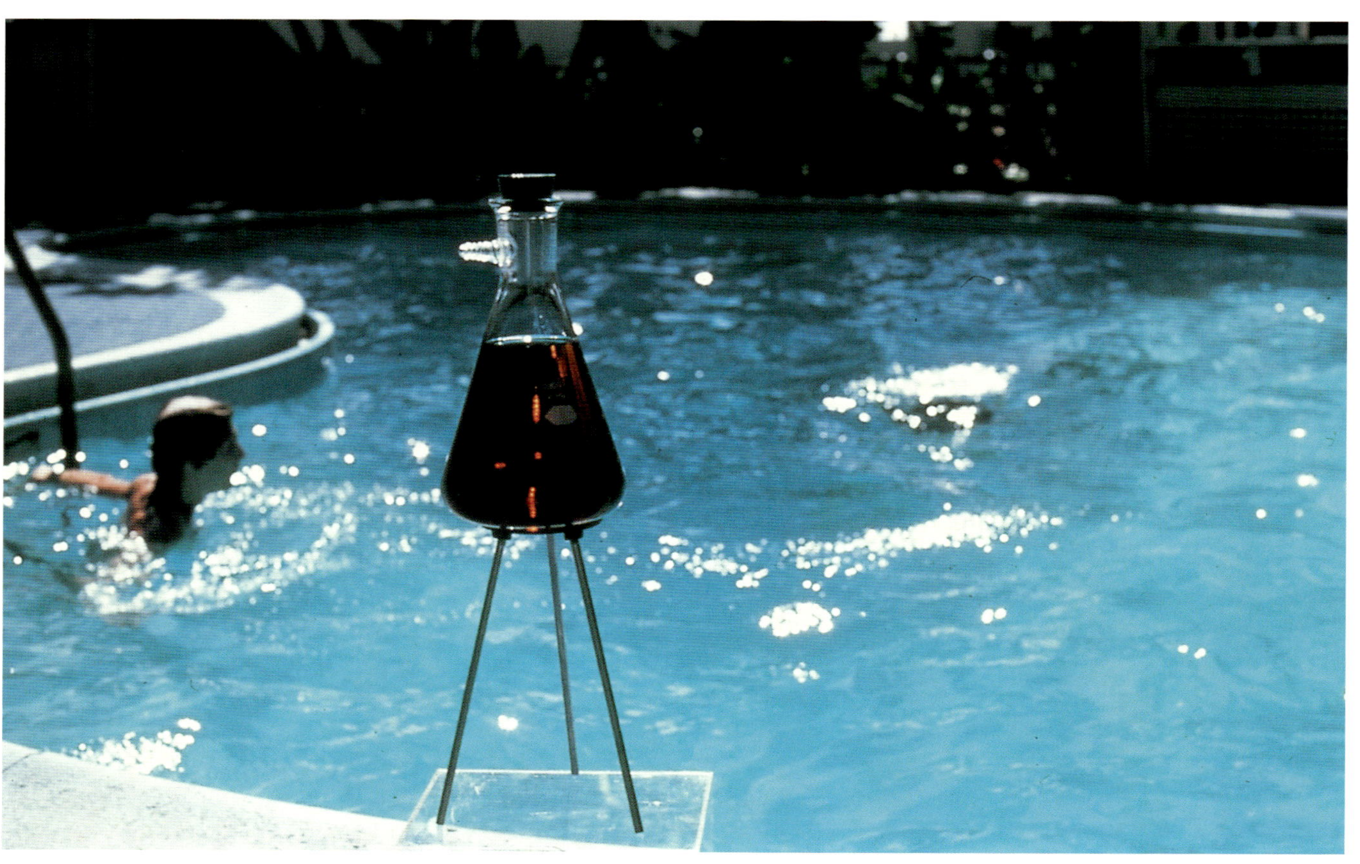

Ten Different Brown Liquors at the Tropicana Motel, LA, 1987

Martha Godfrey, organized a show titled "Room 9" at the Tropicana Motel in West Hollywood. Among her earliest works, visible first in photographs made at the Tropicana, are the series of "culture" pieces. These begin from a position of rejection of all the elements that would conventionally be considered essential for sculpture, beginning with form itself. They are collations of disparate elements suspended together in agar, a form of gelatin that encourages bacterial growth, and allowed to act on each other. *Orchid, Buttermilk, Penny* (1987) is a typically diverse agglomeration, brought together in a pair of petri dishes and presented with great formal elegance. Instability, however, is a given. *Gold, Collagen, and Water-Soluble Fluorescent Dye* (1988) at one point literally exploded out of its glass container. It subsequently had to be chemically stabilized and sealed, after the addition of antibiotics. The process pointed to a tension that in some ways indicated Larner's future direction. Even though the ingredients were inherently unstable, Larner contained them within a flask with a defined, even elegant shape. This reciprocity between the desire for decay and the impulse toward formal resolution is a theme that can be traced throughout her work. Larner herself has indicated her double motivation: "We all want stability, but it's forever slipping away from us, even on the most personal level. I kind of wanted that acceleration of decay." Larner's interest is not only in decay itself; she remains equally engaged with the capture and control of processes that would otherwise continue completely beyond the limits of art. Throughout her series of culture works there is a productive tension between the inherently unstable materials and the coherent form she imposes on them. "In the work I did with cultures, there was something nasty and

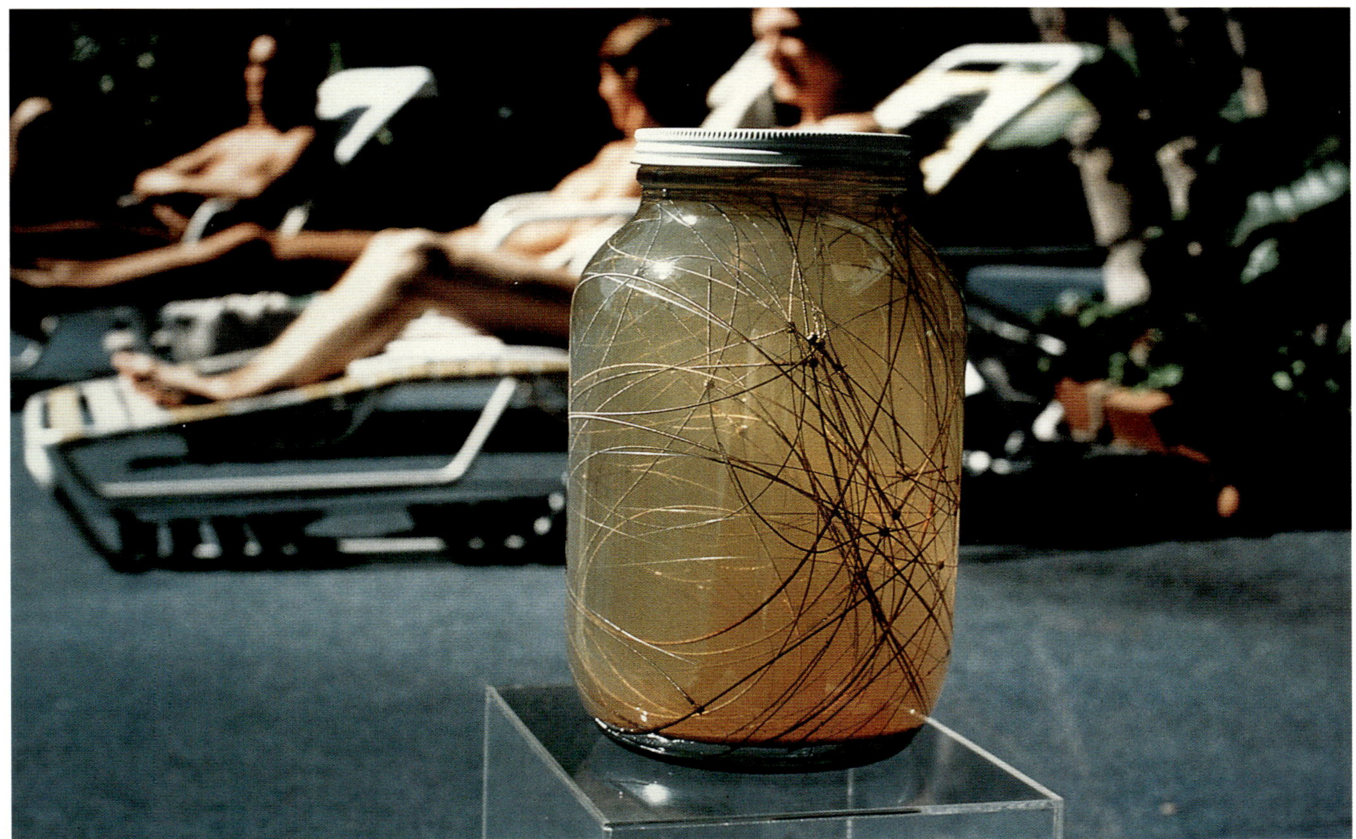

Tropicana Pool Water, Guitar Strings, and Mercury, 1987

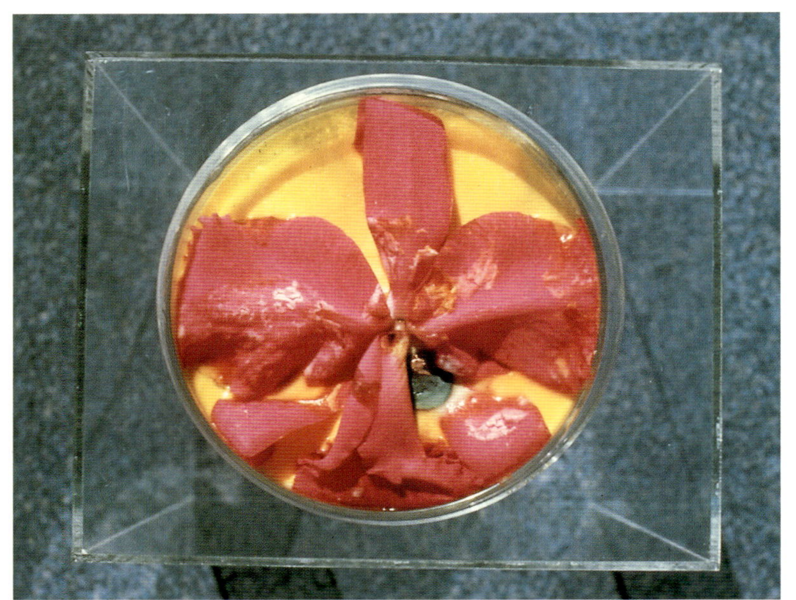

Orchid, Buttermilk, Penny, 1987

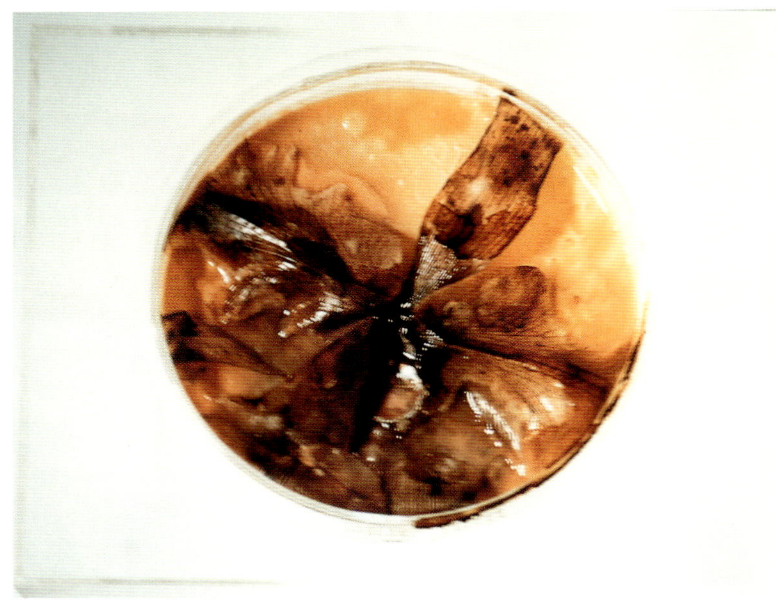

Orchid, Buttermilk, Penny (3 weeks), 1987

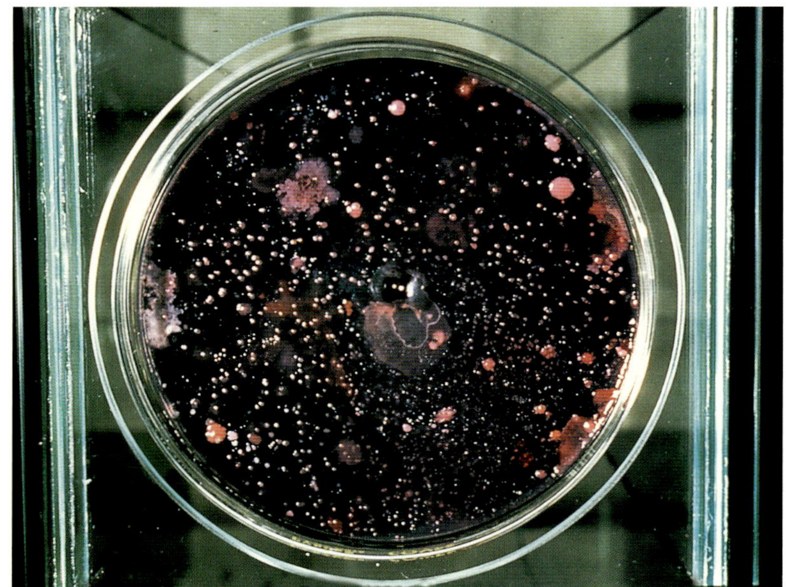

Margo Leavin, 3 Breaths, and an Innoculation, 1987

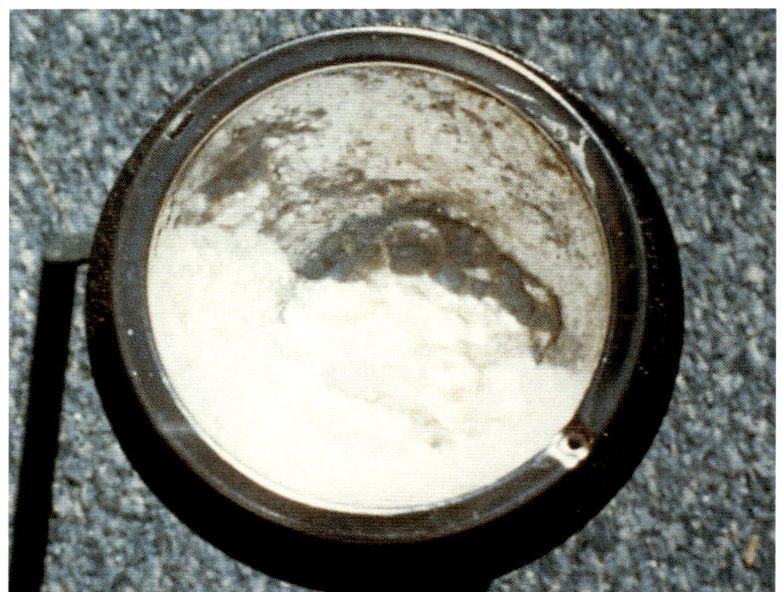

Residue (from all chemicals used in home and studio for six months), 1987

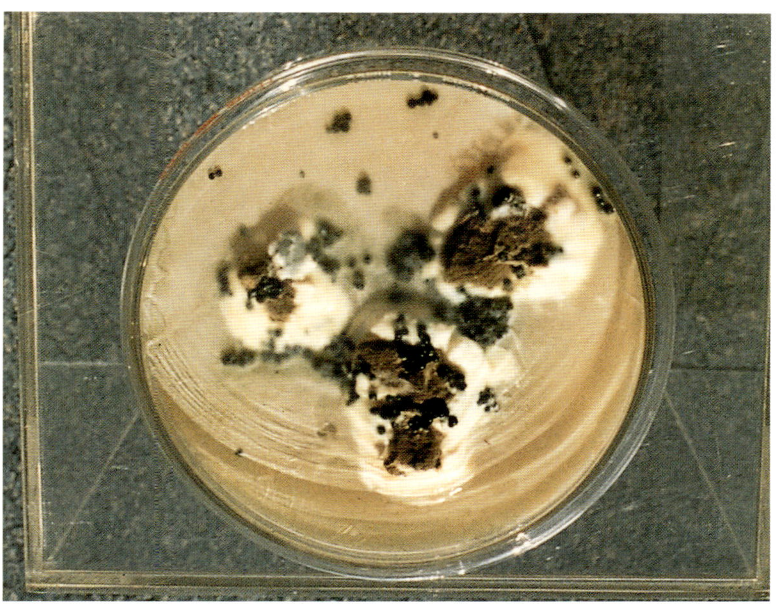

Champagne, Caviar, and Sour Cream, 1987

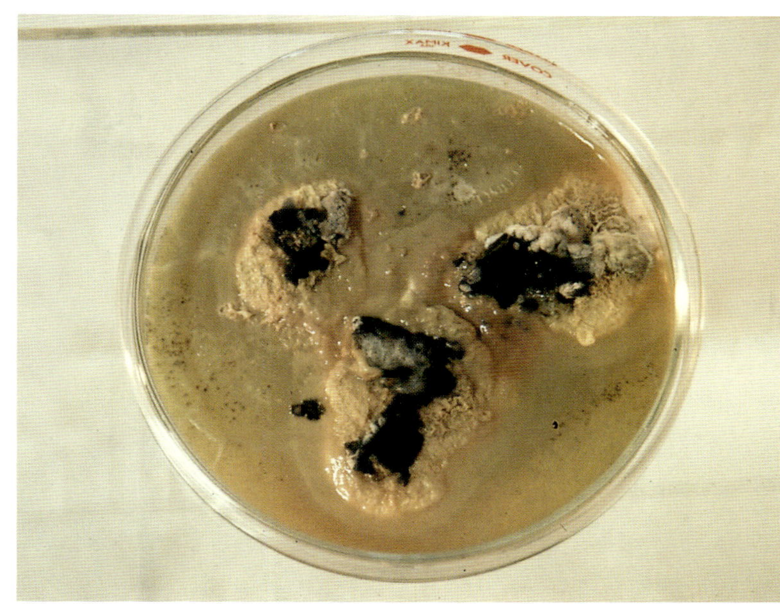

Champagne, Caviar, and Sour Cream (3 weeks), 1987

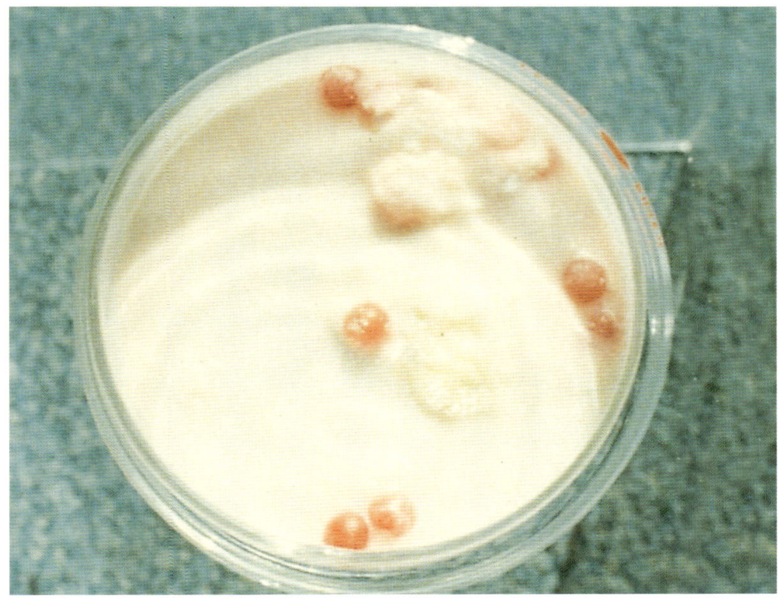

Whipped Cream, Heroin, and Salmon Eggs, 1987

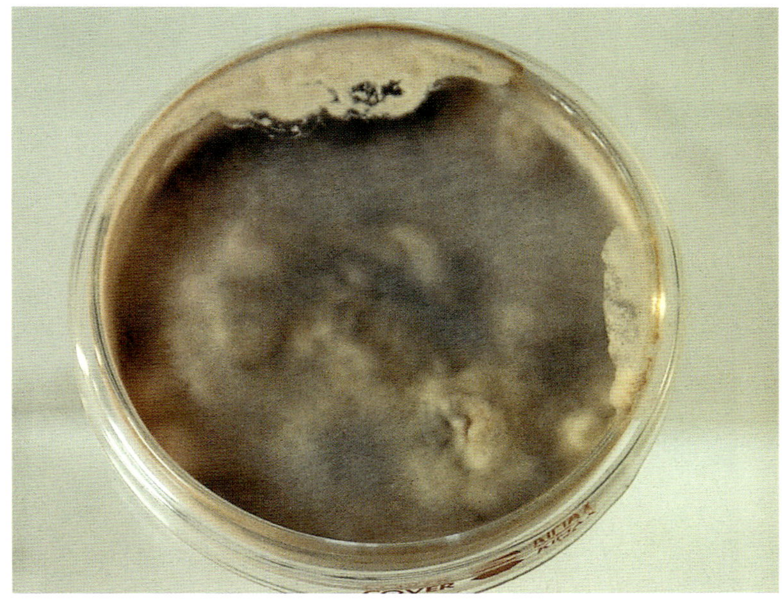

Whipped Cream, Heroin, and Salmon Eggs (3 weeks), 1987

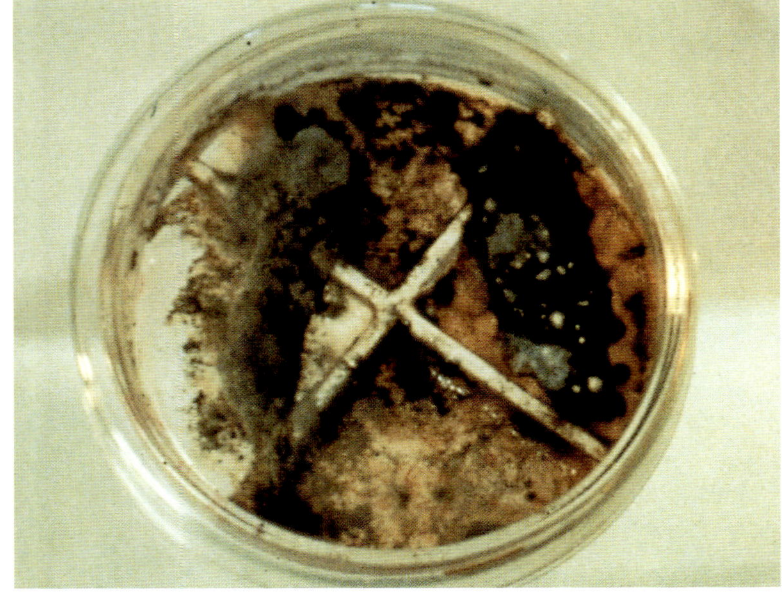

Tea and Honey (3 weeks), 1987

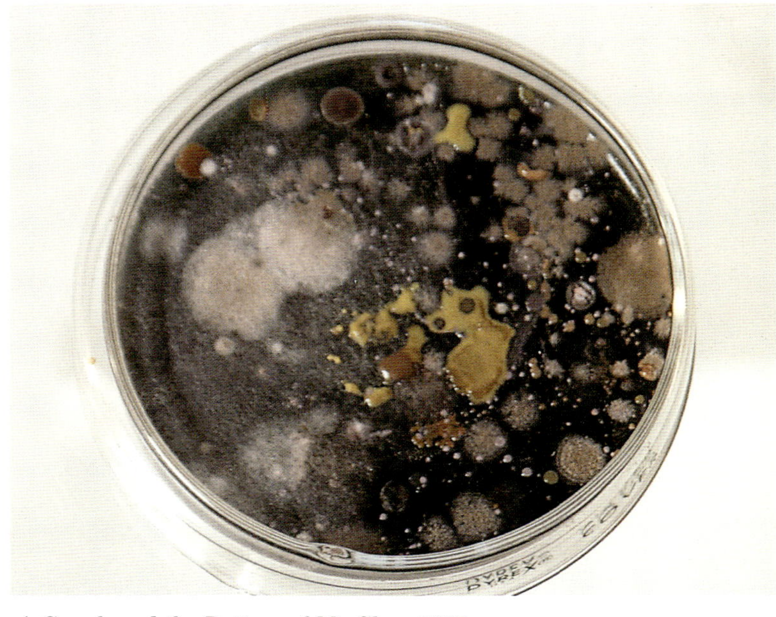

A Cough and the Bottom of My Shoe, 1987

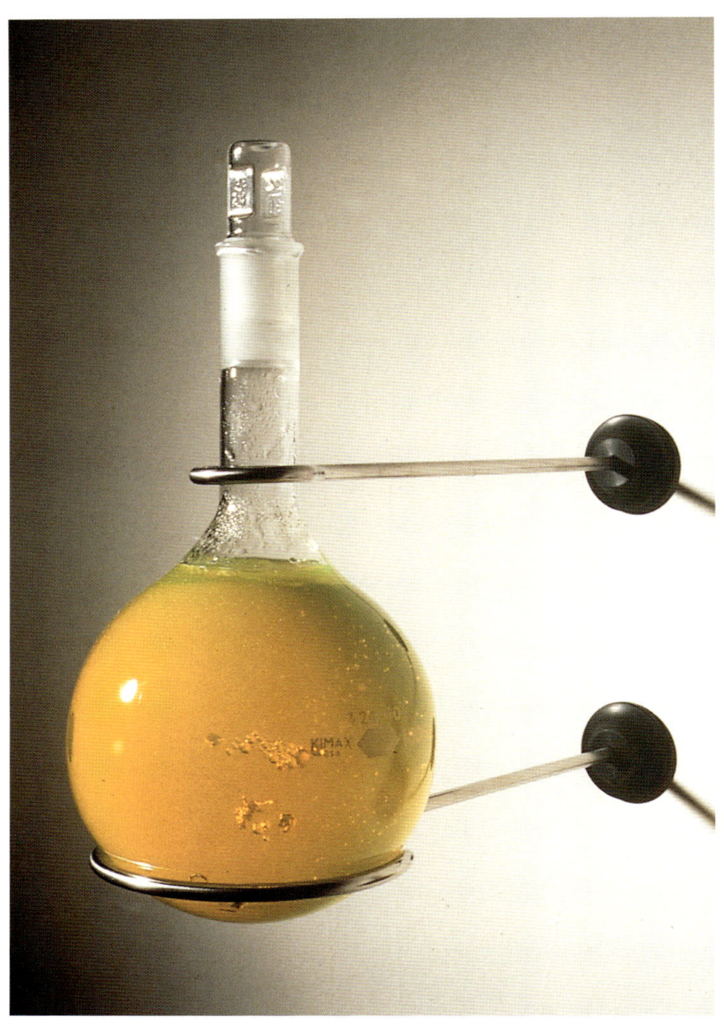

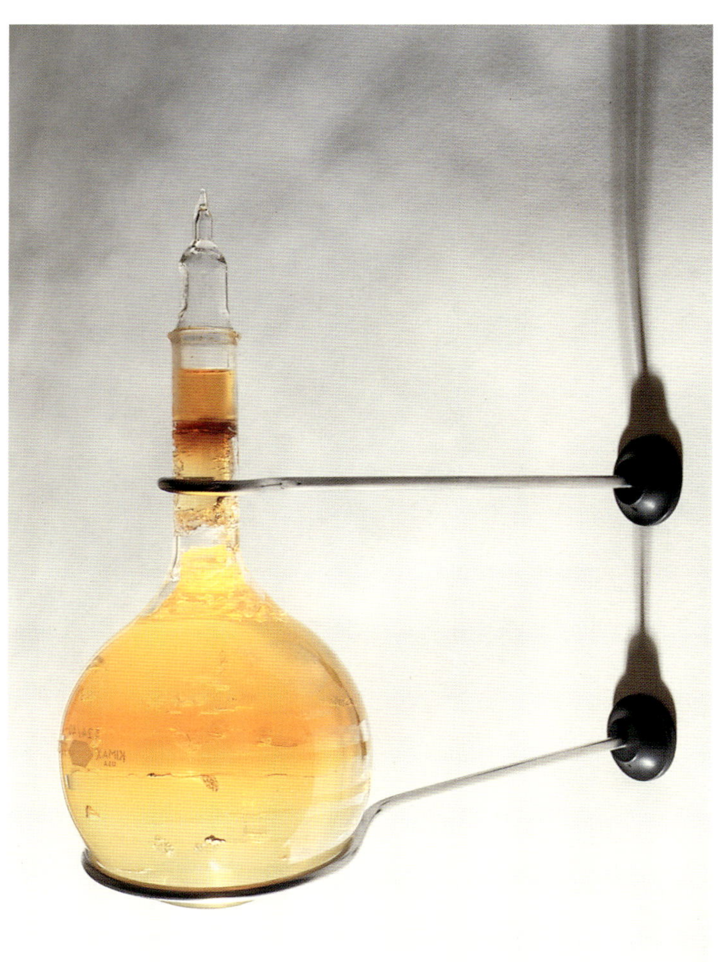

Gold, Collagen, and Water-Soluble Fluorescent Dye, 1988

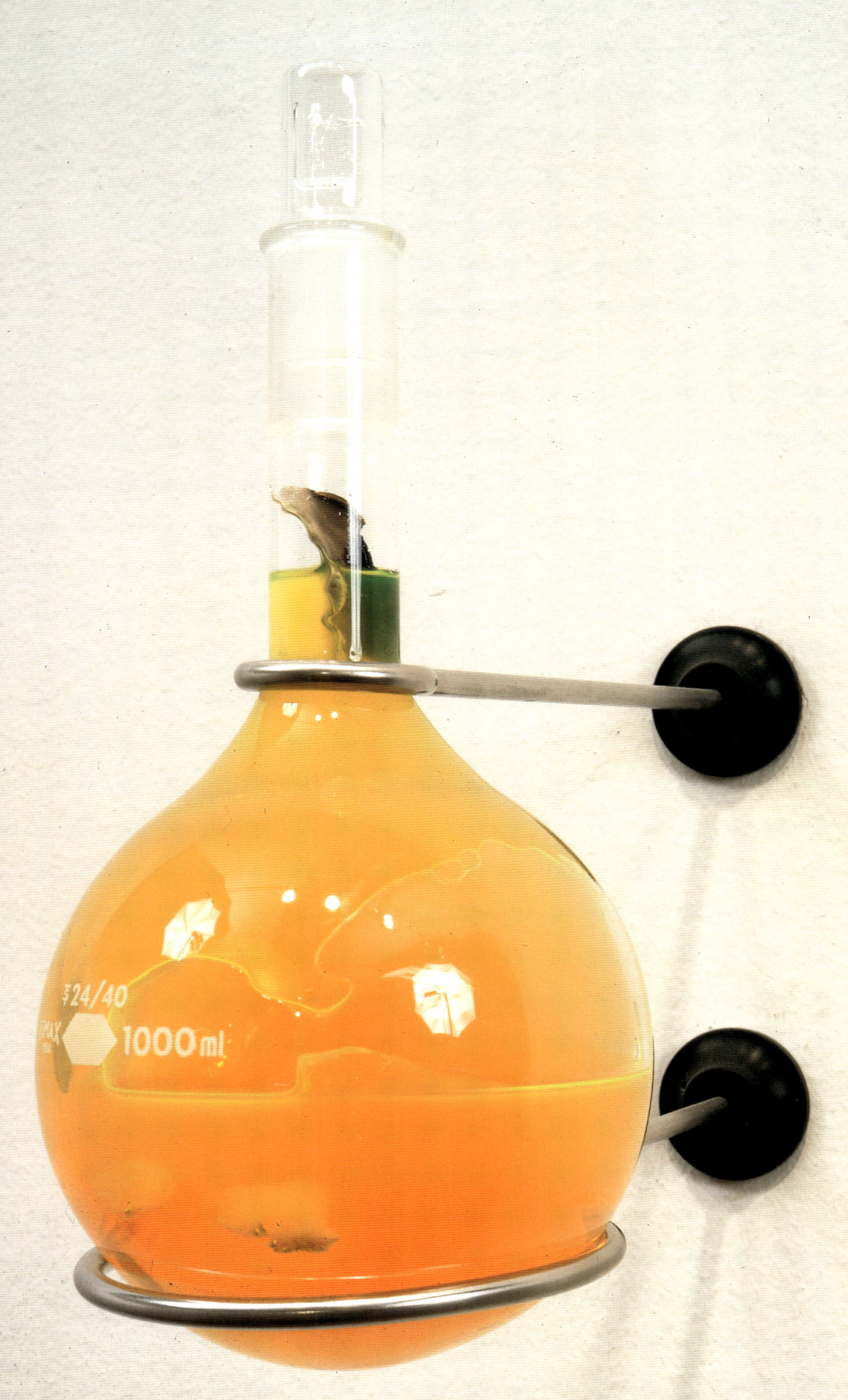

disgusting about the rotting thing. But then it cleans itself up and it dries up. The wet, gooey, bacterialized substance isn't as intense once it becomes a memory. In one way, this is disappointing because the thing has died. In another way, it is a relief because it no longer threatens with its infections."[7] At a certain point, the culture is said to "bloom," a term that, like the word "culture" itself, Larner enjoys for its multiple potential meanings. At the end of the process, however, the putrefying mass stabilizes and becomes an object: an art object.

This work of Larner's invokes a tradition of the formless now associated primarily with the work of Georges Bataille, although it extends far beyond the work of those directly familiar with his writings. "*Formless,*" he wrote, "is not only an adjective having a given meaning, but a term that serves to bring things down in the world…. Affirming that the universe resembles nothing and is only *formless [informe]* amounts to saying that the universe is something like a spider or spit."[8] Spit is in fact one of the most common activating ingredients in Larner's cultures. Spit is doubly important: it represents not only the invocation of something almost

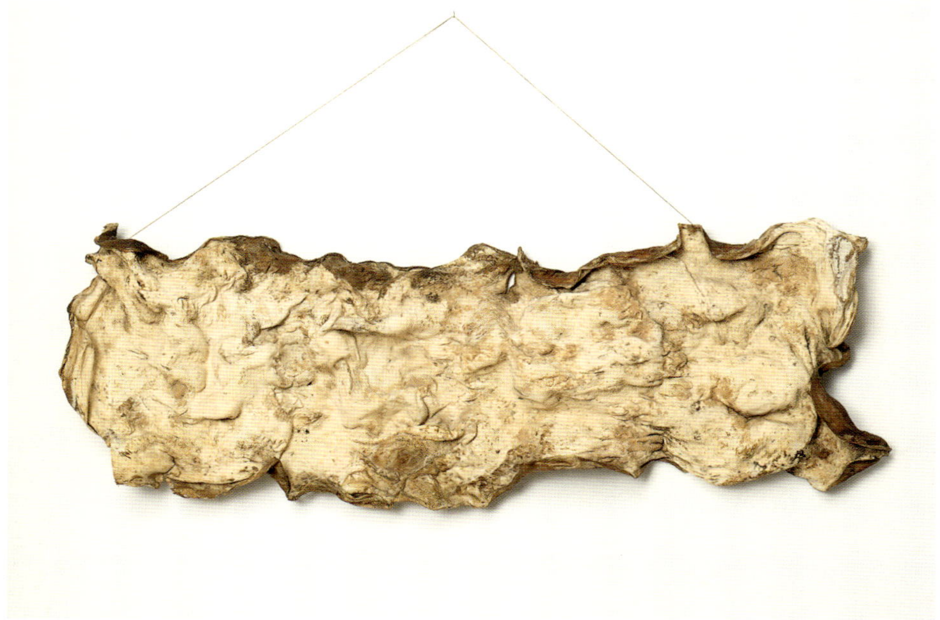

entirely worthless, it also sets into motion a bacterial process largely beyond the artist's control, and is thus a further rejection of form itself. The element of degradation is crucial here. For Bataille the formless is important partly because it has the capacity to "bring things down in the world." *No M, No D, Only S & B* (1990) rejects the authority of mom and dad in favor of sisters and brothers, only to slump inertly on the floor. In the case of *Gold, Collagen, and Water-Soluble Fluorescent Dye*, the use of gold, valuable both literally and symbolically, emphasizes the reductive element present in the culture series. Everything, sooner or later, will decline into formless mush. For Freud, of course, the symbolic value of gold was excrement.

The most direct precedent for Larner's "culture" work is that of Gordon Matta-Clark. He was a forerunner of Larner's in his use of agar as a base for putrefying cultures, into which he introduced heterogeneous and profoundly anti-sculptural materials such as milk, honey, and chicken broth. He also literally fried photographs together with gold leaf until they melded into a single entity. Dieter Roth's many works in chocolate are also a relevant precedent. Slightly

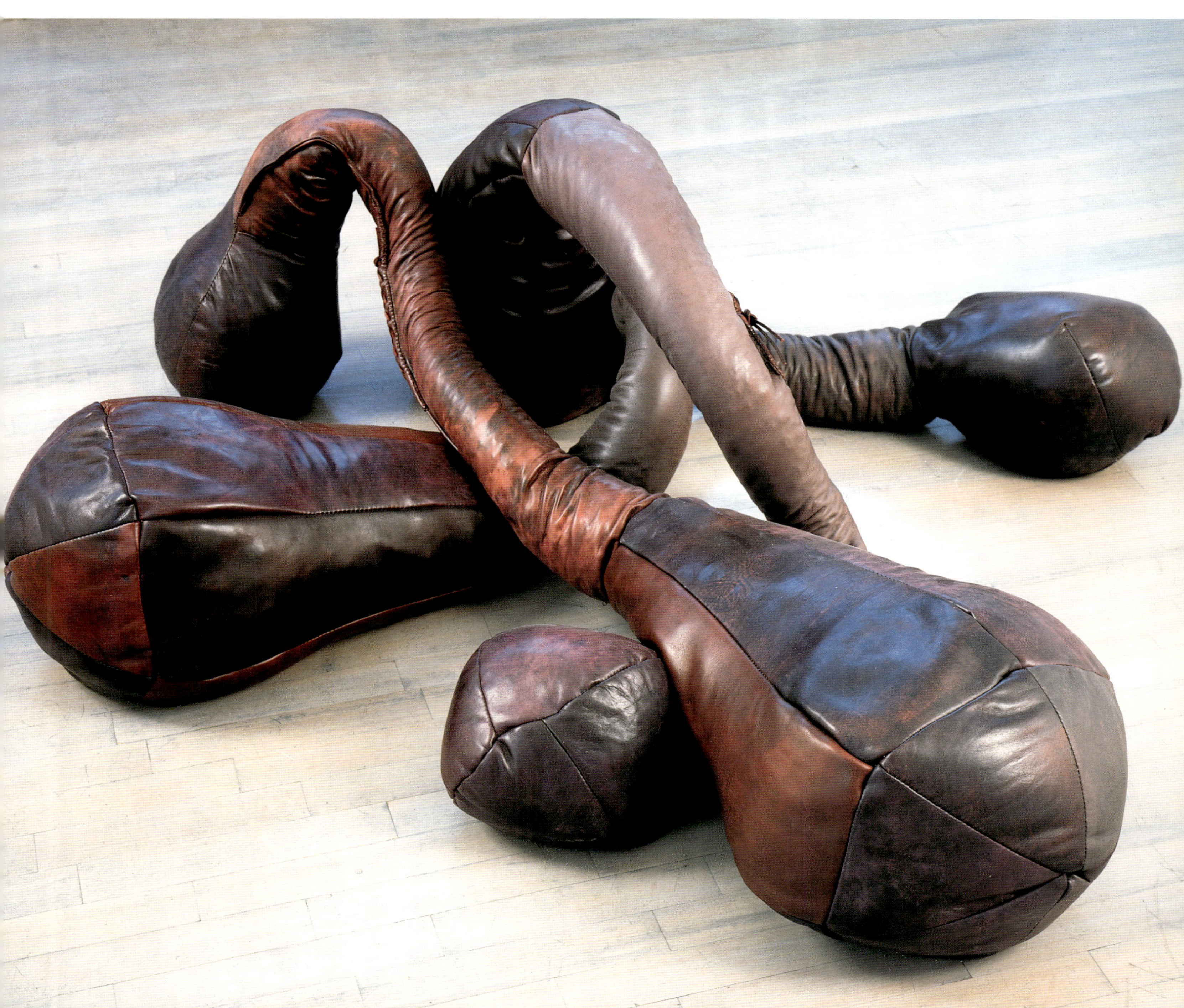

more distant ones are Robert Rauschenberg's *Dirt Painting (for John Cage)* (c. 1953), consisting of dirt and mold and contained in a frame like a regular painting, or his series of untitled gold paintings (1953–55), in which gold leaf is crudely applied to a deliberately rough surface largely made up of old newspapers. Rauschenberg's interest in decay in these works is clearly linked with the idea of bringing down, whether the object of degradation is a prized material like gold or the equally prized idea of painting itself. It was during this time, of course, that Rauschenberg made his *Erased de Kooning Drawing* (1953), an ambiguous gesture part homage, part debasement, with the result carefully encased in a gold-leafed frame.

Larner's own version of Rauschenberg's homage to de Kooning might be *Something I Got Out of the Museum Here in L.A.* (1989), a glass vial fished out of a pit excavated as part of Chris Burden's *Exposing the Foundation of the Museum* (1986-88) at The Museum of Contemporary

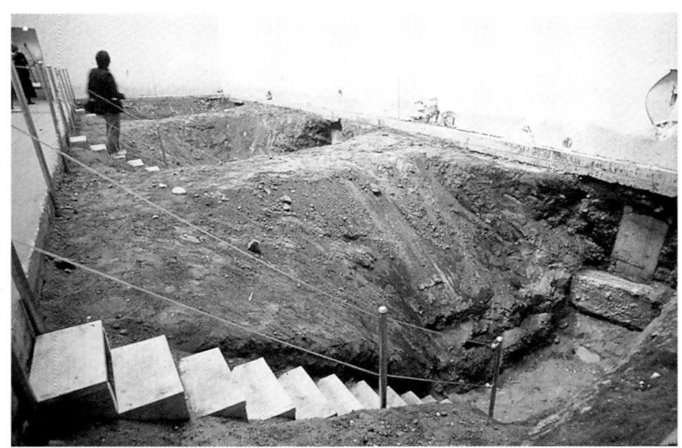
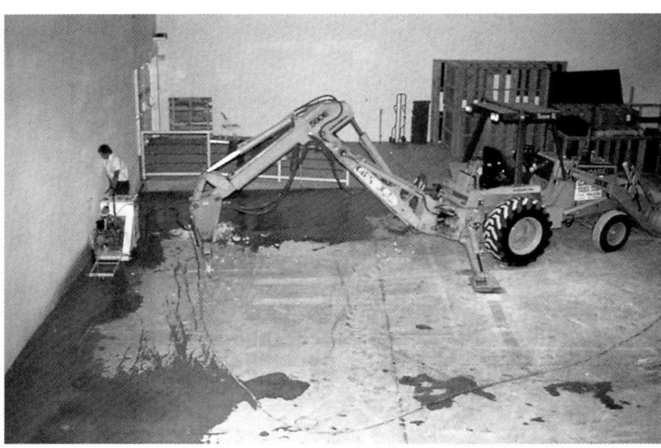
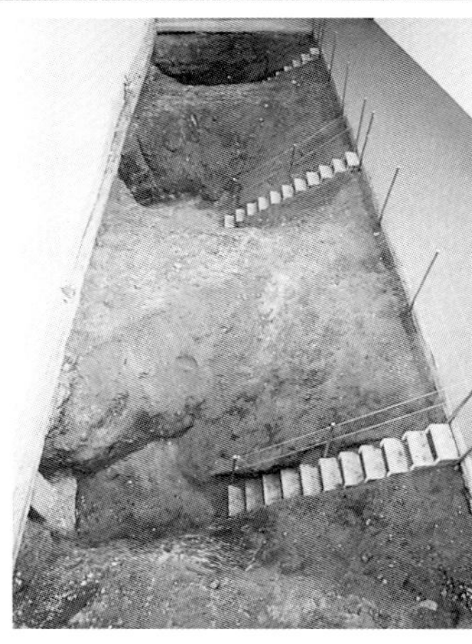
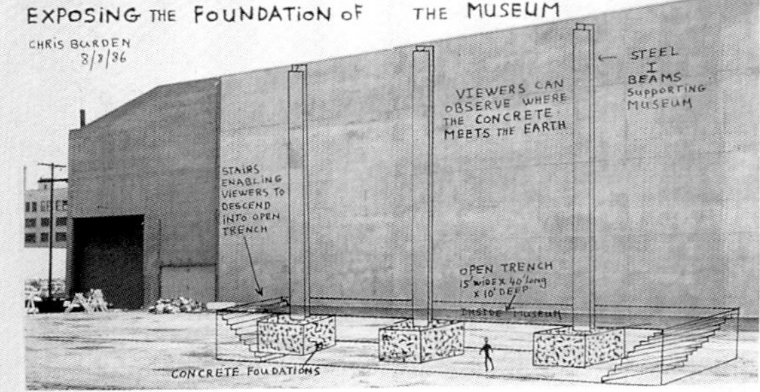

Chris Burden, *Exposing the Foundation of the Museum*, 1986-88

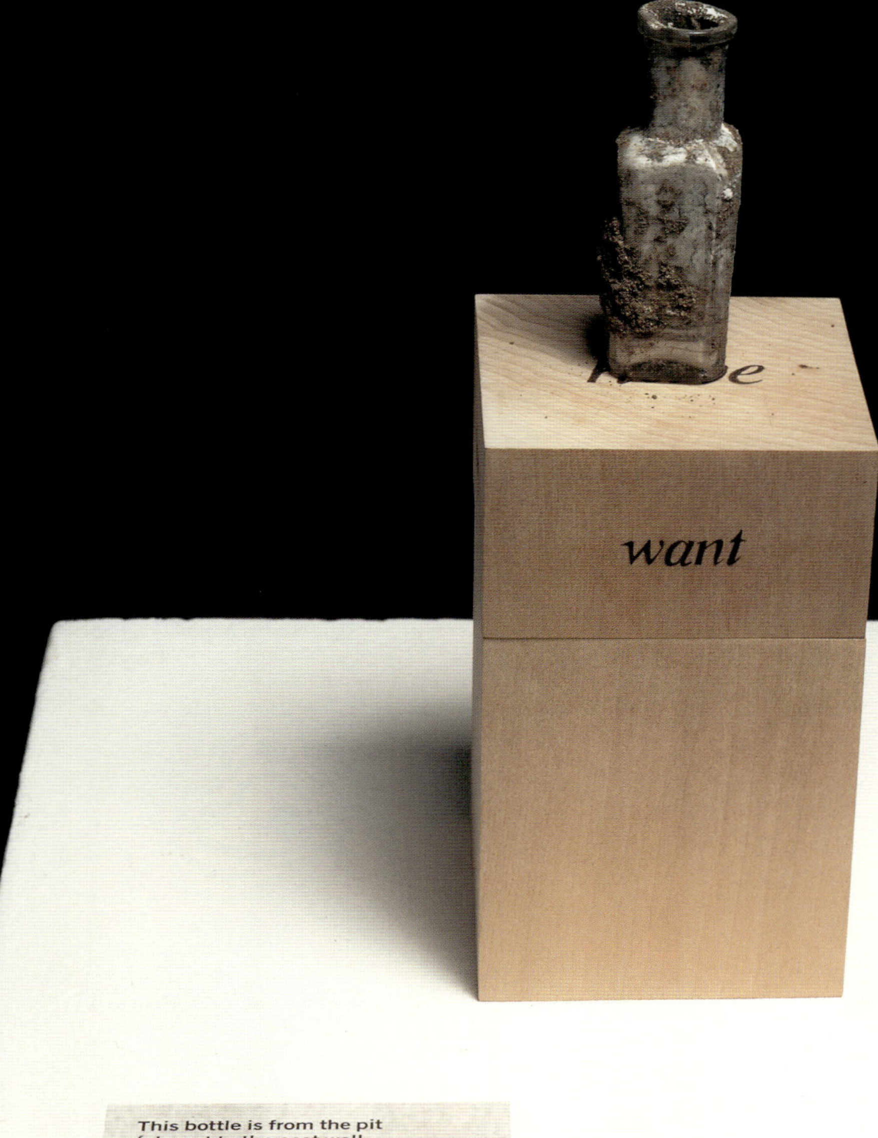

Something I Got Out of the Museum Here in L.A., 1989

Art, Los Angeles. The vial is presented with great formality on a wooden stand. A later work that returns to a similar theme is *Park* (1996), in which a forty-foot-long agave tree, also known as the "century plant," is tipped over sideways (pointedly bringing it down from an erect vertical to a flattened horizontal) and converted into a base from which other, more modest plants can grow. *Park* has something in common with the three *Upside-Down Trees* that Robert Smithson made in 1969. Larner clearly shares Smithson's fascination with entropy and the acceleration of natural processes of decay. It is notable, however, that for Larner it is not enough to topple the tree, to deprive it of its upward orientation. Her fallen tree rests on a concrete base, yet is itself a base for new growth, a development with which Smithson would have been unlikely to sympathize. While he was happy to arrest the entropic process at a given point, he showed no inclination to use what remained as a base for new creation.

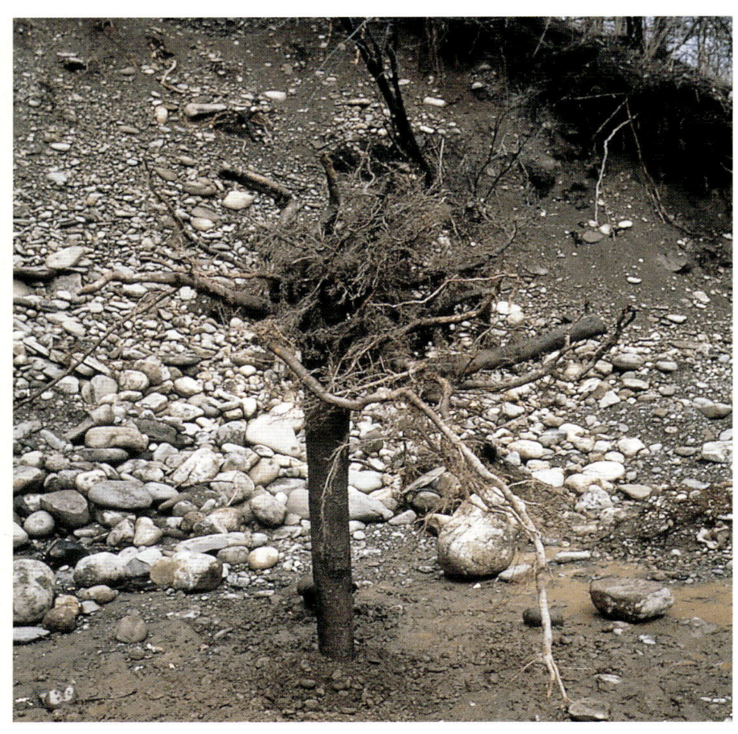

Robert Smithson, *First Upside-Down Tree*, 1969

Park, 1996

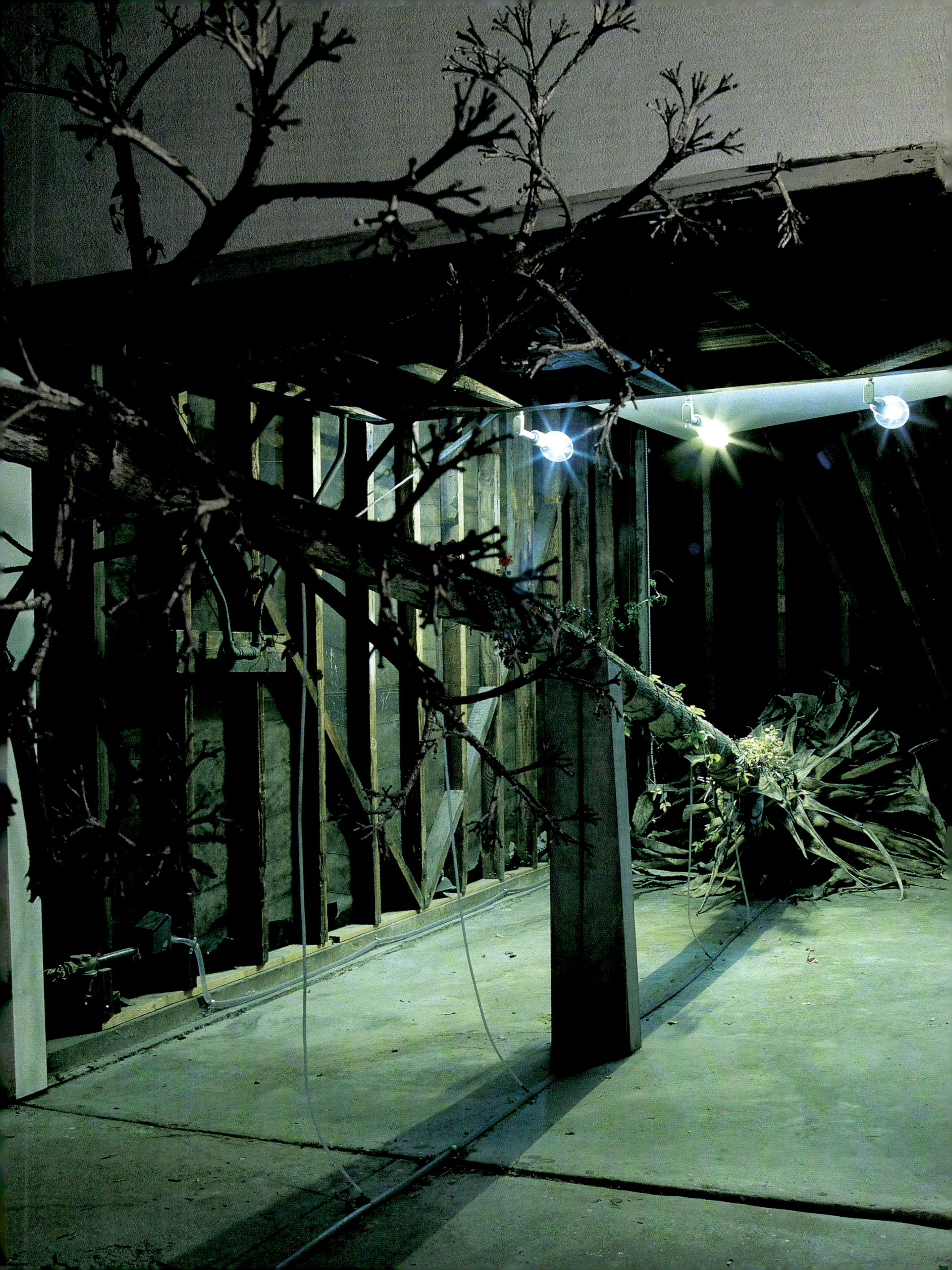

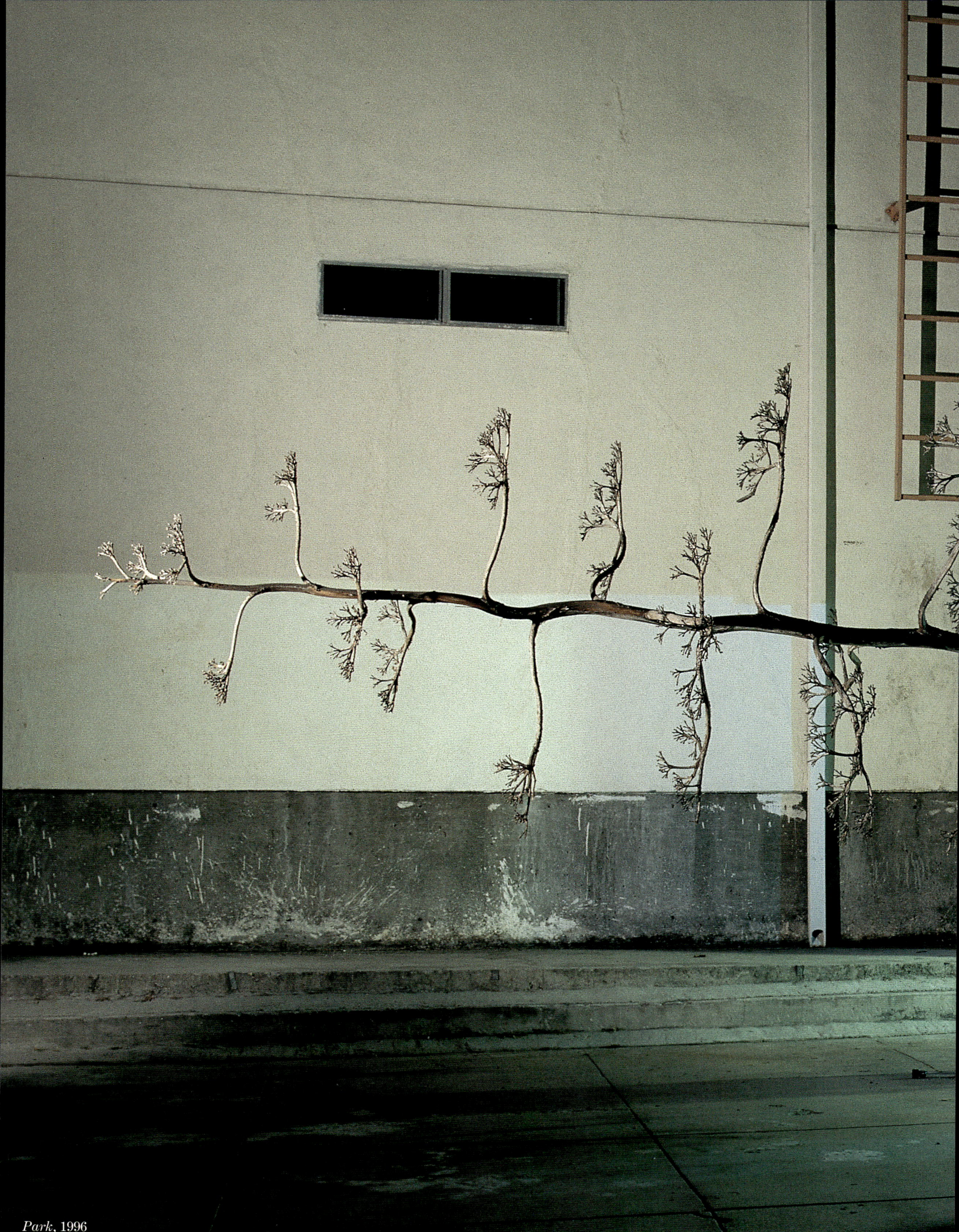

Park, 1996

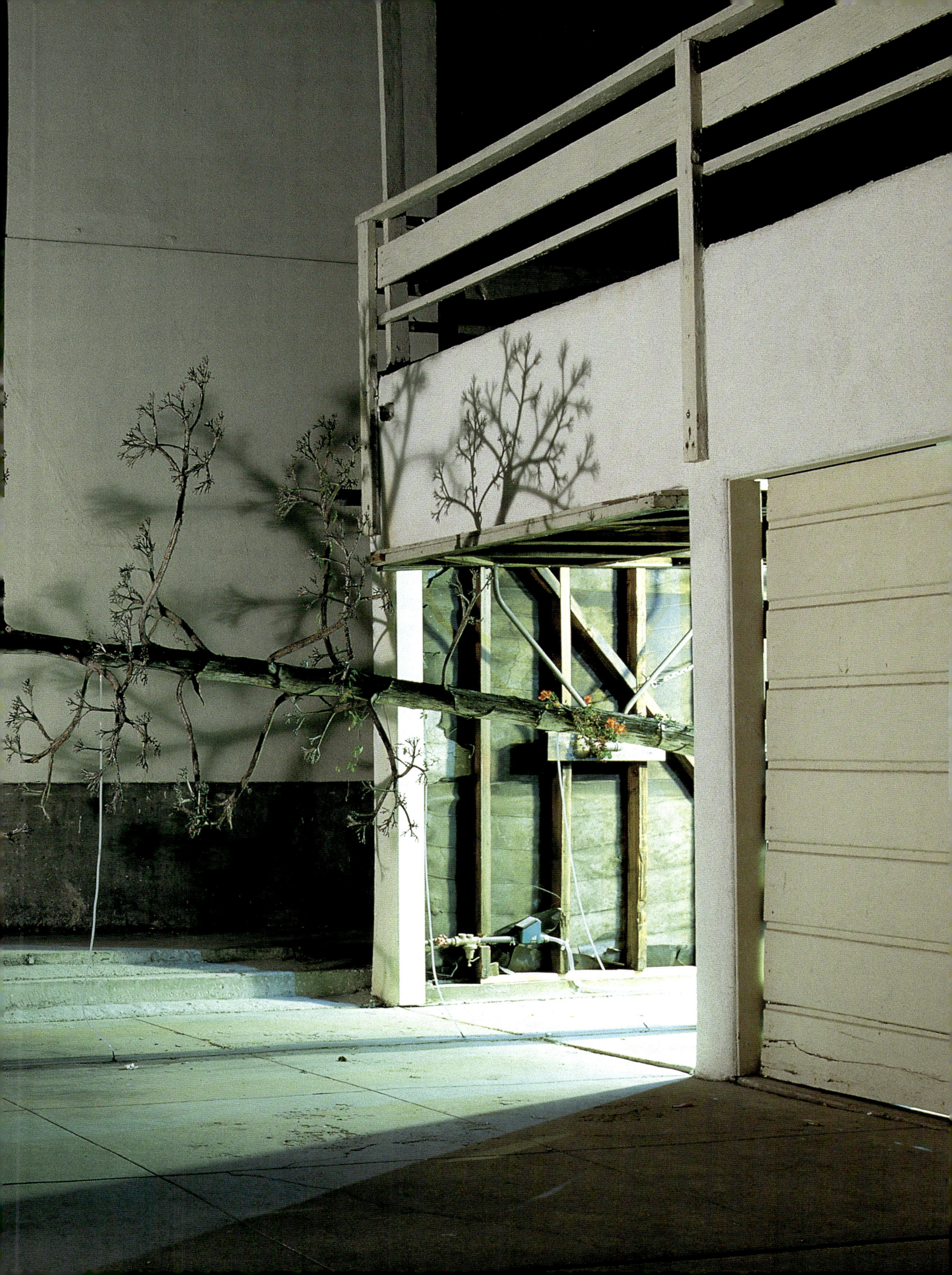

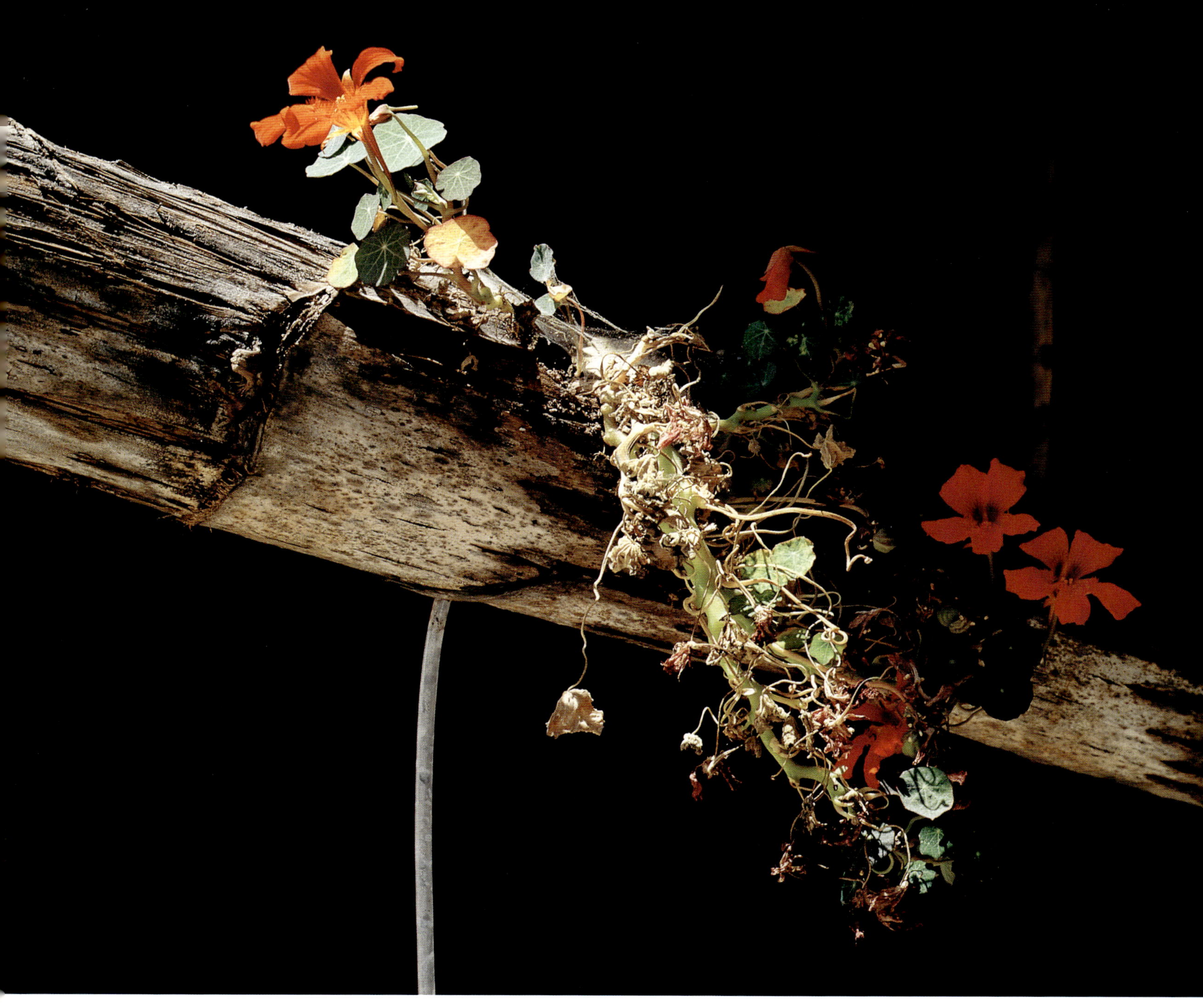

Park (detail of nasturtium), 1996

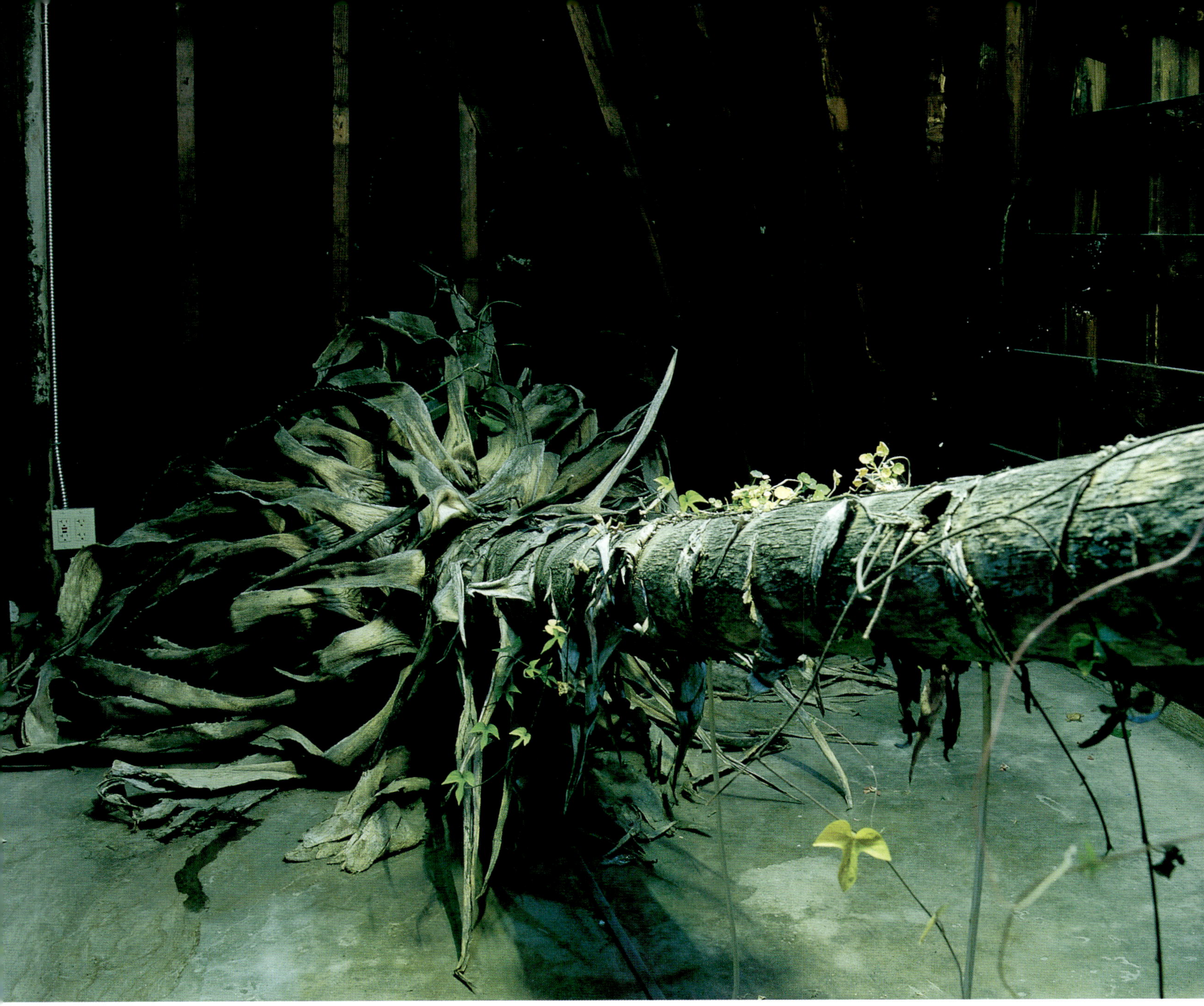

Park, 1996

Early in the twentieth century, Constantin Brancusi had found himself deeply engaged with the bases for his sculptures to the point that they asserted an individuality that challenged the sculptures themselves, even as they remained in a sense subservient to them. The idea of any kind of literal base for sculpture, however, had largely faded from the forefront of art by the late 1960s. Sculpture, or "three-dimensional work," was by then much more likely to take its place directly on the floor, which became a crucial element in the articulation of the work. Where a base appeared at all, it was more likely to be in the kind of conceptual parody staged by Piero Manzoni, whose apparently inverted plinth was announced as nothing less than a base for the entire planet.

The role of the sculptural base, however, was to play a decisive part in Larner's development. The base is one of those traditional signifiers of sculpture that Larner's practice seeks to interrogate and redefine. Her bases slowly began to take on greater and greater significance, eventually competing with other elements for supremacy. In *Used to Do the Job* (1987), the lead and sheet-metal base is almost a mirror image of the cube of mixed ingredients that sits on top of it. Among those ingredients, suspended in paraffin wax, are materials used to cast bronze sculptures and those used to make bombs. Larner gives the base for this volatile concoction an equivalent presence to the potentially explosive "sculpture" on top of it. The "base" for this sculpture can also contain it, and thus can be considered as both a kind of storage crate and as the shell casing for the sculpture in its incarnation as a bomb. Her continuing struggle with the very value of sculpture is evident.

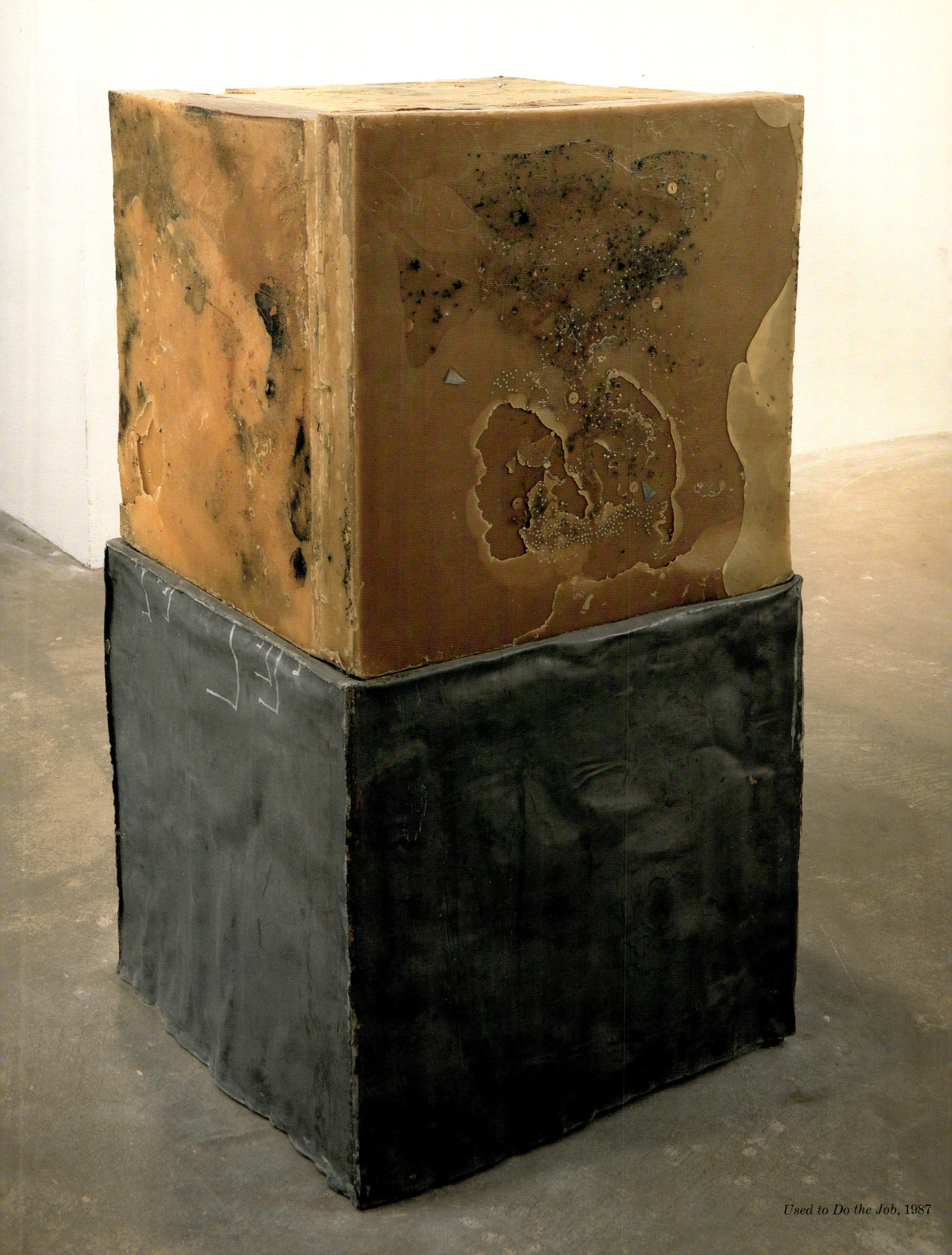

Used to Do the Job, 1987

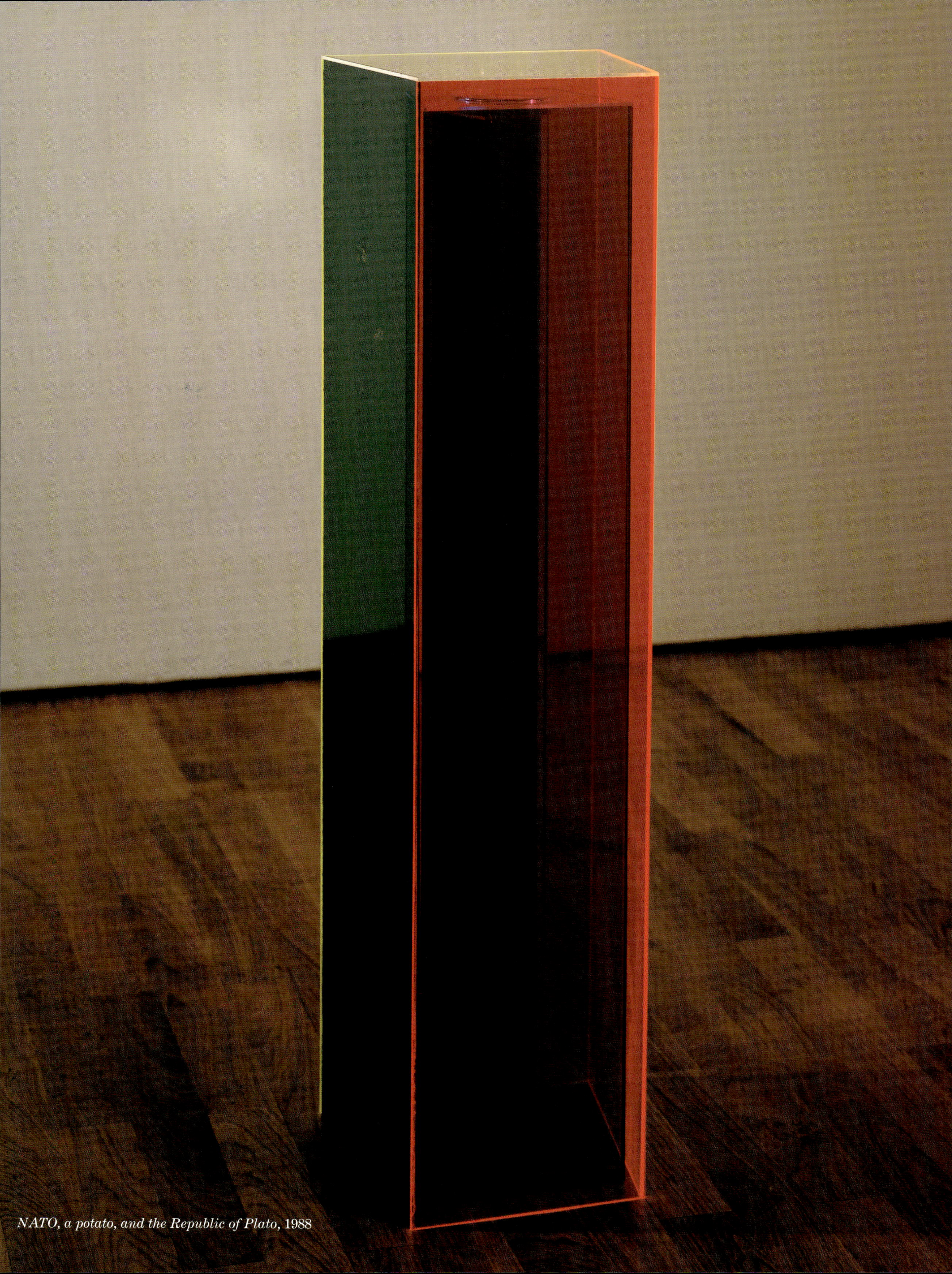

NATO, a potato, and the Republic of Plato, 1988

Among the culture pieces, *NATO, a potato, and the Republic of Plato* (1988) represents another important transitional step. For this work, which has its origins in a culture scraped off the front doors of NATO headquarters in Brussels, Larner constructed a multi-colored Plexiglas base inspired in part by the flags of the various countries that constitute NATO. The elaborate development of this base in particular prefigured her subsequent move towards a much more concrete and formal direction. This was not a pre-determined decision. Instead, characteristic of Larner's working process, the move emerged from her practice in the studio. "The bases were nothing at first," she says, but "then they got really elaborate, and the culture almost became the inspiration for the base. It was like I was making a sculpture inspired by the culture." The pragmatic decisions prompted by the process of making bases for other work began to generate new questions for Larner. She felt unable simply to ignore them, and they

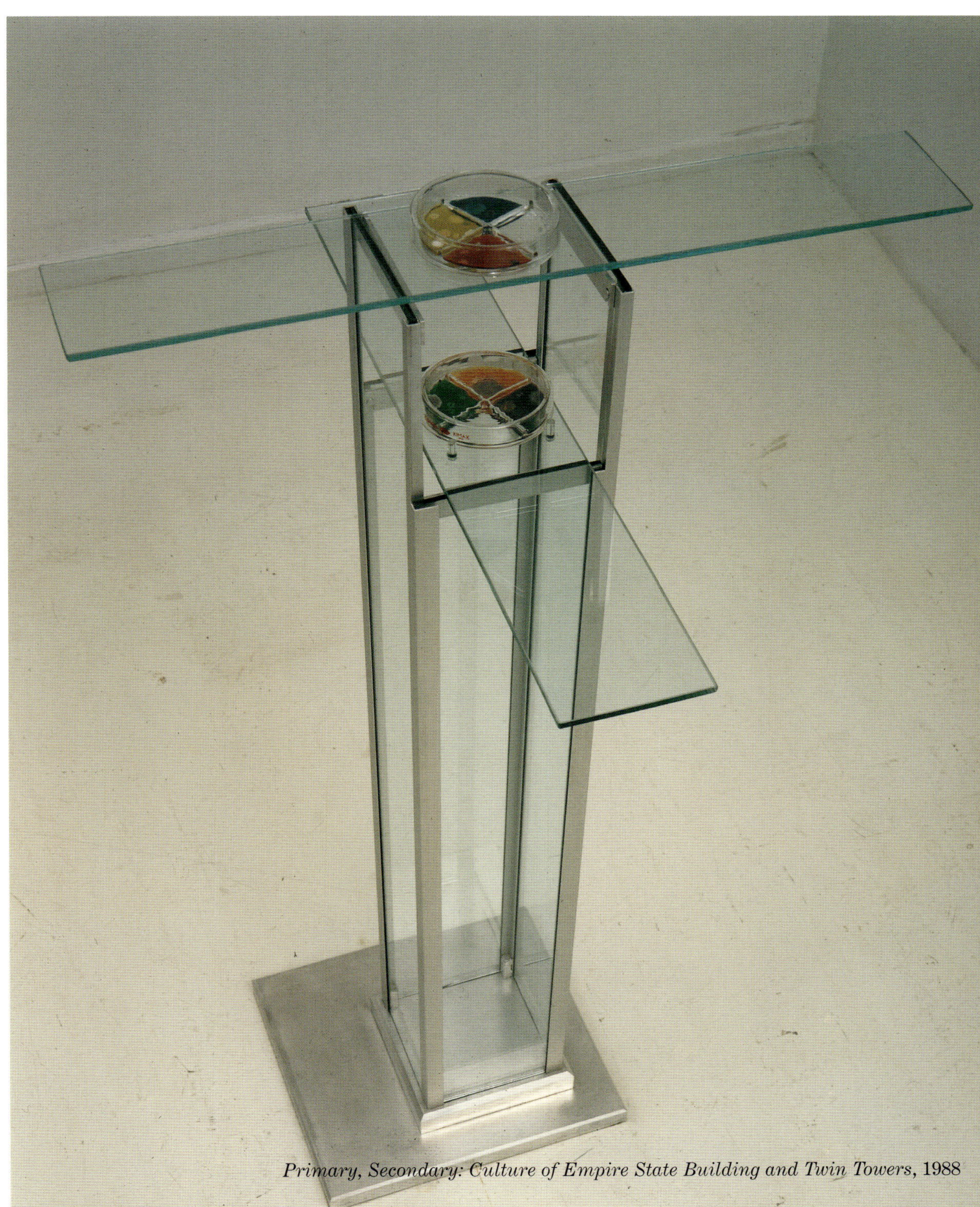

Primary, Secondary: Culture of Empire State Building and Twin Towers, 1988

began to manifest themselves with increasing force. Whereas artists such as Judd or Serra had decisively rejected bases in favor of an unmediated relationship with the floor and walls, Larner continued to find the idea of them intriguing. Her exploration of the subject kept delivering new issues that she found herself unable to put to one side. "These basic sculptural ideas just kept coming up, and I had to keep making decisions about them, like how do I set this thing to occupy exactly the space it should be in. They were little bothersome things at first and then they turned into the whole deal." Although Larner initially wanted to take care of these things so that she could move on, at a certain point it became clear to her that her response to "basic sculptural ideas" was in fact at the heart of her work.

The issue of the base had been worked through enough that Larner could make a floor-based work. *Bird in Space* (1989) is an arch of nylon cord sewn with silk. Although it does not

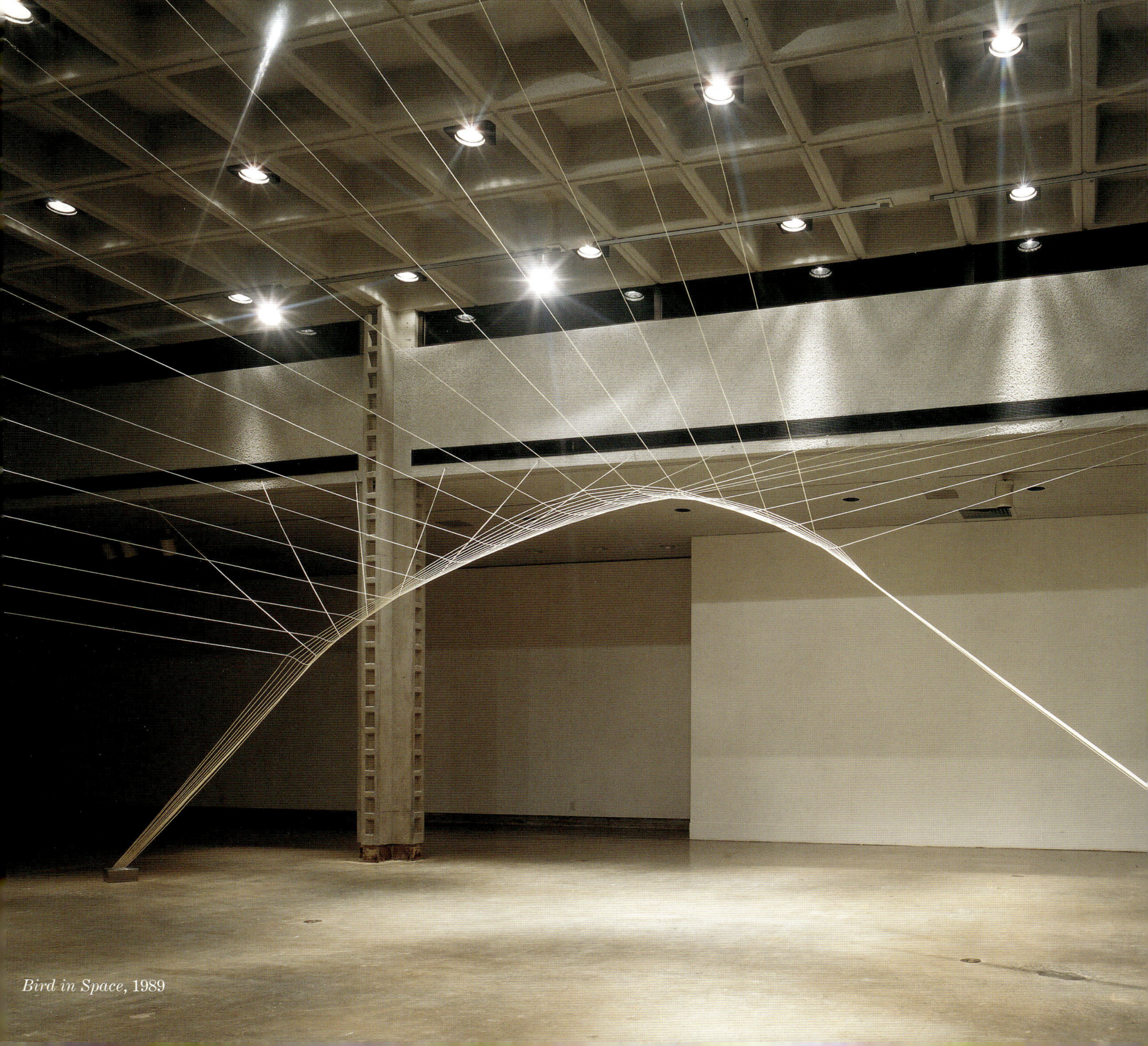

Bird in Space, 1989

engage with decay as previous works did, it employs other means to cut against conventional expectations for sculpture. It is not a work that sits squarely on the floor but seems instead to be in the process of taking off. It convincingly occupies a substantial amount of space, yet it does so with materials that are all but weightless. Only the small stainless-steel blocks that anchor the soaring form to the ground prevent it from being evanescent. The lines demarcated by the cord are "drawn" by the tension held by the weights, but the overall linearity of the piece also suggests lines more conventionally defined—lines drawn on paper, lines that occupy a two-dimensional plane rather than a three-dimensional space. The fact that the piece as a whole drives these apparently two-dimensional elements into unequivocally three-dimensional space is one of its great and intriguing strengths.

Larner's title deliberately invites comparison with Brancusi's *Bird in Space* (1928), an

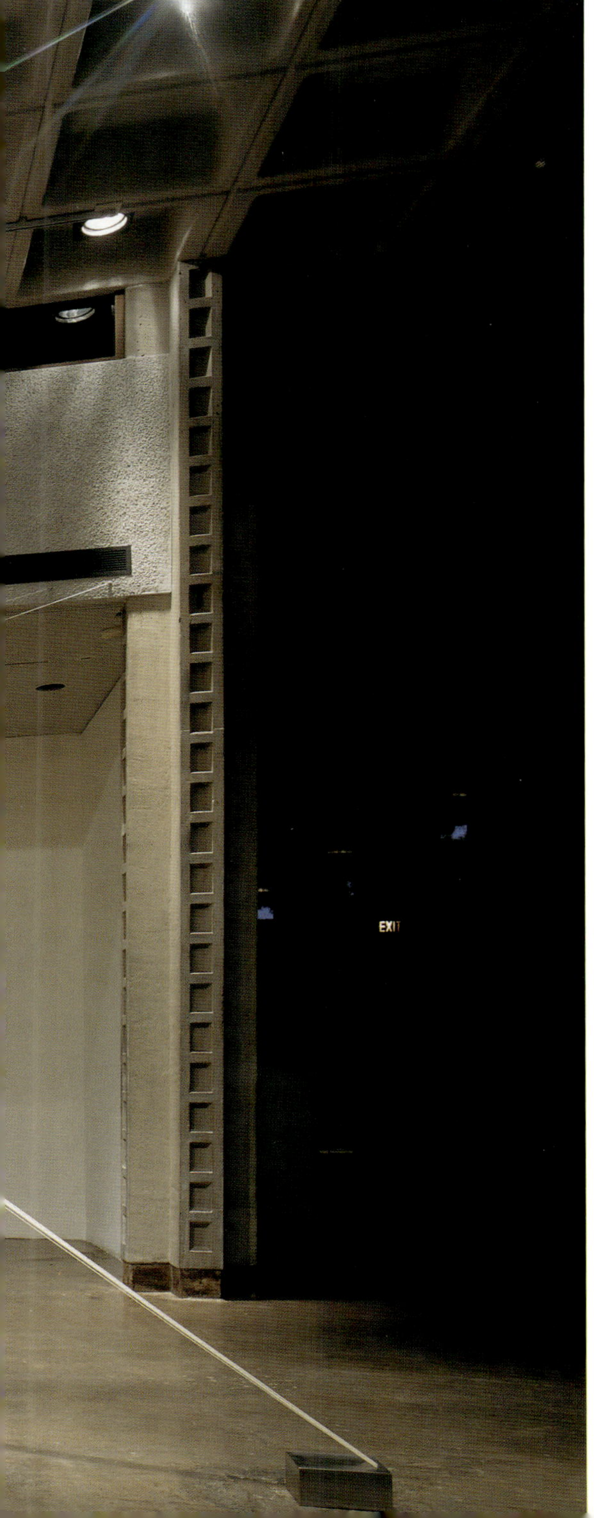

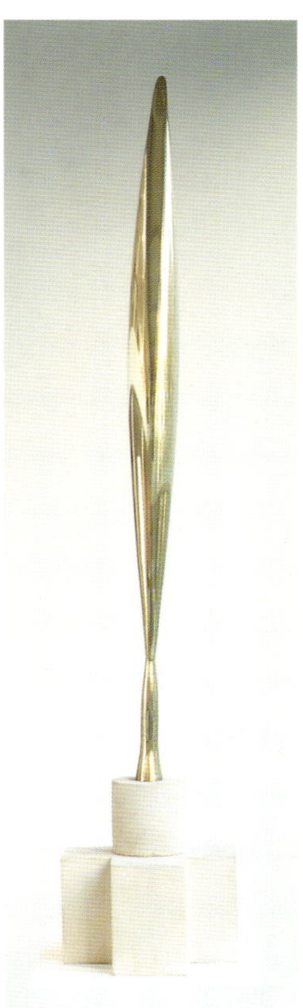

Constantin Brancusi, *Bird in Space*, 1928

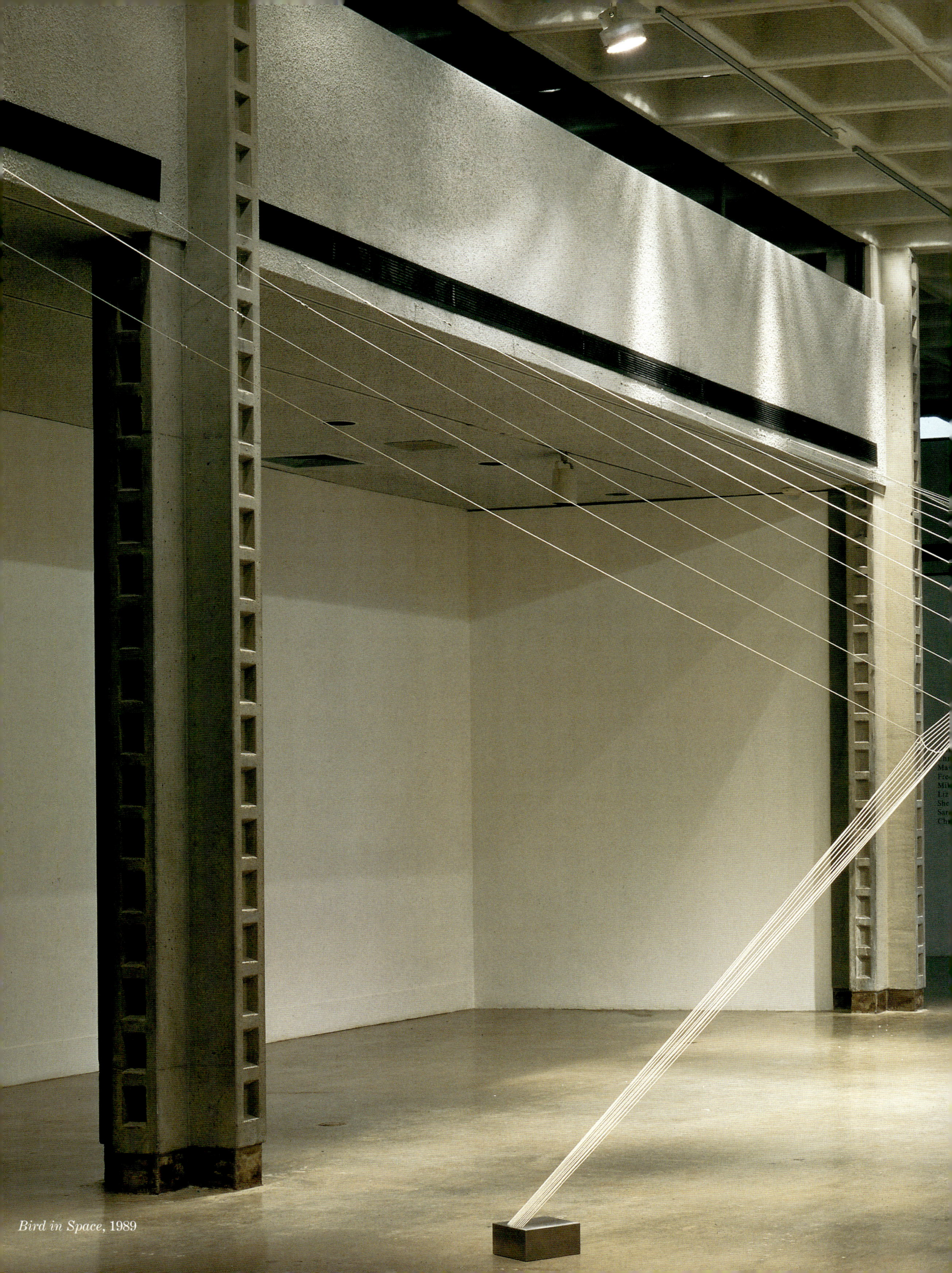

Bird in Space, 1989

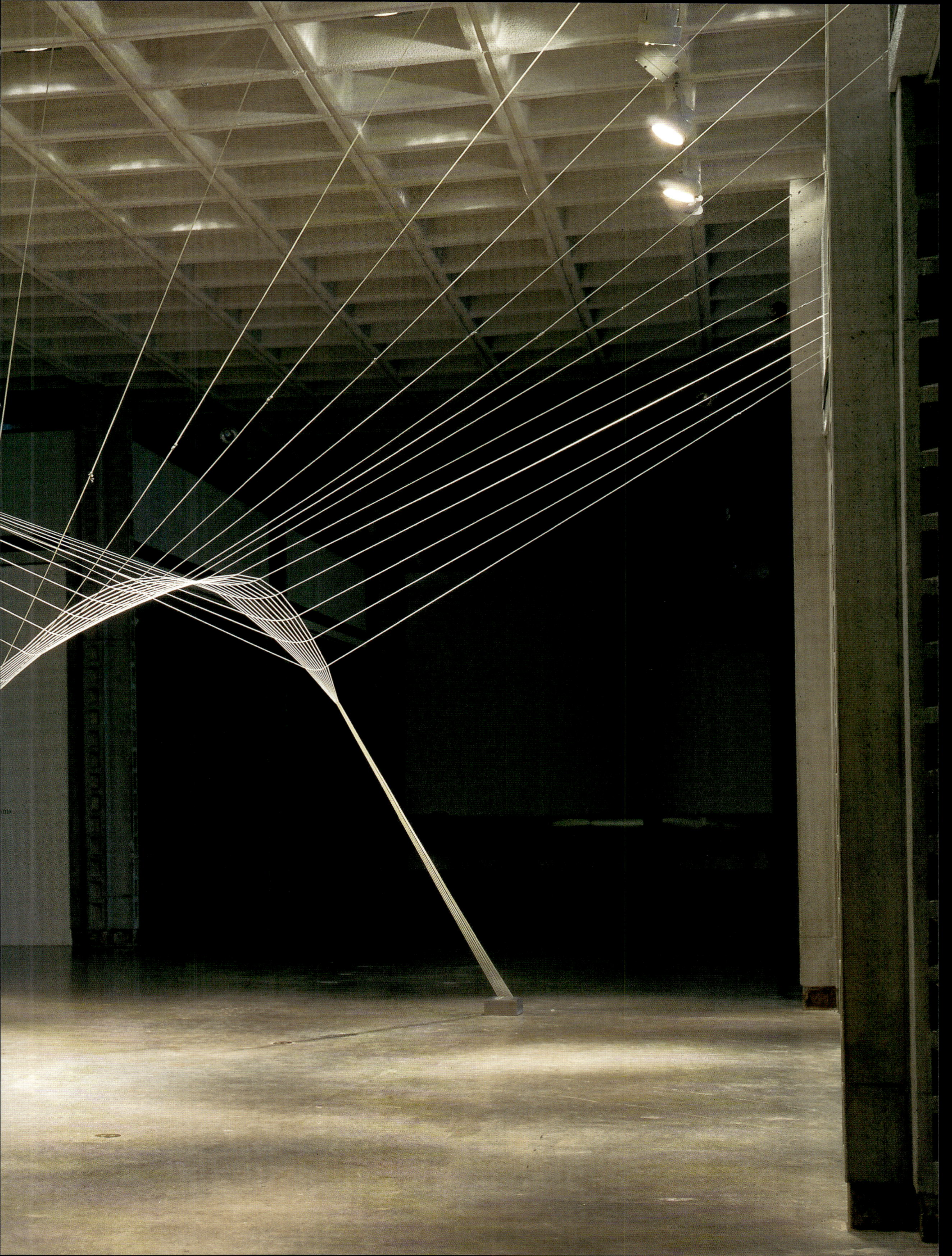

invitation, incidentally, that indicates the range of Larner's interest in the history of investigations of space through sculpture. It is true that both works successfully capture a sense of fluid motion through the air. The differences between them, however, are profound. The aerodynamic form of Brancusi's sculpture seems to slice through the surrounding atmosphere. Its combination of weight and sleekness make it as well balanced as a good knife. Brancusi's form is the essence of sculptural self-containment, whereas Larner's seems to be expanding outwards to the point of disintegration. This element of fragility, often present in Larner's work, does not mean that her sculpture lacks resolved form. Her *Bird in Space* is as complete as Brancusi's. It does mean, however, that Larner is willing to include in her work the possibility of its own breakdown and fragmentation.

The use of fabric and knotting in Larner's work suggests a relationship to the reclamation of "women's work" by feminist artists during the 1970s, as well as the work of their immediate predecessors, such as the rope constructions of Eva Hesse. The connection is a real one. "I'm not an overtly political artist in the usual sense," Larner says, "but I think the world has been made by men, and I think that it reflects that visually. Space has been built, carved, and thought through by men, and that's how we understand space, that's how we understand the world. I'm trying not to copy the forms of men." In this endeavor, Larner has been repeatedly drawn to materials that hover on the verge of rejecting form altogether, or at least that resist easy apprehension as coherent and self-contained form. Her expansive *Head, Torso, Foot* installation of 1989 evokes a body, but not a rigid, controlled body. A sprawling mix of collaged and woven

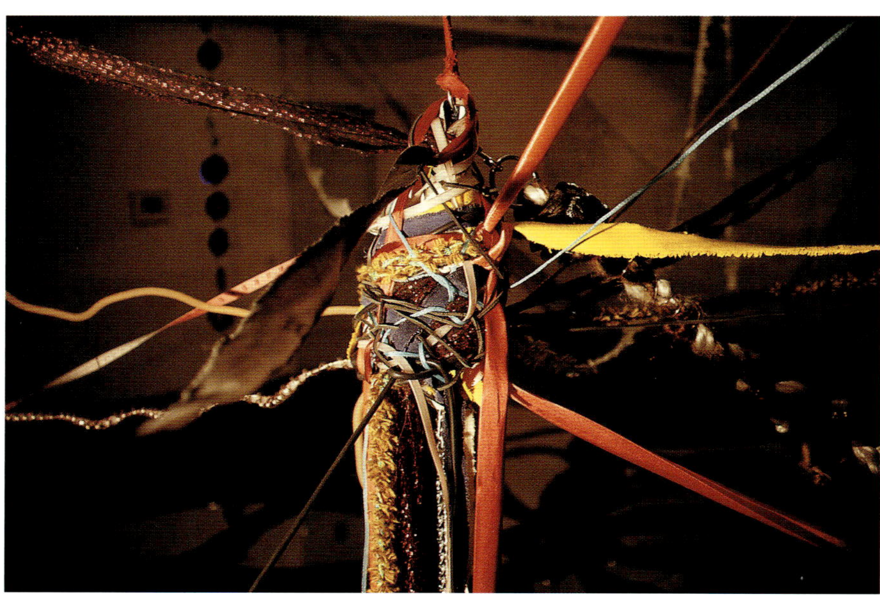

Come Together (detail), 1990

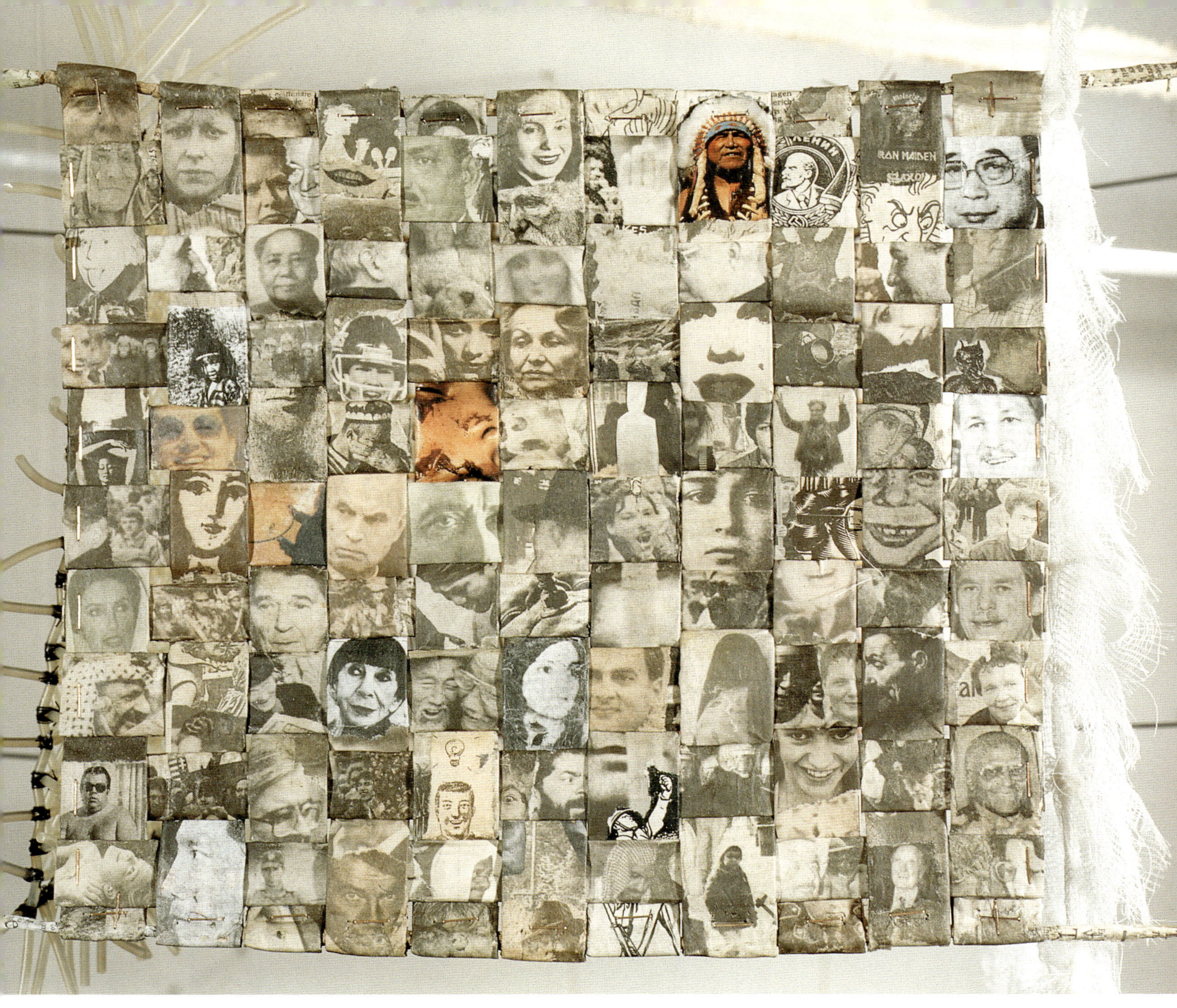

Head, Torso, Foot (detail, *Head*), 1989

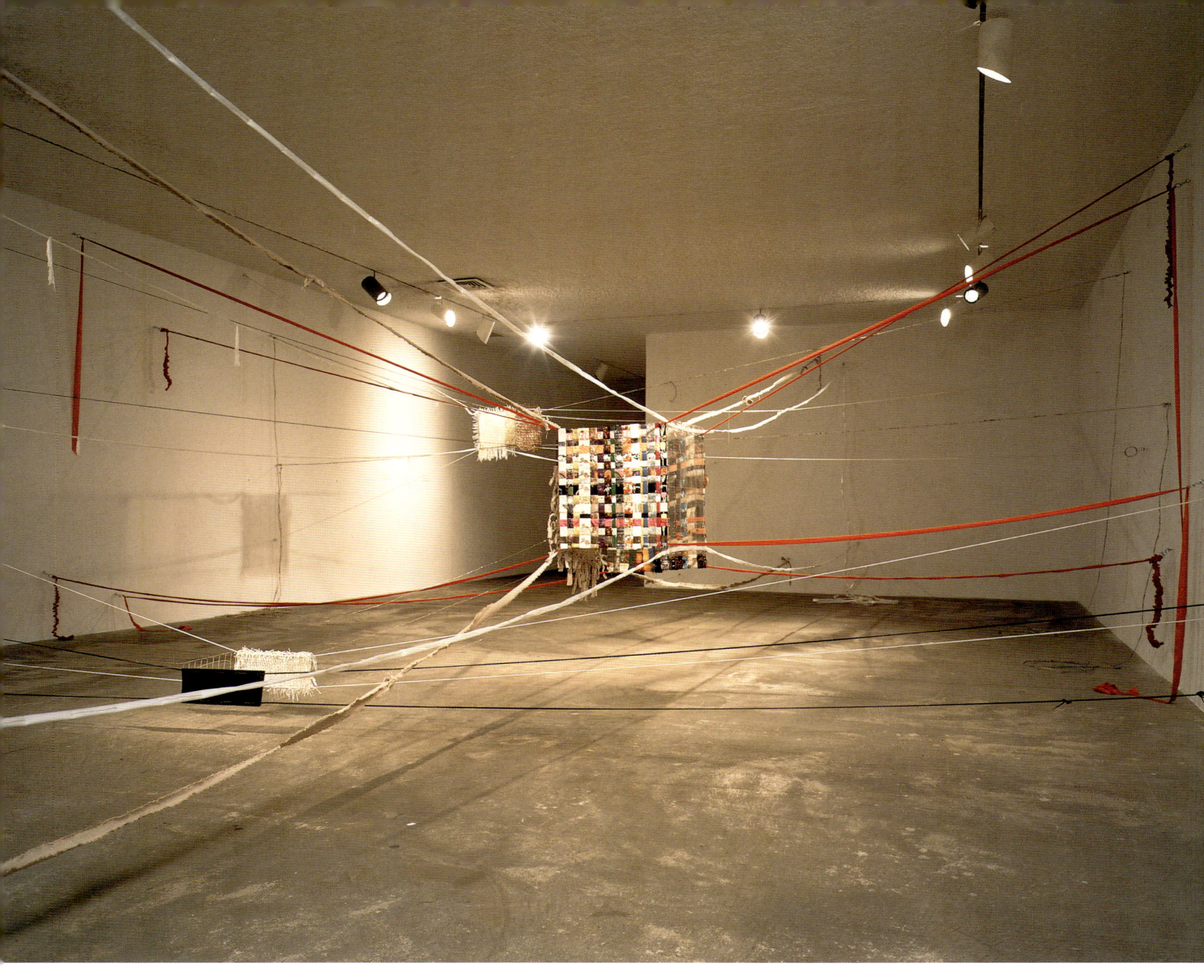

Head, Torso, Foot, 1989

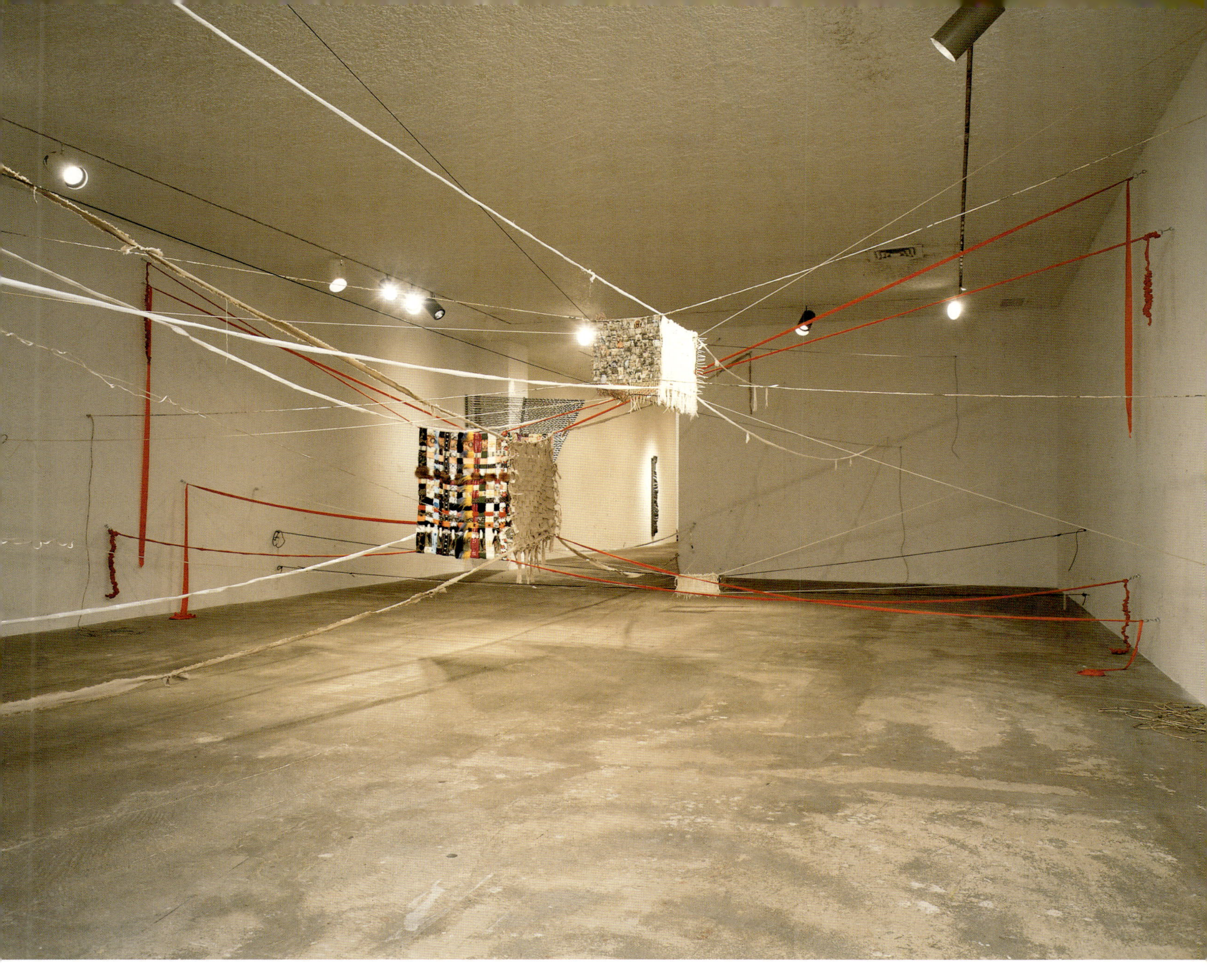

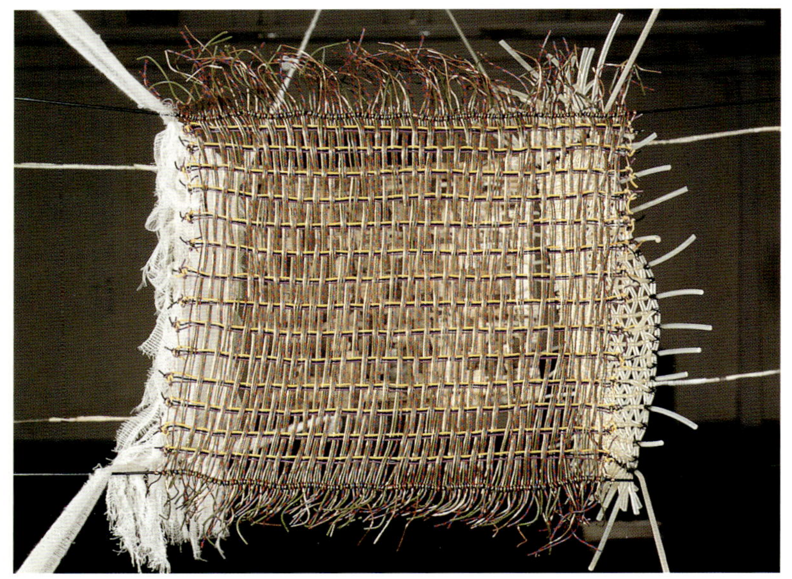
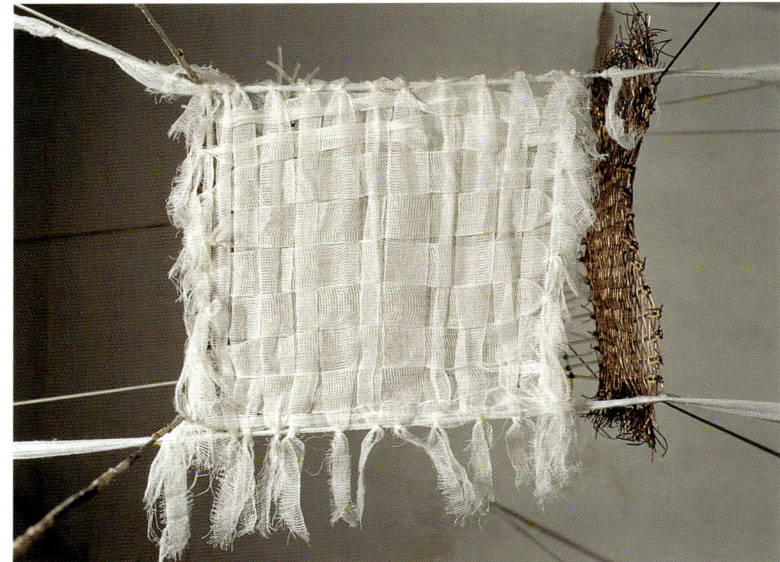
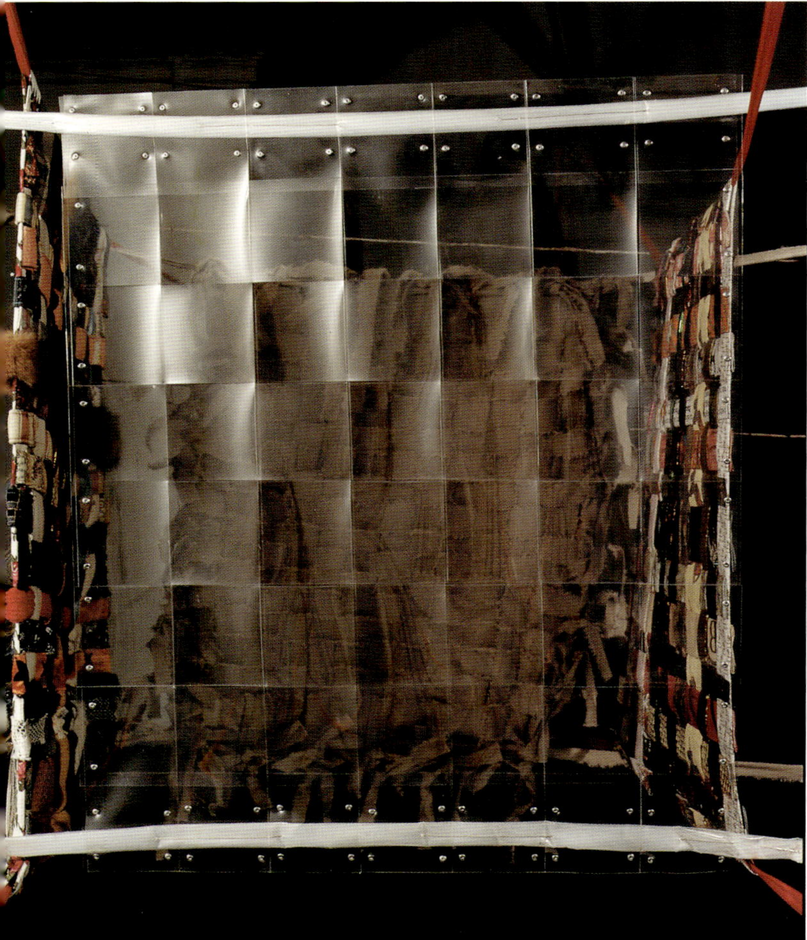
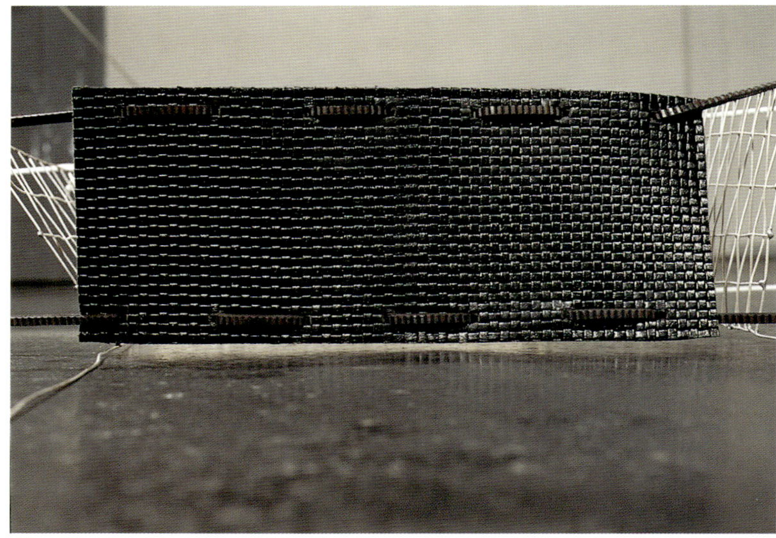

Head, Torso, Foot, 1989
clockwise from top left: detail, *Head*; detail, *Head*; detail, *Foot*;
detail, *Torso*

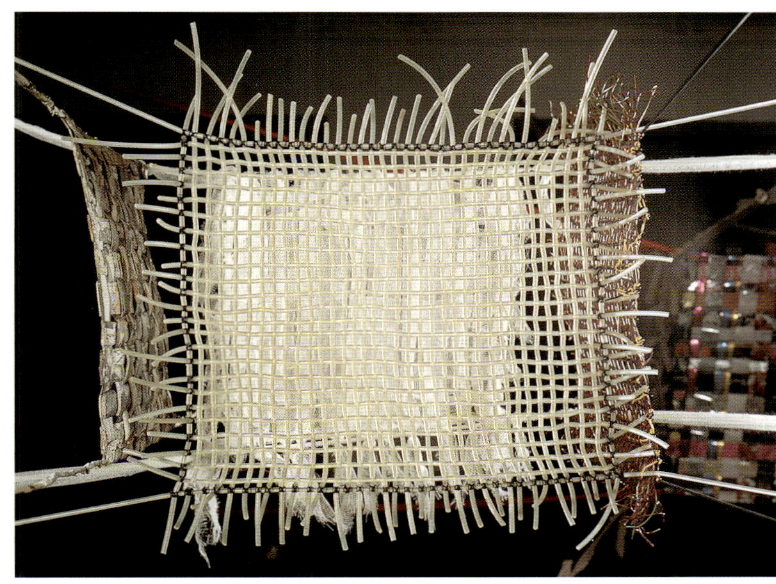

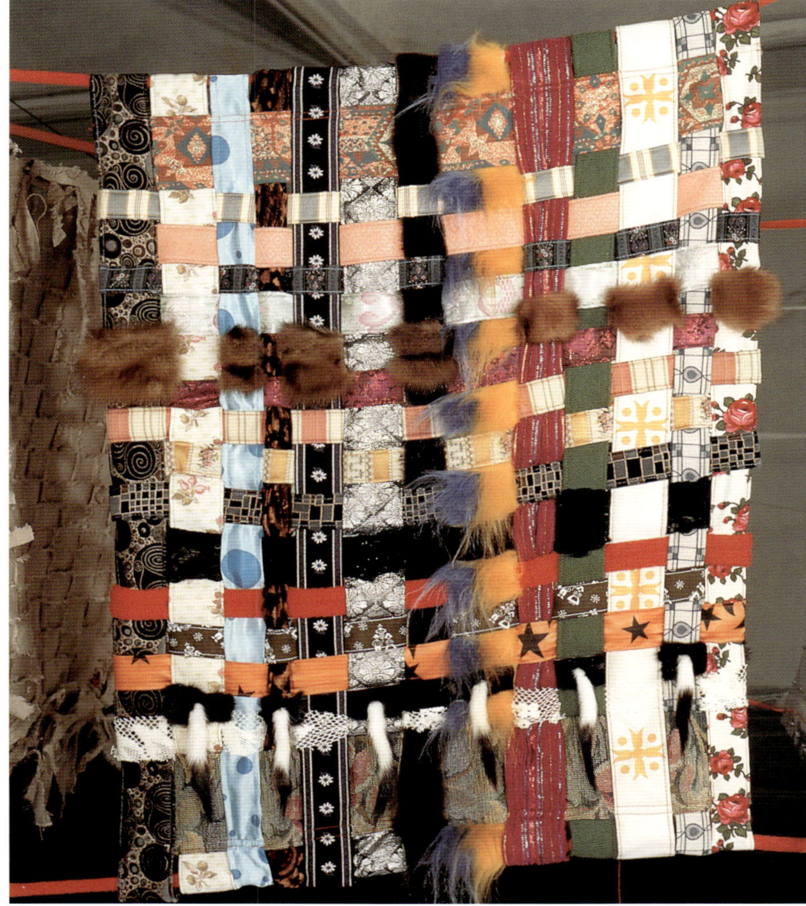

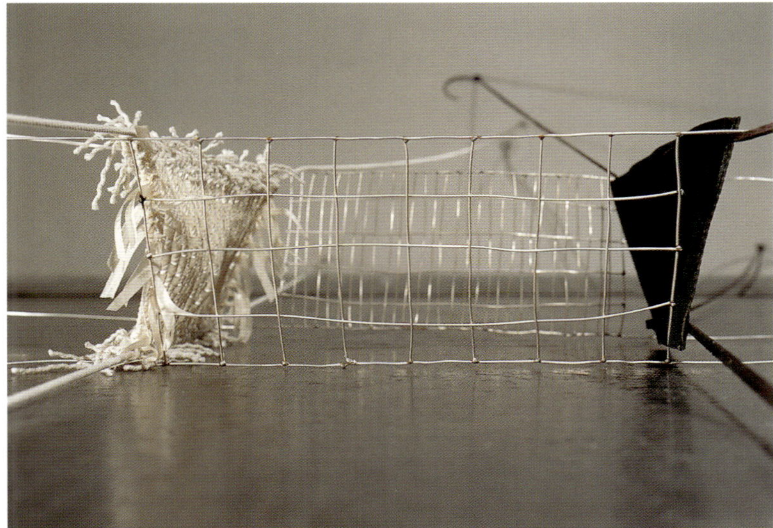

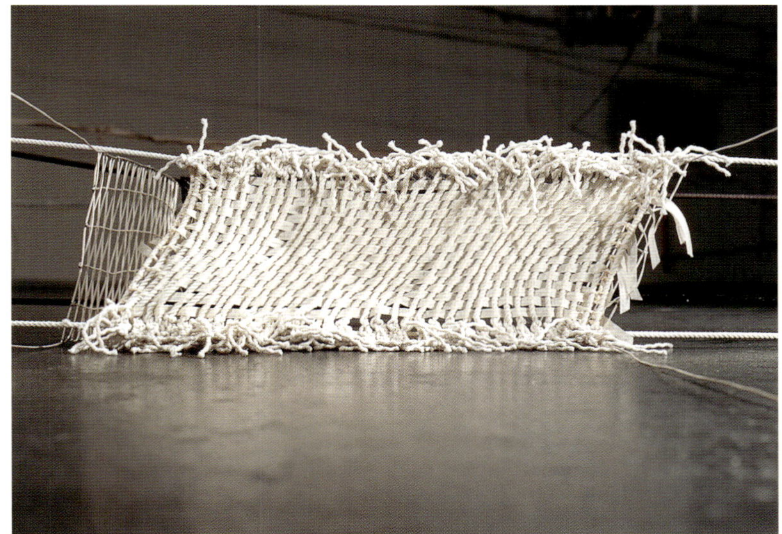

clockwise from top left: detail, *Head*; detail, *Torso*;
detail, *Foot*; detail, *Foot*

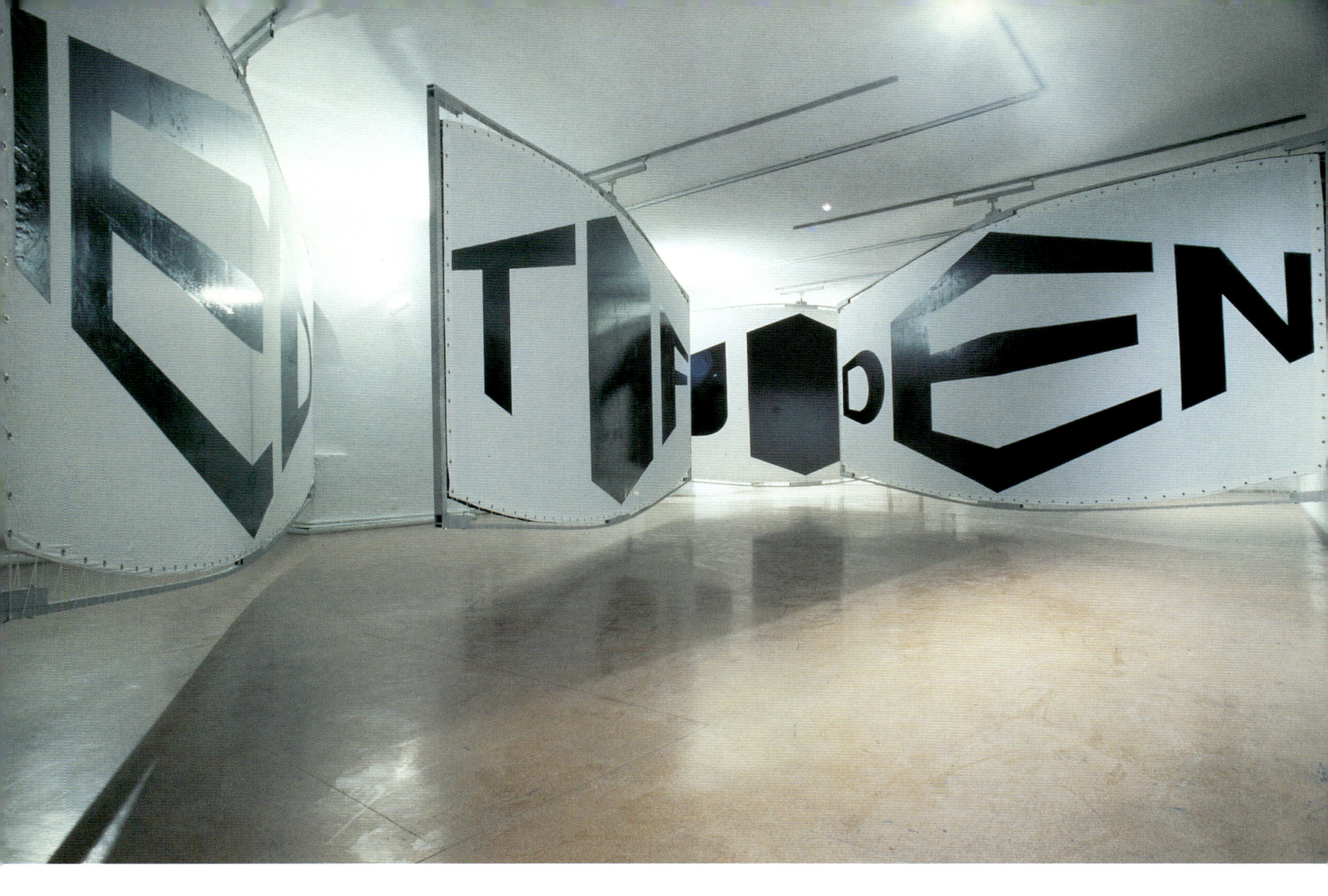

DDEEFIIINNTU, 1999

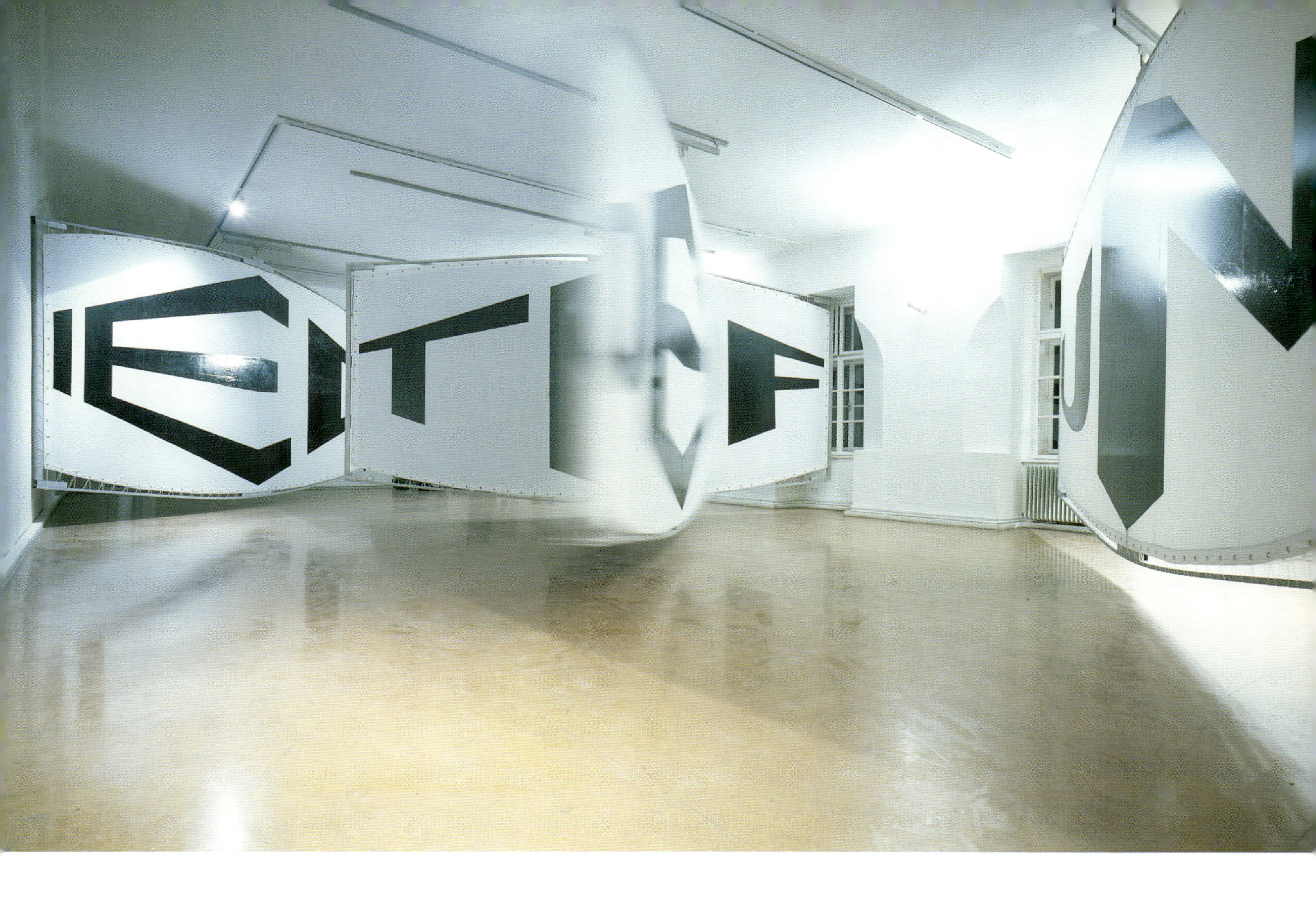

elements suggests instead a body simultaneously expanding and fragmenting, the antithesis of the idea of the (male) human body as fundamental measure of all things. In *DDEEFIIINNTU* (1999) the letters that make up the word "unidentified" are rearranged alphabetically in the title, but in the sculpture are free to rotate through the space in endless combinations. "I still want to have an object," she acknowledges, "but I don't want a recognition of form—the external shape of the object—to be the primary element of my sculpture."[9]

If many of Larner's sculptures seem capable of abandoning the particular confines of their form, they seem equally capable of proliferating without limits. Although her sculptures do of course have defined dimensions, it is easy to imagine her twelve-foot long *Chain* (1988) continuing downwards indefinitely. *Chain* is unequivocally vertical, unusual in Larner's sculpture, but because it hangs from the ceiling rather than rises up from the ground it implicitly rejects

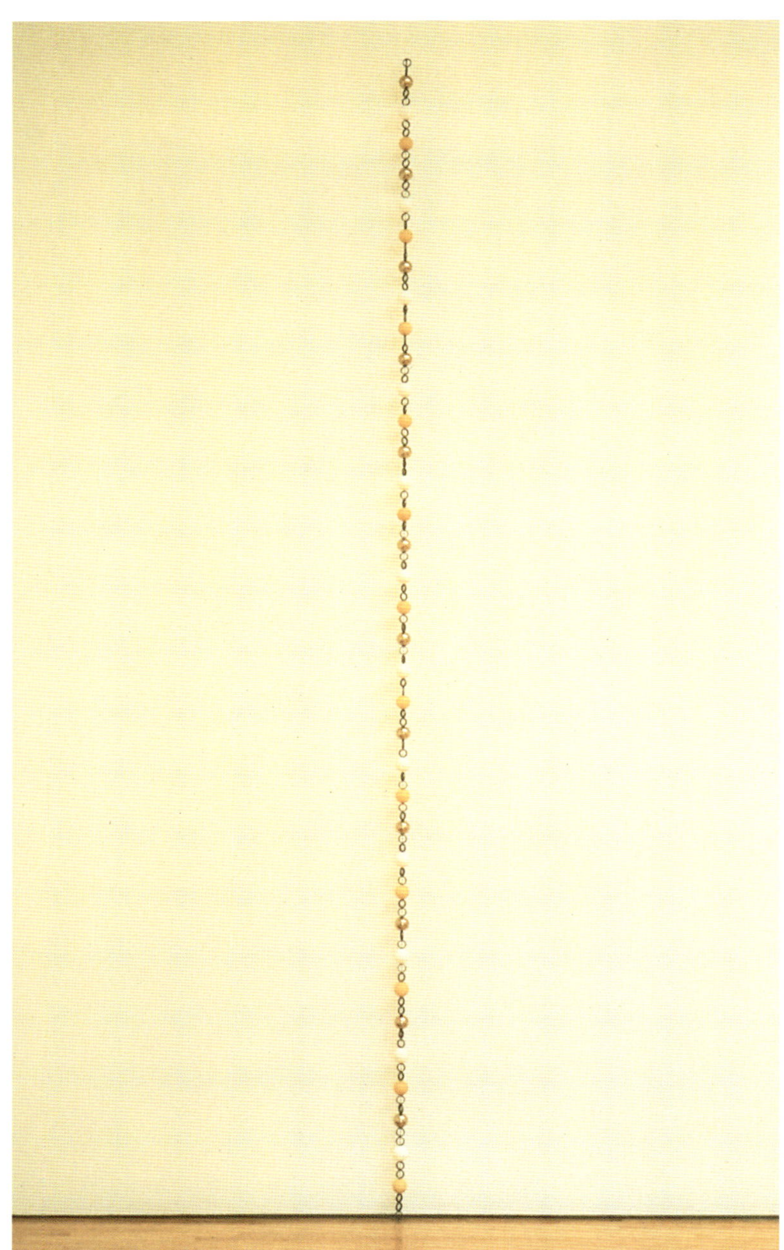

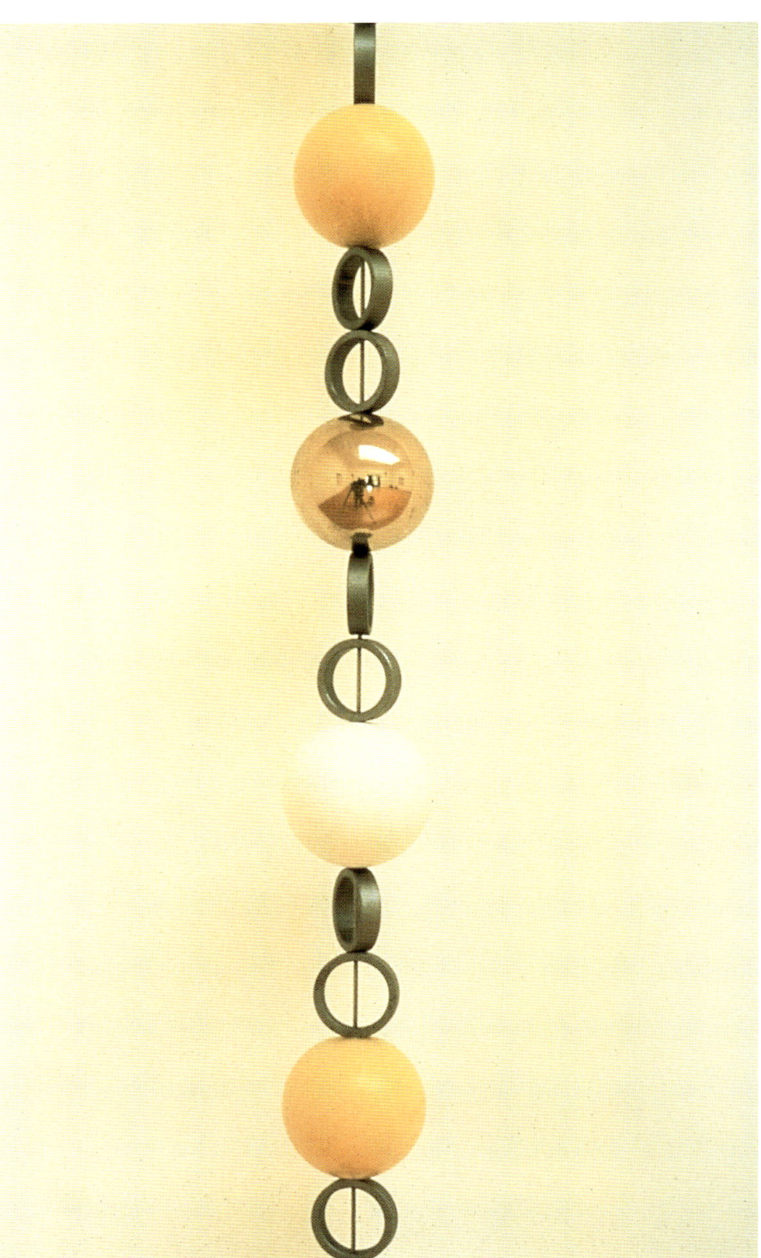

Chain, 1988

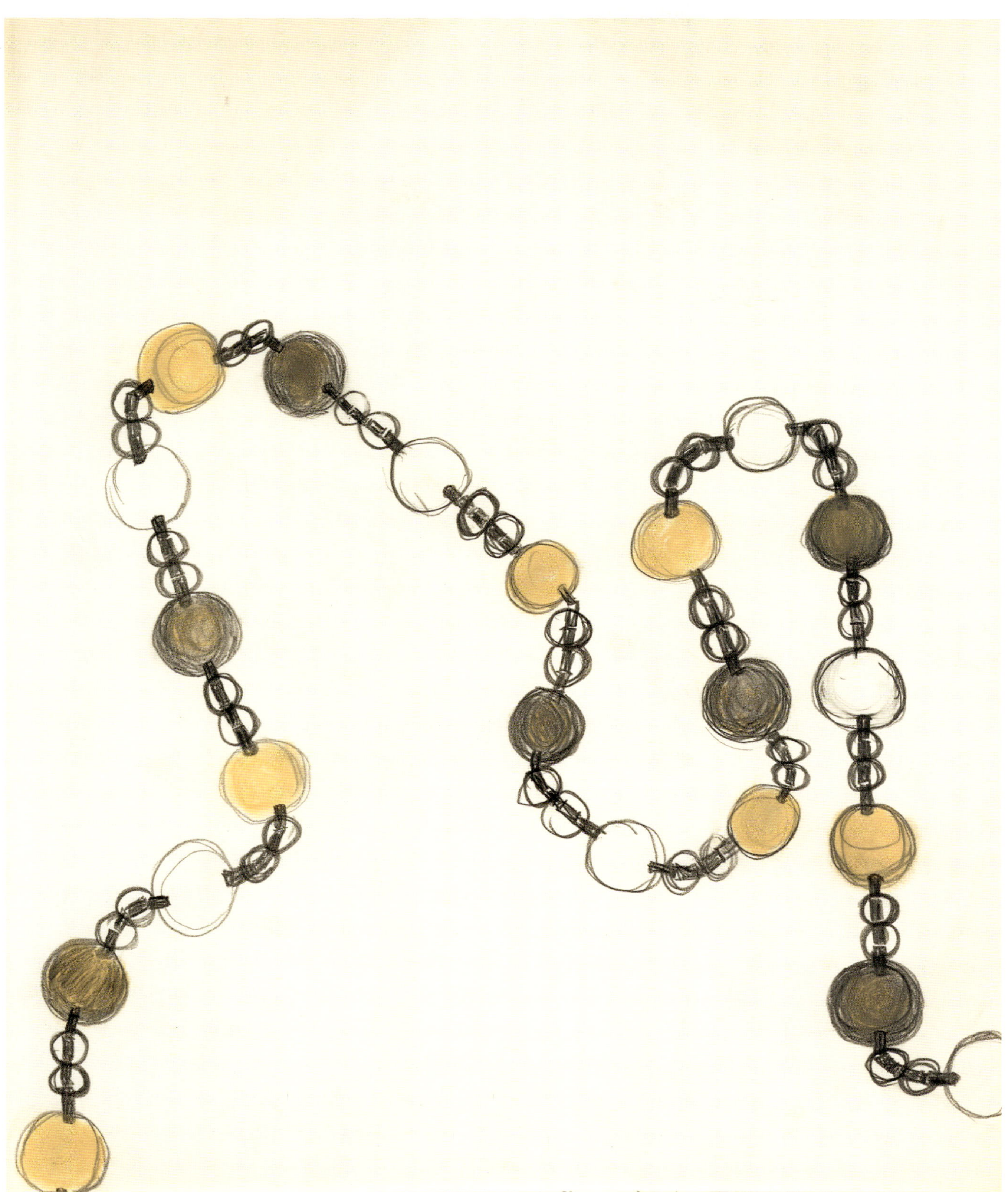

Untitled (Study for Chain), 1987

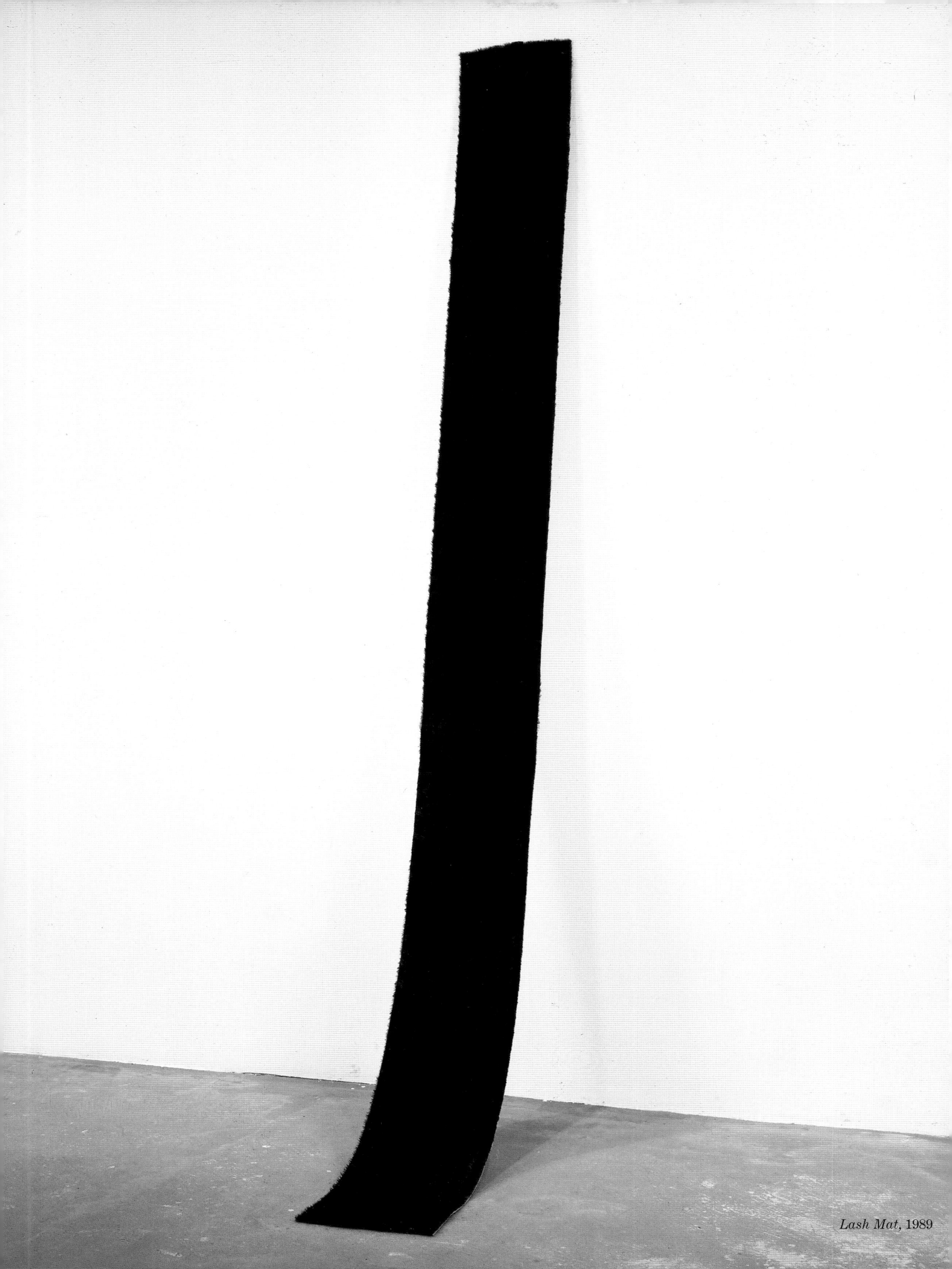

Lash Mat, 1989

any suggestion of monumentality. Where we might conventionally expect it to be rooted, it melts away.

Her *Lash Mat* (1989), however, sags against the wall, suggesting that it might soon slip all the way down to the horizontal. The horizontal implies a lack of rigid boundaries or a spreading out in all directions that rejects boundaries altogether. The sense of a kind of anti-monument is only emphasized by the deliberately incongruous use of (almost satirically flimsy) false eyelashes as its primary medium. The eyelashes are in part an homage to Louise Nevelson's famous eyelashes, but their patterning is derived from a painting by Bridget Riley. Riley's paintings, of course, set up an optical effect that resists stability. Eyelashes could well take their place alongside Bataille's spider, or spit, as emblematic of the ephemeral and formless, albeit here given a very contingent form by Larner.

Another work, *Out of Touch* (1987), also implies a potentially unlimited running on. *Out of Touch* consists of sixteen miles of surgical gauze, wrapped around itself to a diameter of four feet, until it becomes almost a Platonic ideal of the sphere. One of the key reference points for the work is Marcel Duchamp's "mile of string" installation at the "First Papers of Surrealism" exhibition of 1942. (Duchamp had originally planned to use sixteen miles of string.) In this case, however, Larner reverses the relationship that her work had to Brancusi's *Bird in Space*. This time her strategy is to condense rather than to fragment. Where Duchamp's installation ran amok throughout the gallery like a huge and uncontrolled spider's web, Larner's sixteen miles become a concentrated essence of the solid. The work's solidity, however, derives from the

Out of Touch, 1987

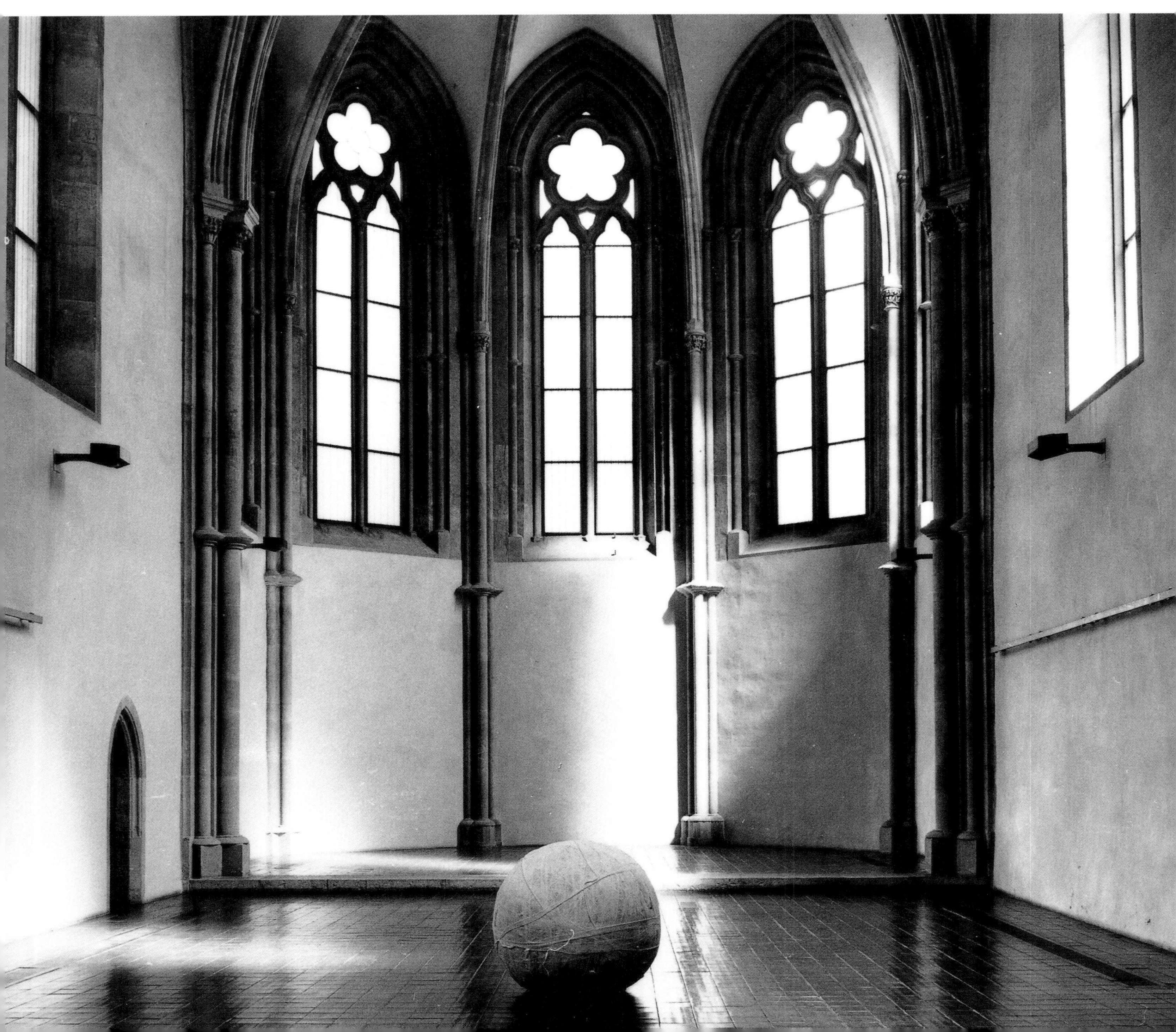

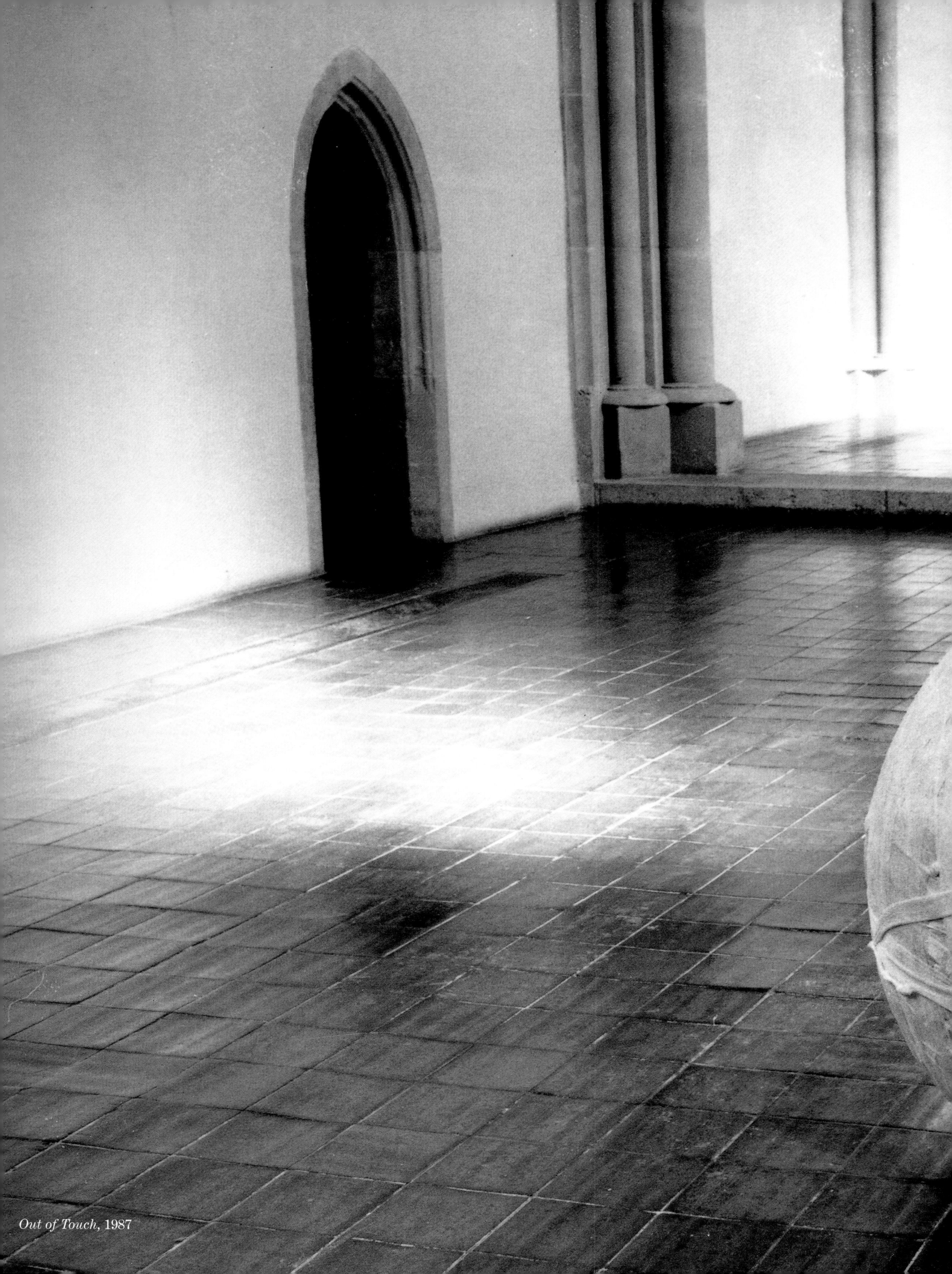

Out of Touch, 1987

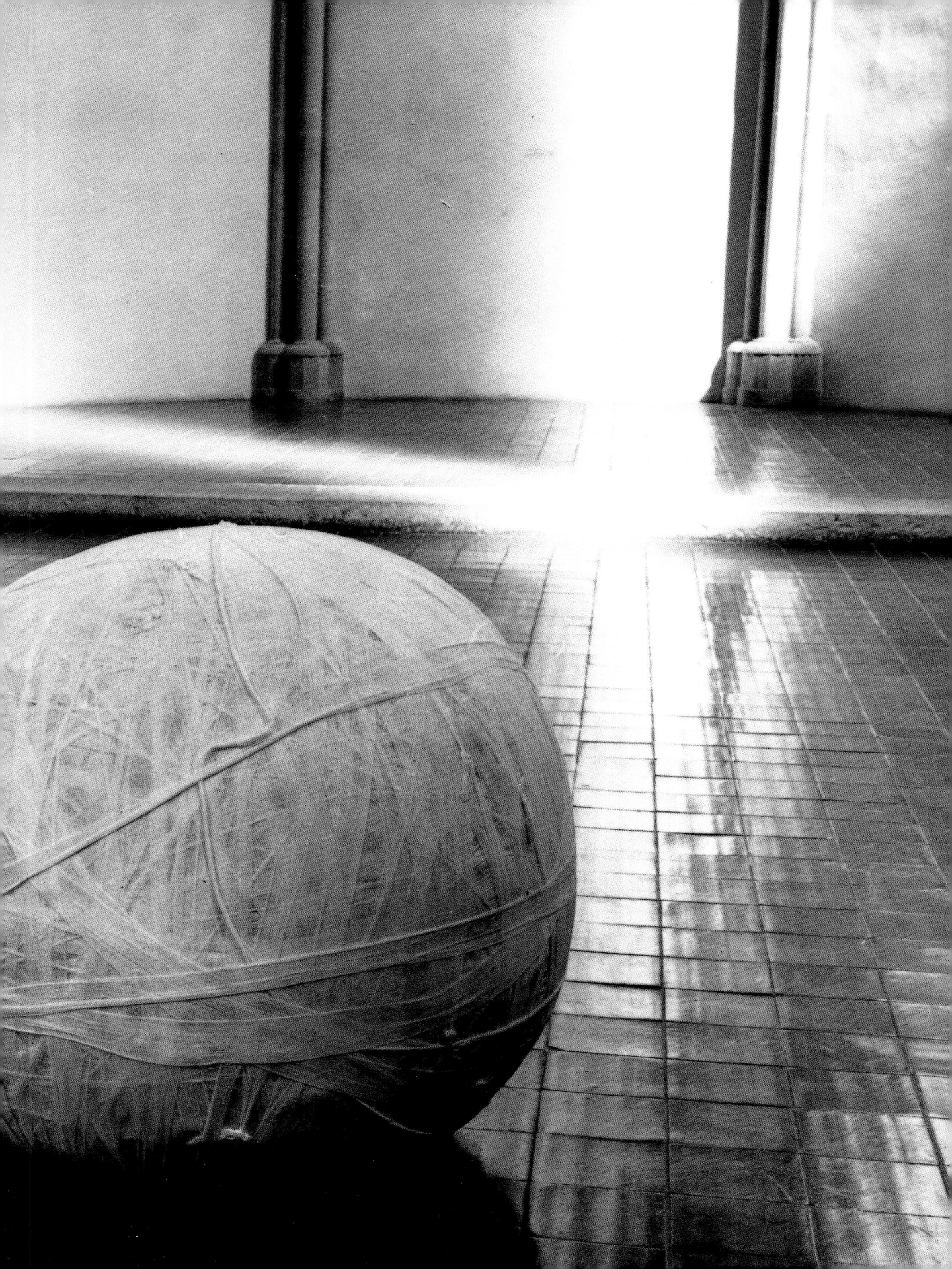

extension of a line, an extension so extreme that the two-dimensional is converted into an inescapable three-dimensional presence. Larner actually adds gauze to the work with each exhibition to freshen it: the work actually still, very slowly, grows. An almost pure line here generates pure volume. Density and mass are counterintuitively subsumed under line.

A more recent piece, *I thought I saw a pussycat* (1997–98), revisits the concept of the unlimited, but with a looser line. Here, a conglomeration of looping forms not only seems as if it could be extended indefinitely but, especially when seen from afar, challenges the viewer's ability to judge its scale, thus introducing a further level of instability. *I thought I saw a pussycat*, like much of Larner's more recent work, brings together ambiguous line and ambiguous blue-green color to create a work that is simultaneously very present in the space yet puzzlingly difficult to pin down. It is in fact rather like the cartoon character Tweety Bird, whose signature

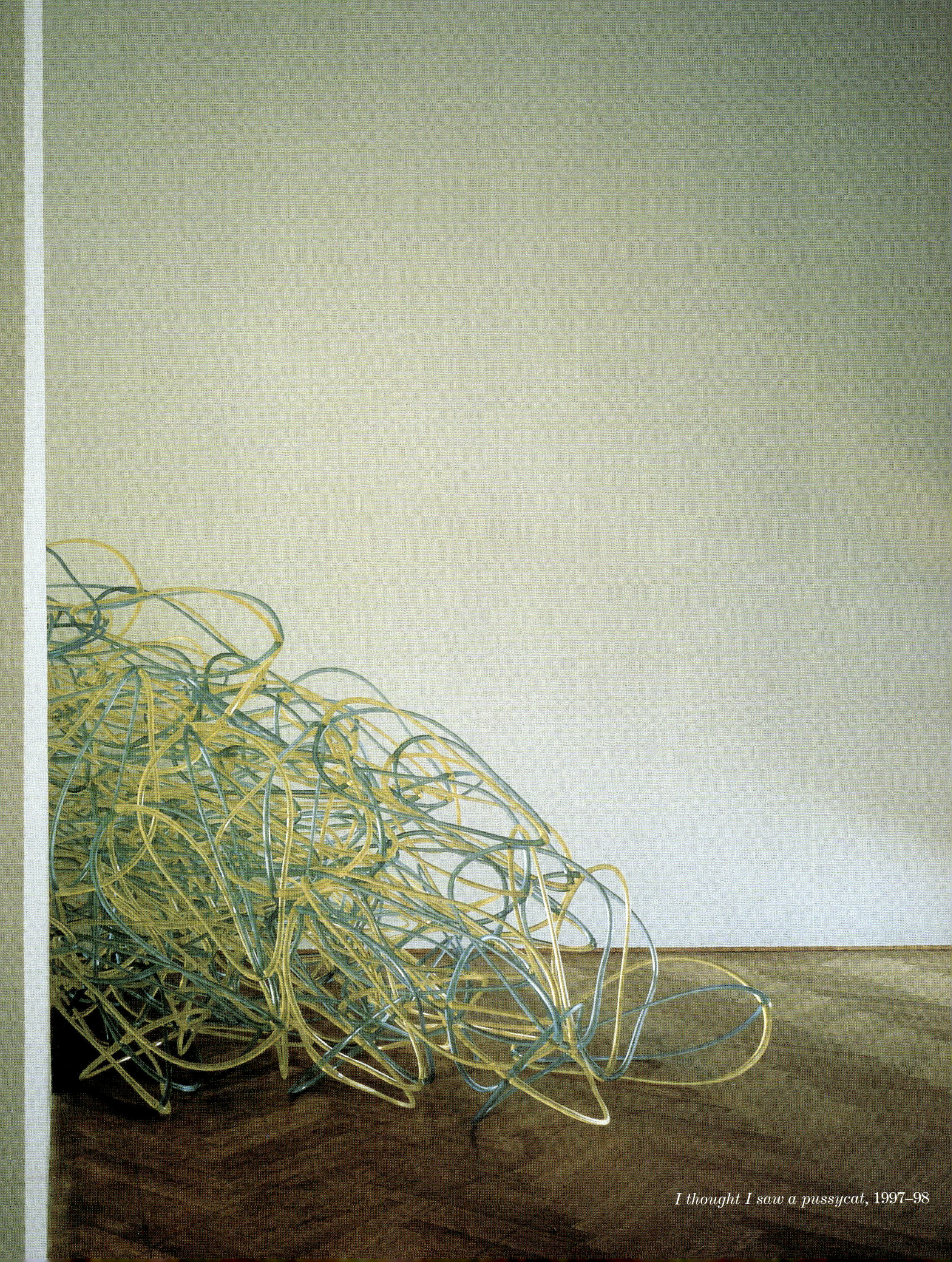

I thought I saw a pussycat, 1997–98

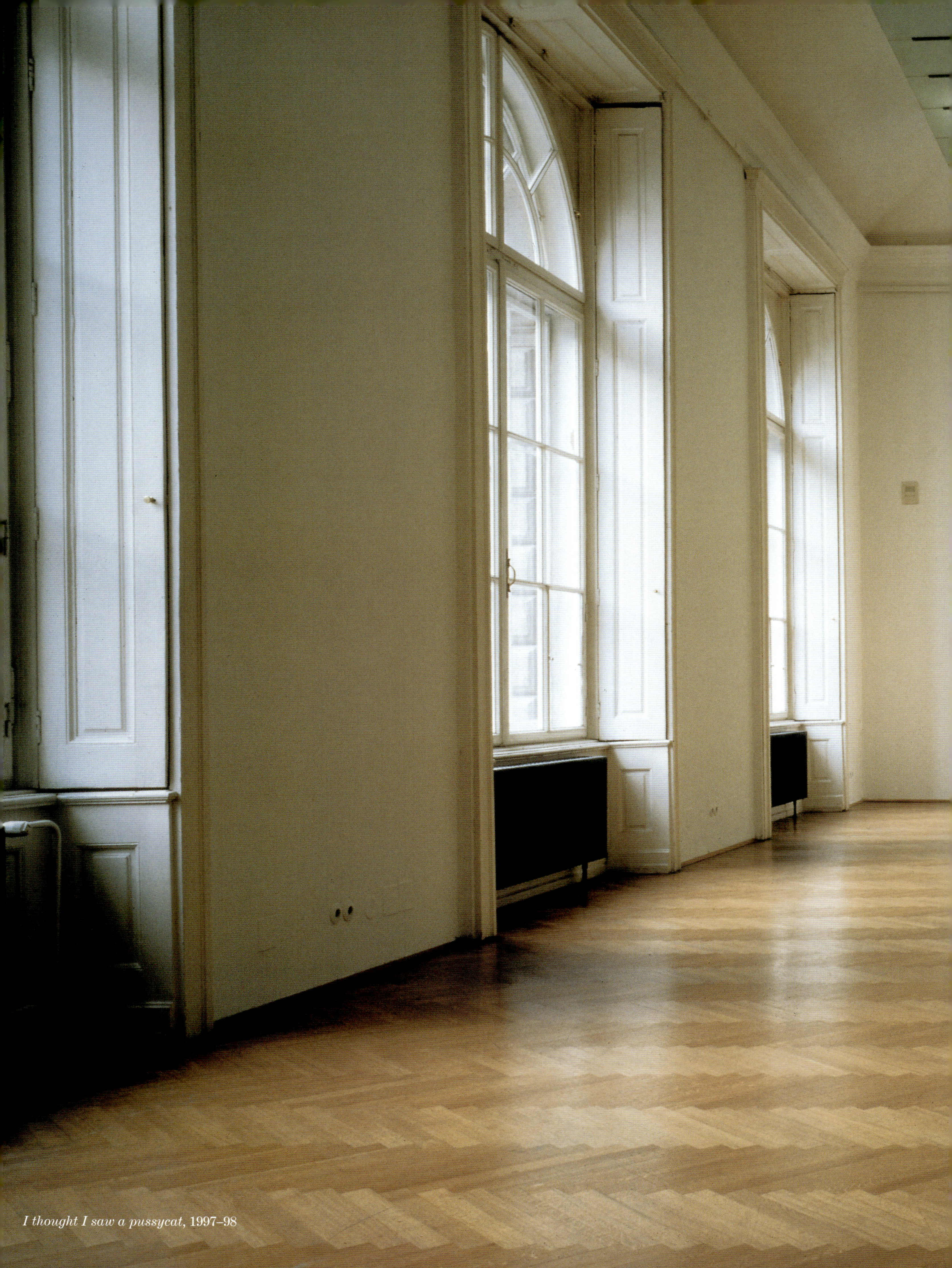

I thought I saw a pussycat, 1997–98

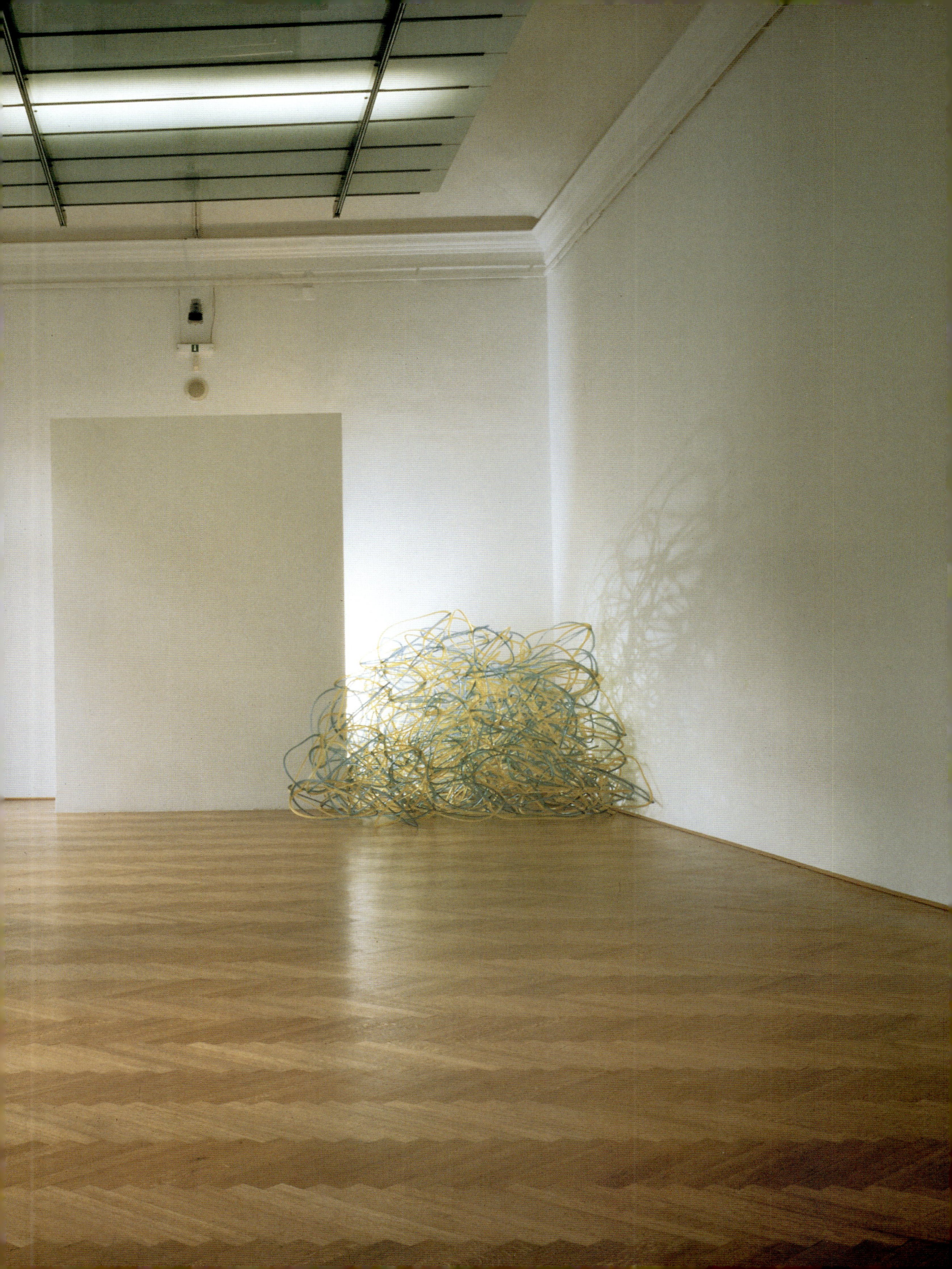

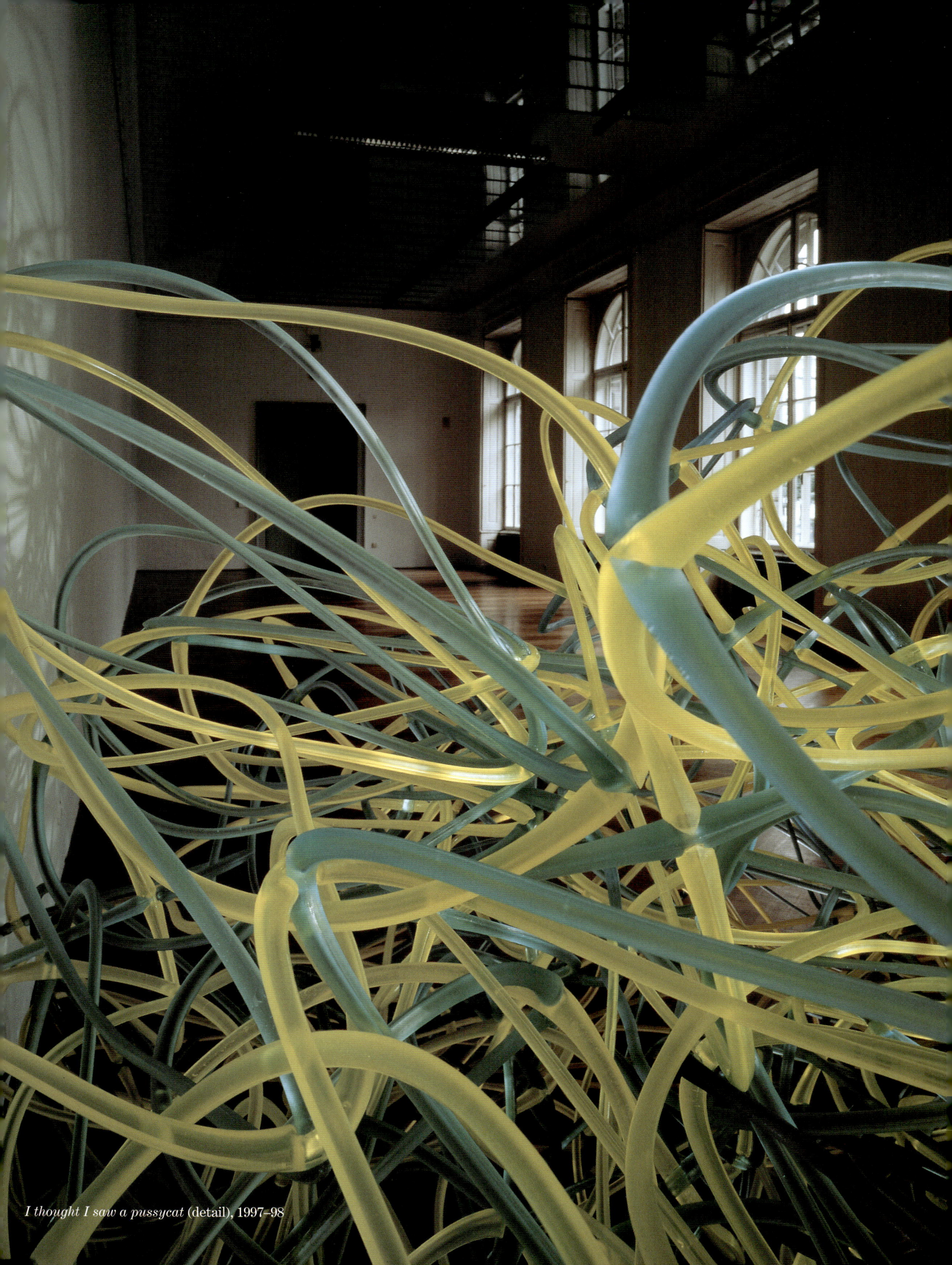

I thought I saw a pussycat (detail), 1997–98

phrase gives the work its title. For his nemesis Sylvester, Tweety Bird is always very much present, yet slippery and hard to grasp. The piece is actually quite rigid, as its components are cast in a hard, translucent polyurethane, but it is often perceived as soft and pliable.

Larner's use of line to create volume constantly tempts critics to discuss her work in terms of drawing, but it is mistaken to imagine drawing itself to be the departure point for her sculpture. Comparisons, often made, to the calligraphic paintings of Brice Marden are frustrating to her. "I can see it, but it makes me feel sad," she says. "It makes me feel that people aren't getting this. It freaks me out if people are seeing my work as a kind of picture. Because that is precisely what my work does not do. Marden's work is profoundly flat; it's profoundly about the fact that you can't get on the other side." At the same time, she recognizes that "There is something in the way the sculptures look that does look like drawing—the way a kind of pressure

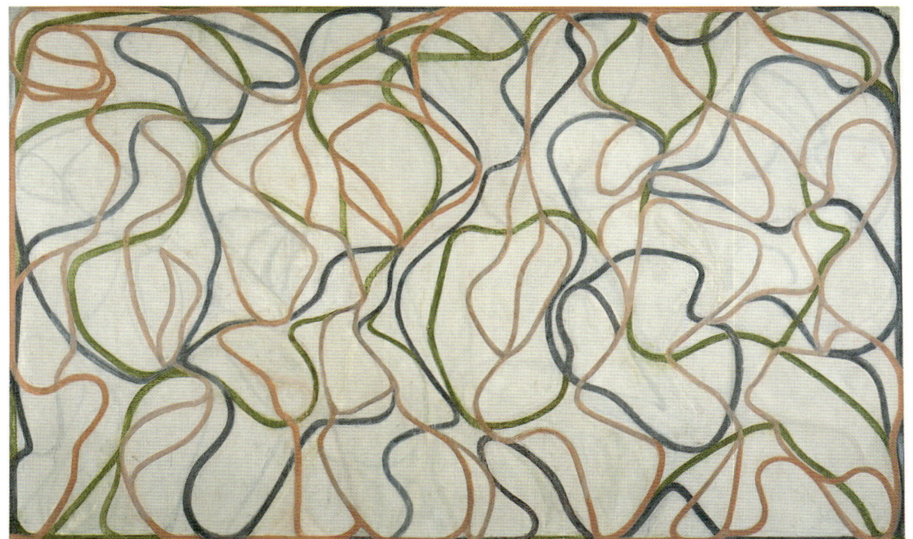

Brice Marden, Study for the Muses (Eaglesmere Version), 1991–94/1997–99

can make the drawn line thicker or thinner. The relationship is there, but I see it more in terms of the thickness or thinness creating a space inside the space that the thing exists in. That space might be contrary to what you would have initially perceived it as if it were blocked out as something massive." Line is thus primarily a way of articulating real space, rather than the creation of any kind of illusionistic space on a flat surface. "It's easy to be illusionistic in drawing," she says. "It's harder in non-representational sculpture." Larner does make drawings herself, but they are mostly planning drawings, technical and color studies for work that remains fundamentally sculptural.

Sometimes line becomes a way to generate planes without mass, without any sense of solidity. This is perhaps most evident in the series of works that make use of metal chains. In some ways Larner's chain pieces are actually the most related to drawing of all her sculpture,

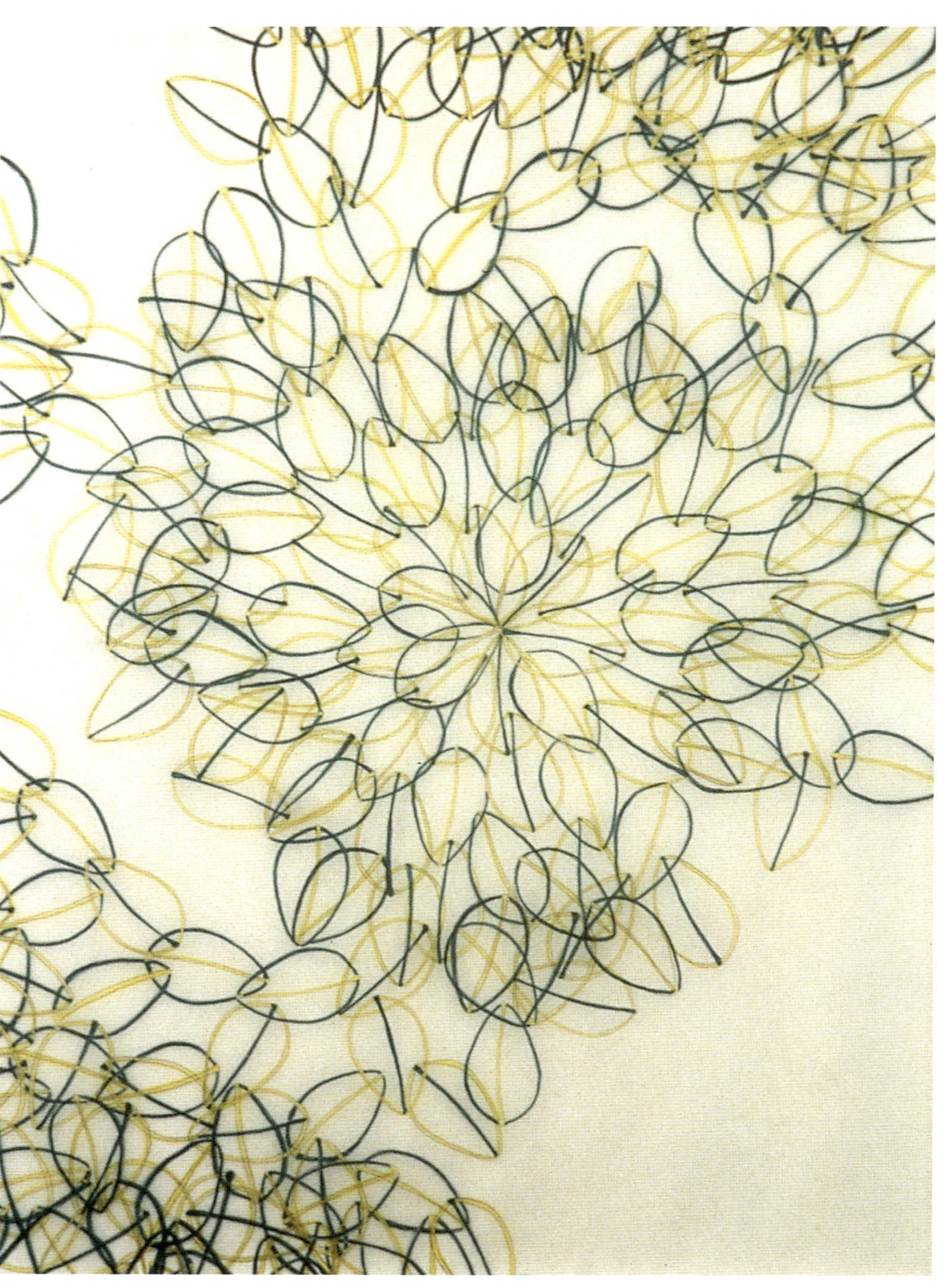

Untitled, 1998

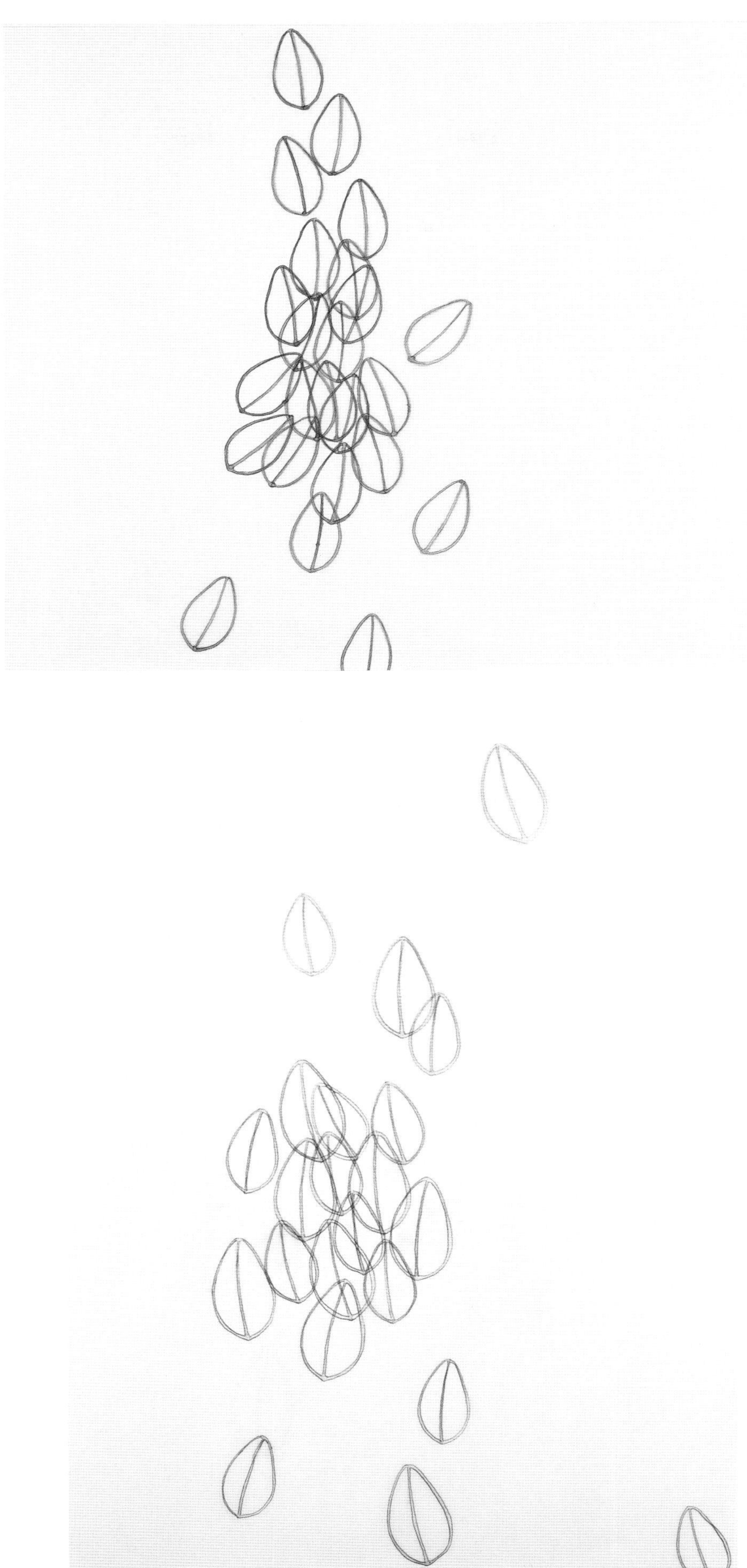

both: *Untitled*, 1999

even though they are also in some ways the most rigid, as high tension converts the formless but strong chains into straight lines. The steel of the chains is also about as close to colorless as Larner gets, again echoing the more or less neutral graphite of a drawn line. In pieces such as *Chain Perspective Reflected* (1990) or its successor, *Forced Perspective (reversed, reflected, extended)* (1992), the chains mark out the contours of real space with the authority of an architect's pencil delineating hypothetical space. They exude the same combination of the ideal and the authoritative that characterizes architectural renderings. Yet at the same time, unlike any drawing, Larner's chains are not at all hypothetical. They really do impose themselves on the viewer's ability to perceive and experience the three-dimensional space that both the chains and the viewer occupy. The use of chains as both chains and lines simultaneously enables Larner to define all the boundaries of the perceived space, yet at the same time have it remain completely permeable. In the case of *Forced Perspective*, a vanishing point remains, but the grid that describes it is reversed. The room in which the work exists begins to seem unrelated to the space within the perspectival grid. The space becomes not merely permeable but almost mobile, seeming to move back and forth depending on the changing position of the viewer. As Kirby Gookin has pointed out, however, the mobility of the viewer is controlled by the parameters of the work: "The first openings are wide enough to accommodate the viewer and invite one to enter the described volume. Because the perspectival recession is constructed rather than illusionistic, however, one's progress is soon thwarted, and a feeling of bodily entanglement and constriction becomes palpable as one proceeds."[10] Larner demonstrates that an overwhelmingly

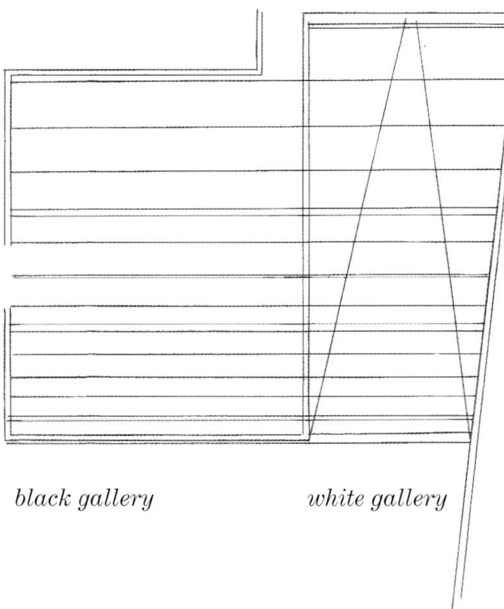

Floor plan of *Forced Perspective (reversed, reflected, extended)*
installation in "Helter Skelter"
The Museum of Contemporary Art, Los Angeles, 1992

opposite top: *Chain Perspective Reflected*, 1990
bottom: *Forced Perspective (reversed, reflected, extended)*, 1992

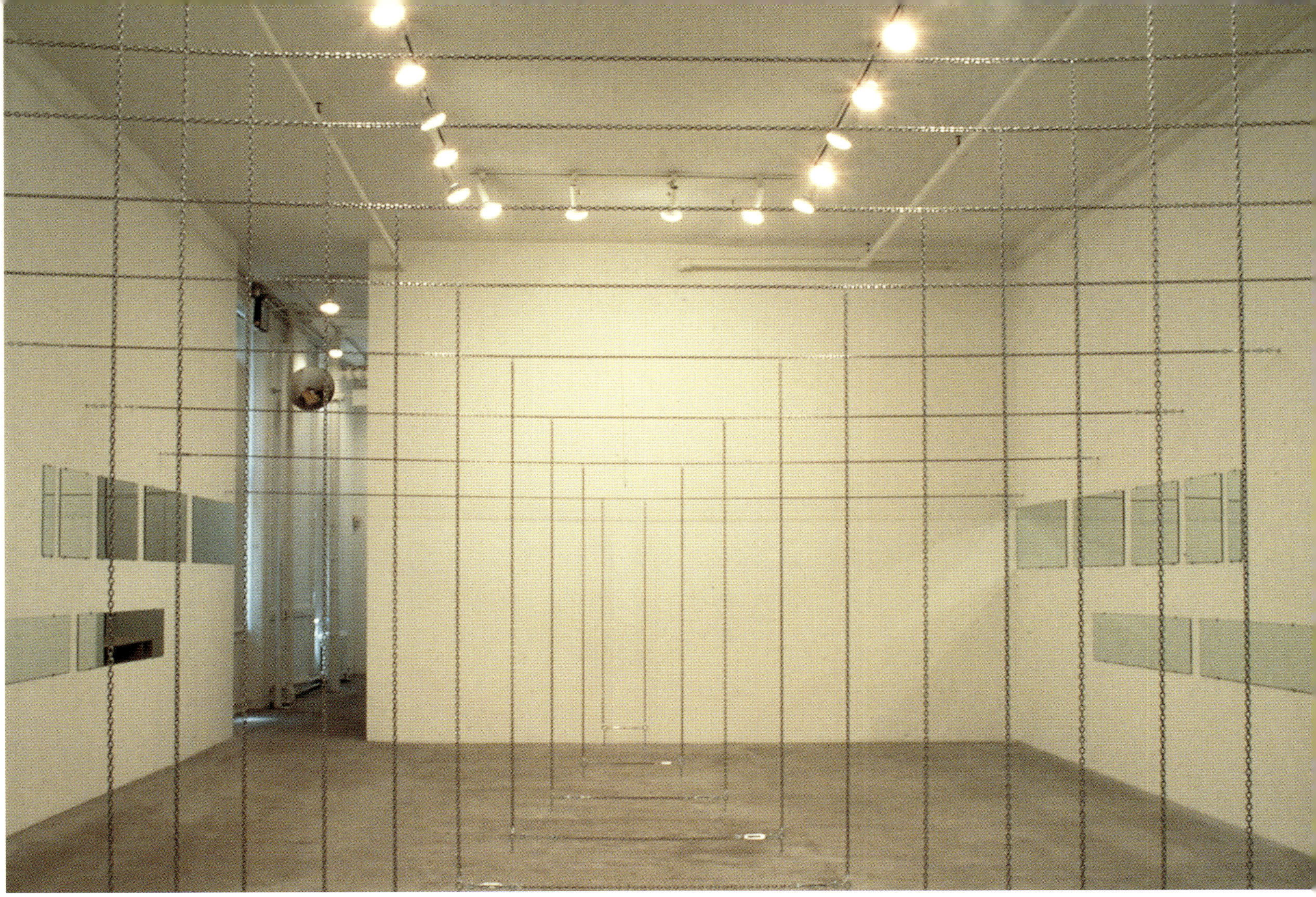

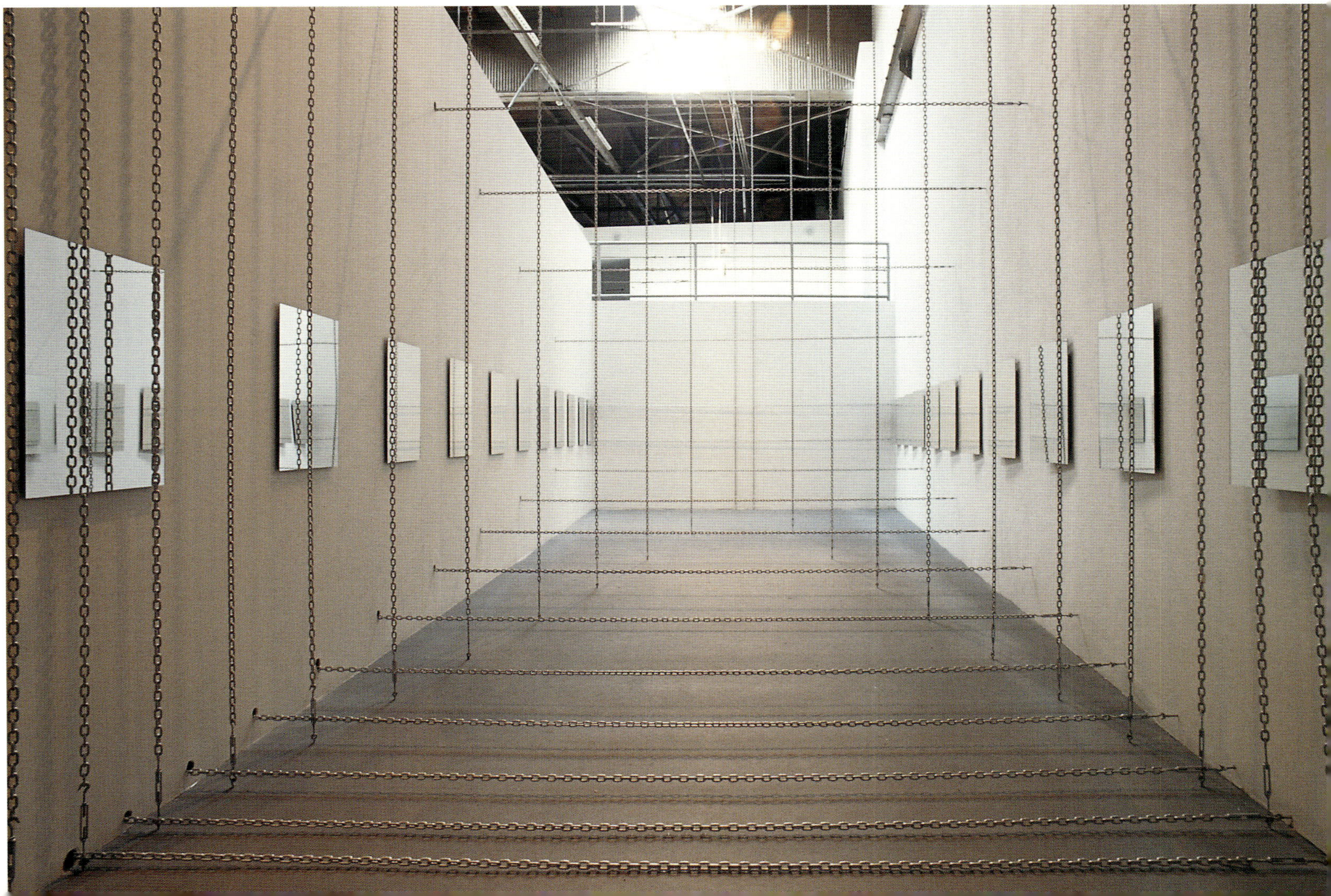

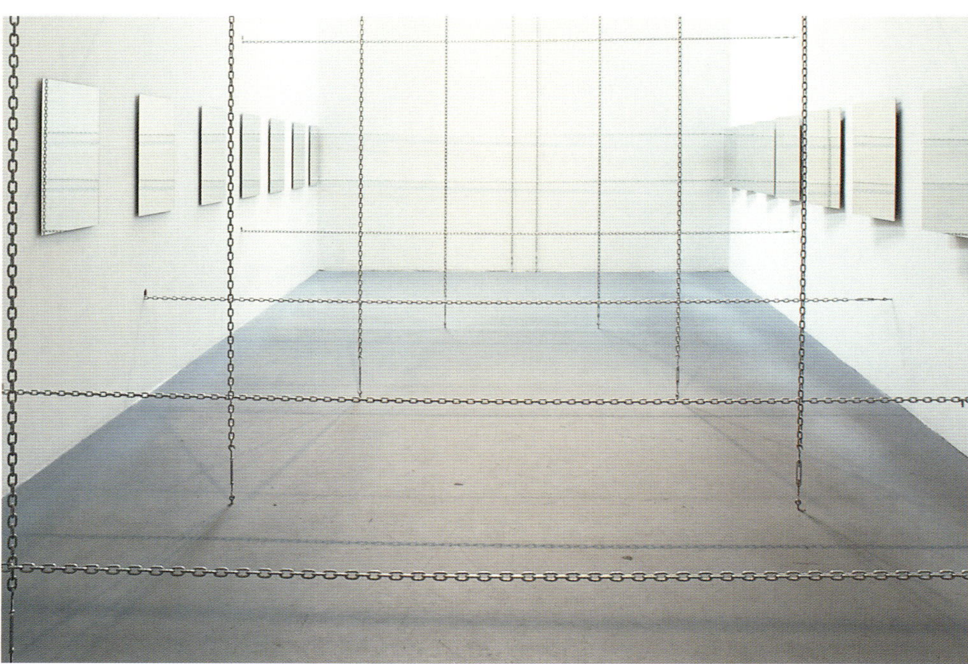

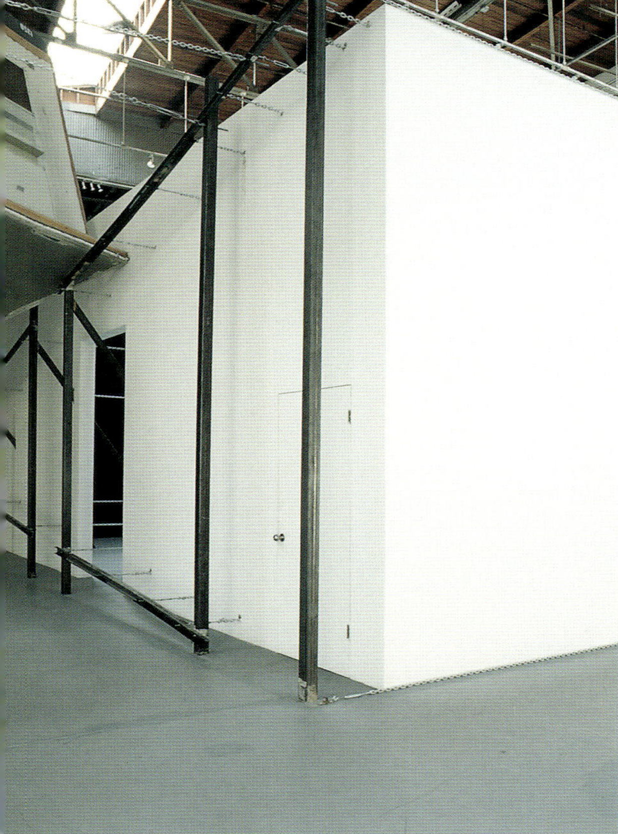

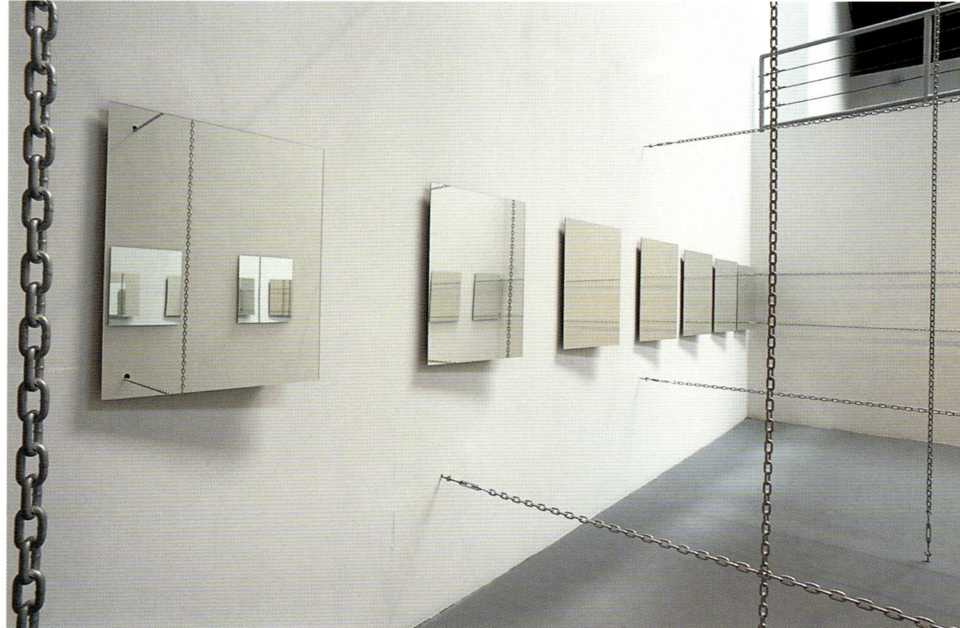

Forced Perspective (reversed, reflected, extended), 1992

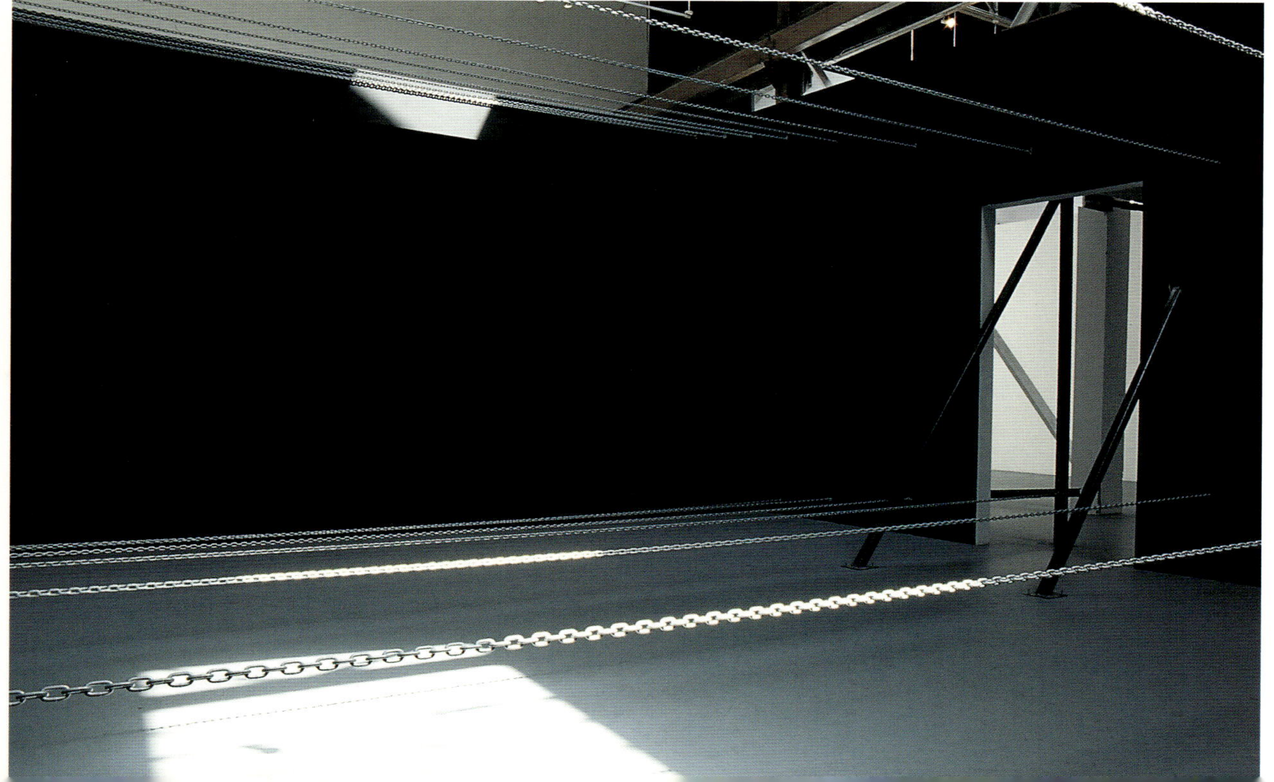

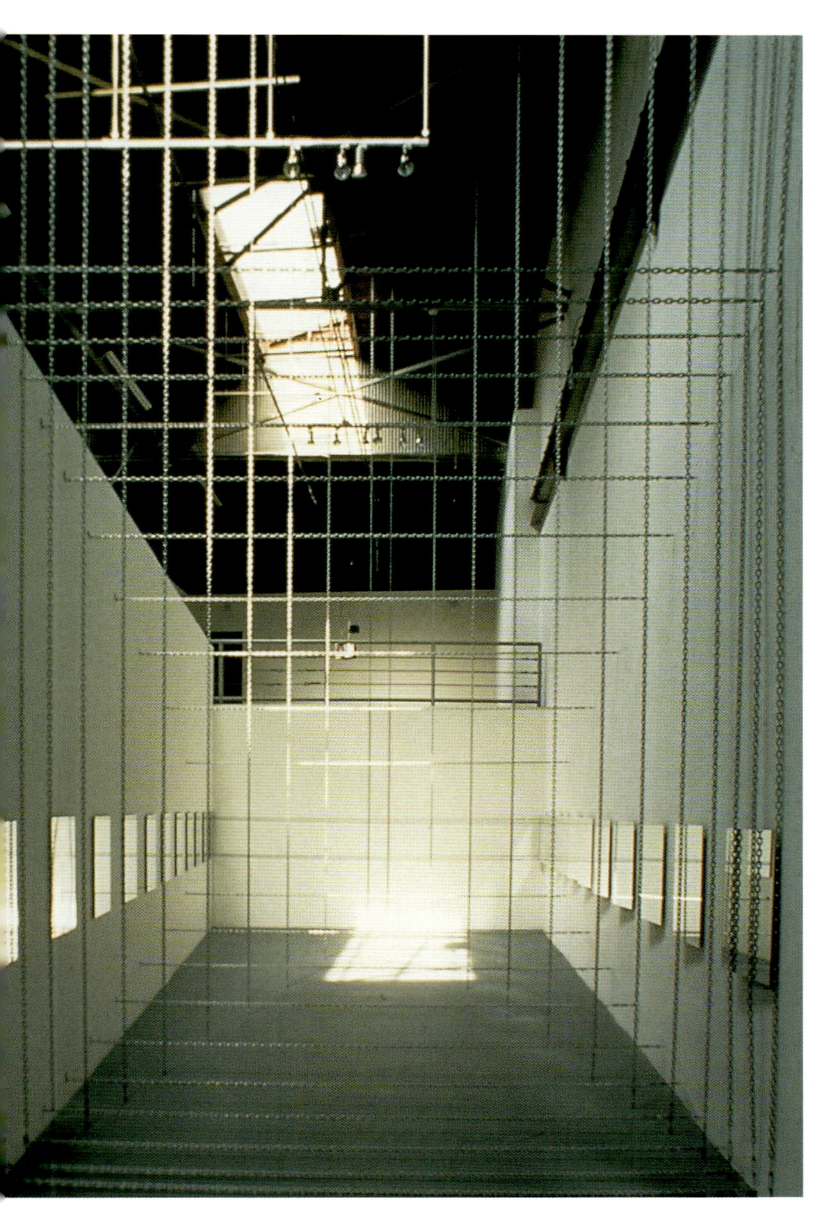
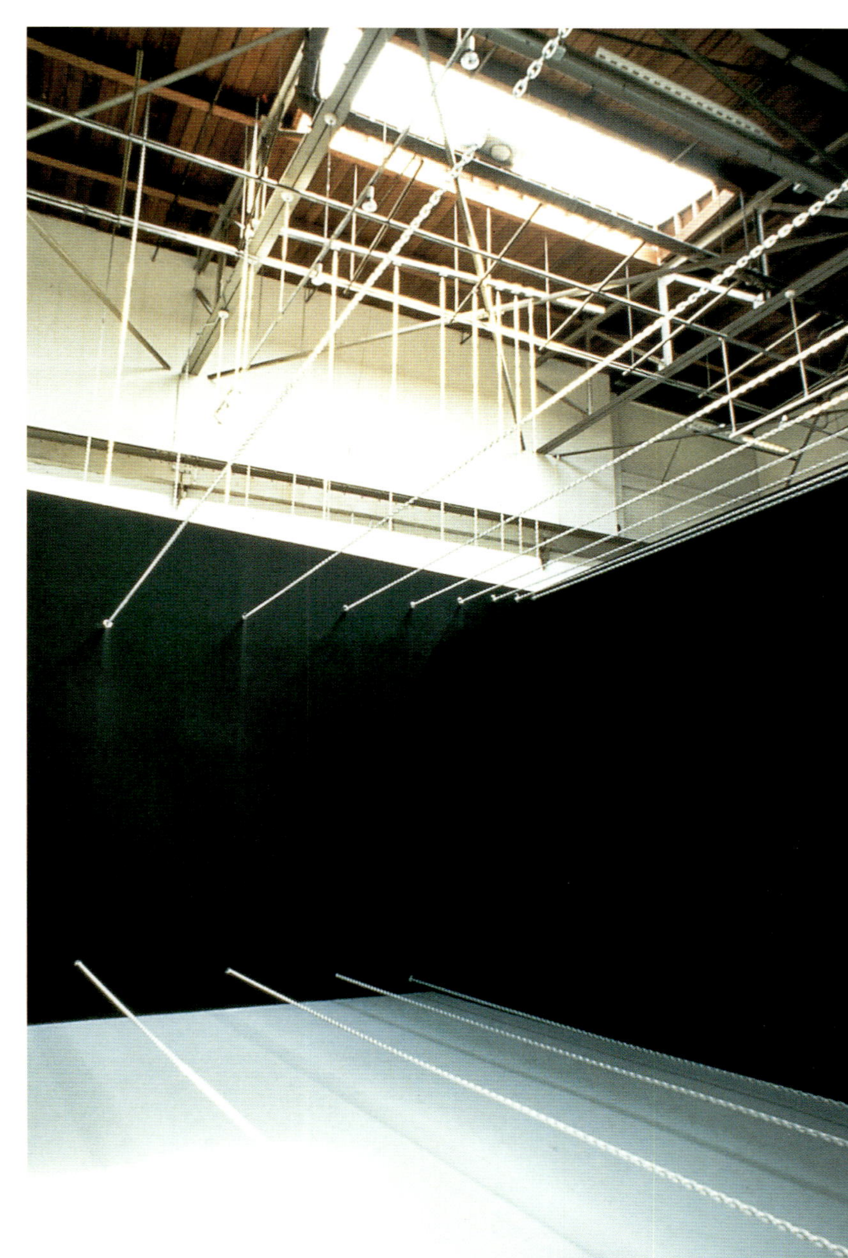
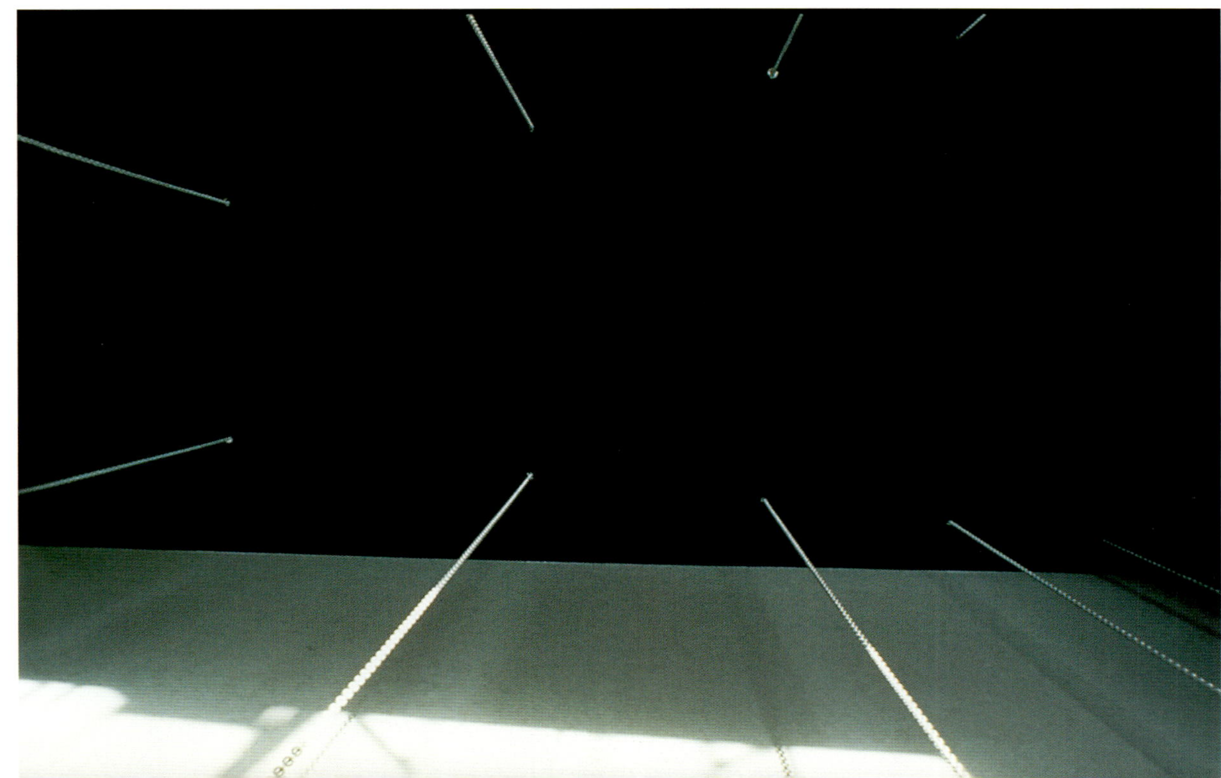

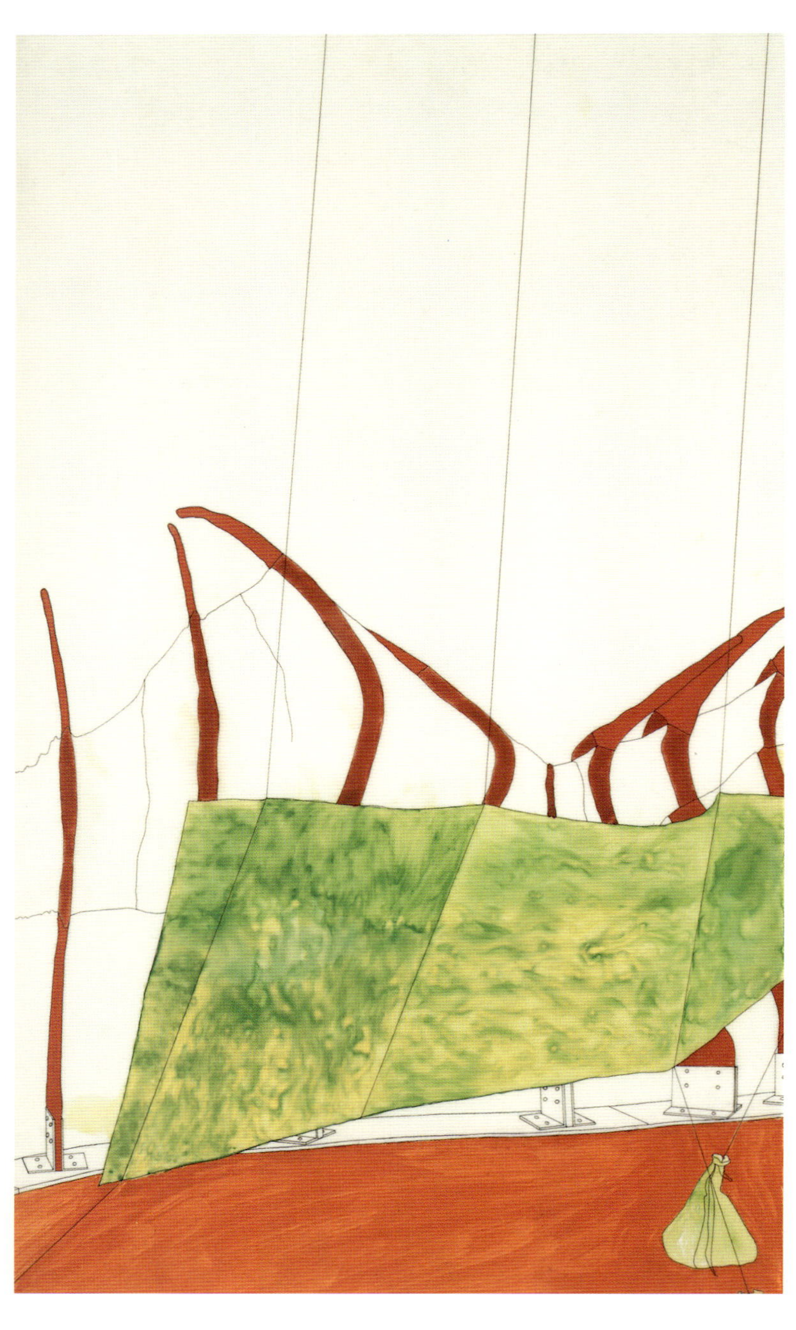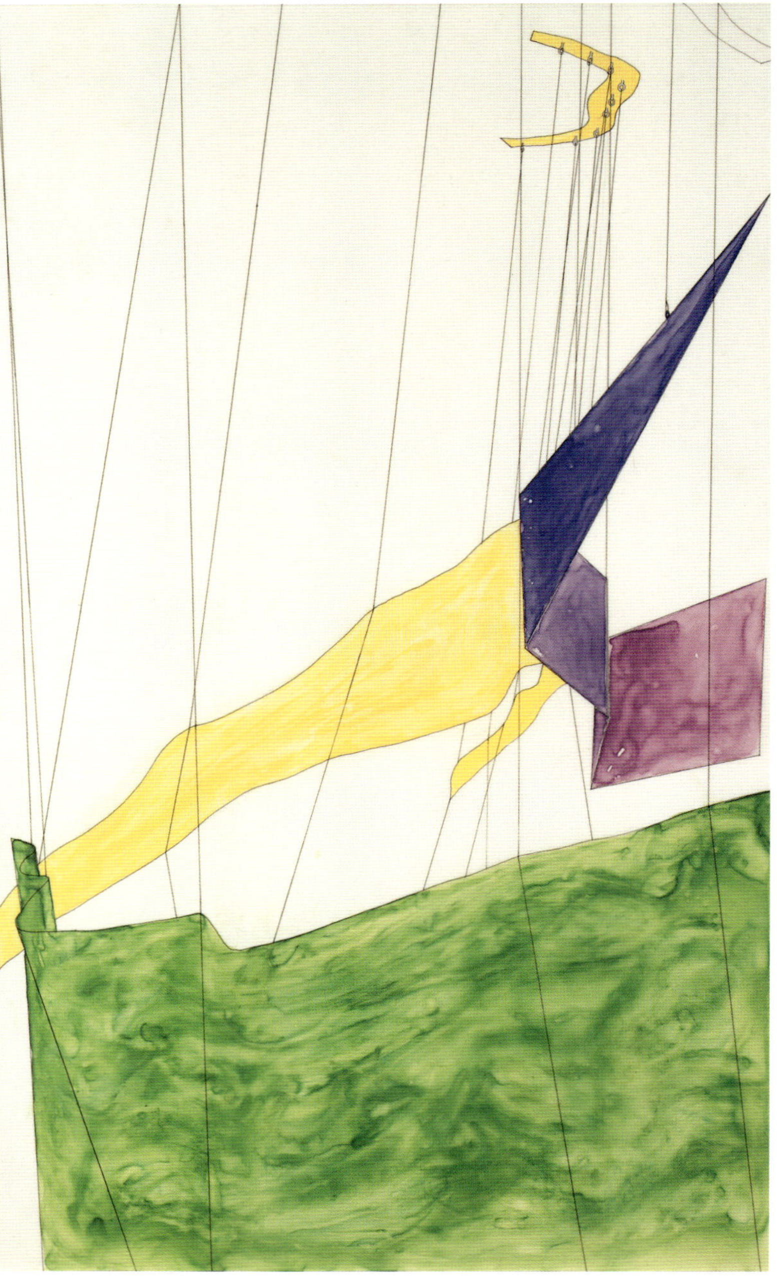

both: *Untitled (Study for Corridors)*, 1990–91

linear construction can take command of a given space without relying on weight or mass.

Line is not Larner's only weapon against monumentality. She also makes use of color to achieve her ends. Color has been a particularly fraught issue for sculpture, caught up in arguments about "pure" form that can be traced at least as far back as neo-classicism and the mistaken view that ancient Greek and Roman sculpture was without color. David Batchelor, in his book *Chromophobia*, traces a long history of "attempts to purge color from culture." He identifies two main ways that the purge has been accomplished:

> In the first, color is made out to be the property of some "foreign" body—usually the feminine, the oriental, the primitive, the infantile, the vulgar, the queer or the pathological. In the second, color is relegated to the realm of the superficial, the supplementary, the inessential or the cosmetic. In one, color is regarded as alien and therefore dangerous; in the other, it is perceived merely as a secondary quality of experience, and thus unworthy of serious consideration. Color is dangerous, or it is trivial, or it is both.[11]

Larner takes on both of these objections to color, and turns them to her advantage.

The aspects of color that are dismissed as "feminine" and so on are employed in conjunction with the debased materials of her culture pieces to heighten their rejection of traditional standards of form and appearance. As Larner describes it:

> Most of the cultures I've made contain three levels of differently colored nutrient media: one level red, one yellow, one blue. I inoculate the prepared plates with whatever it is I'm going to culture. In a day or two, bacteria begins to grow and feed off the nutrient media. When this happens, the colors start mixing wildly, and I get something like a miniature action painting.[12]

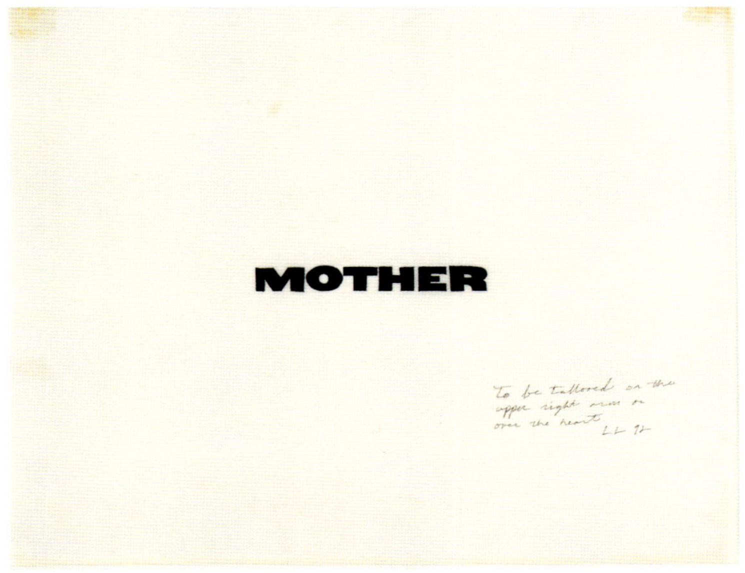

Mother (Tattoo Flash), 1992

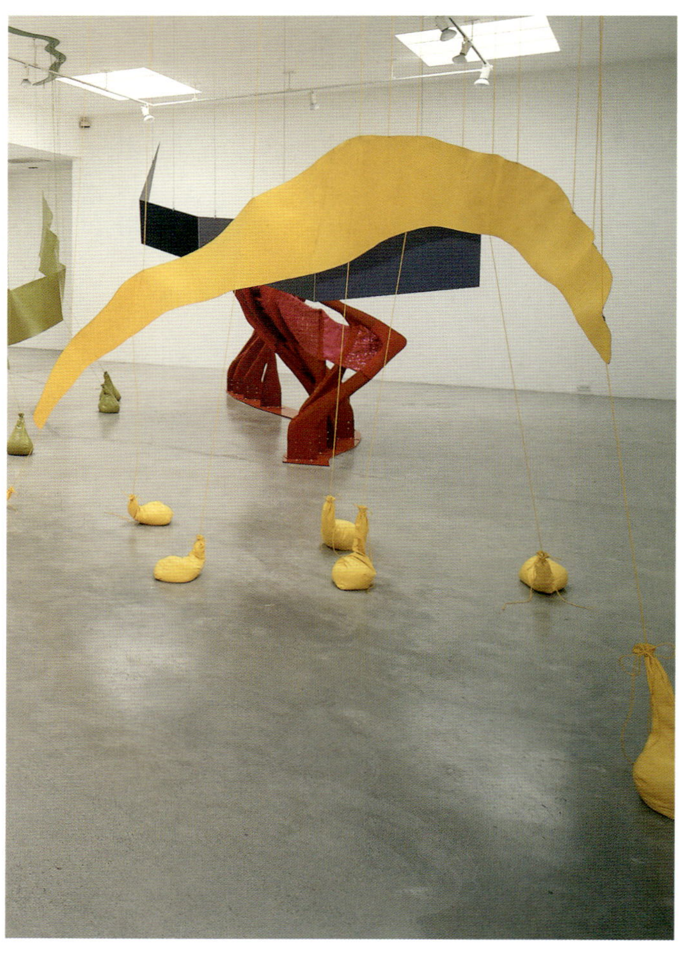

Corridor Yellow/Purple and *Corridor Red/Green*, 1991

She compares her culture pieces, generated at random by bacteria in a decaying culture of primary colors, to action painting, which is emblematic of the triumph of American art. This is evidence enough of the degree to which Larner's work can be read as hostile to established patterns of value. In terms of color, the wild mixing goes hand in hand with the formless, mutating culture itself to reinforce the work's status as a "foreign" entity: an anti-object object.

In sculpture, anti-color bias has been much stronger than in painting, and much of the argument against it derives from the second of Batchelor's two categories: color as "the superficial, the supplementary, the inessential or the cosmetic." Even sculptors who are widely recognized for their use of color, such as Anthony Caro, tend to make use of it largely in this way: as a kind of reinforcement for a more integral manipulation of structural form. Michael Fried, indeed, argued explicitly that there

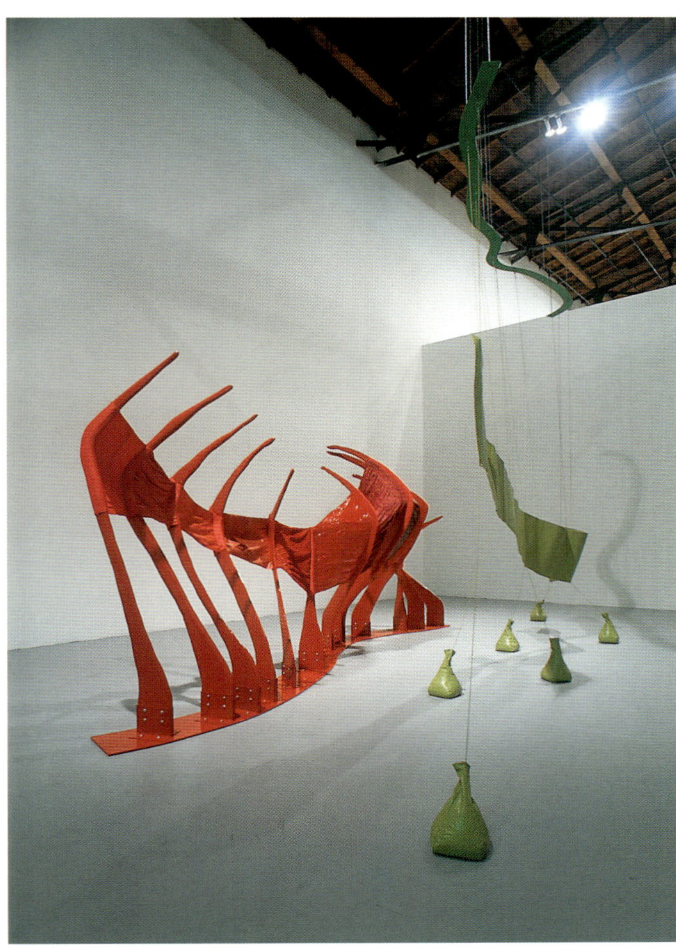

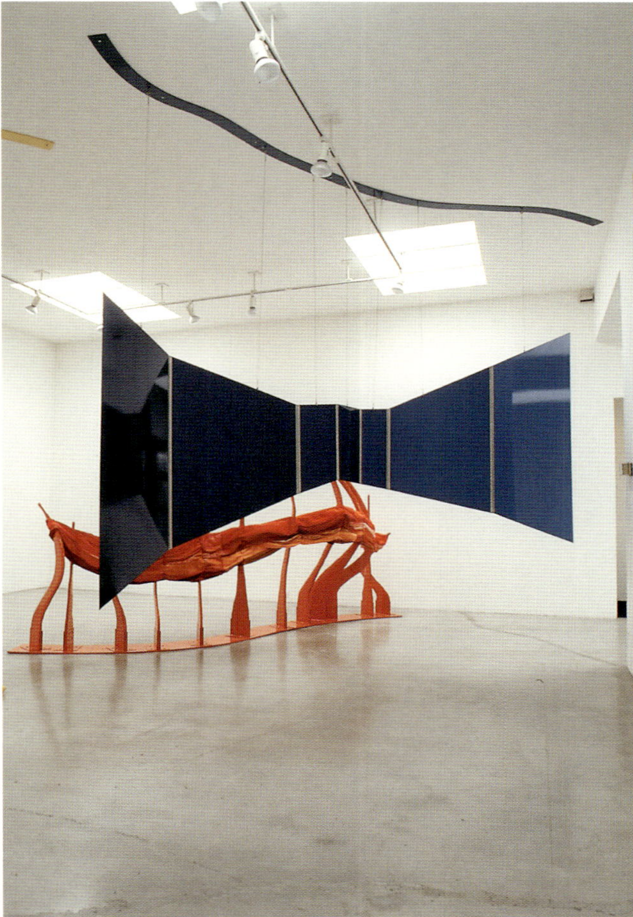

Corridor Red/Green, 1991   *Corridor Orange/Blue*, 1991

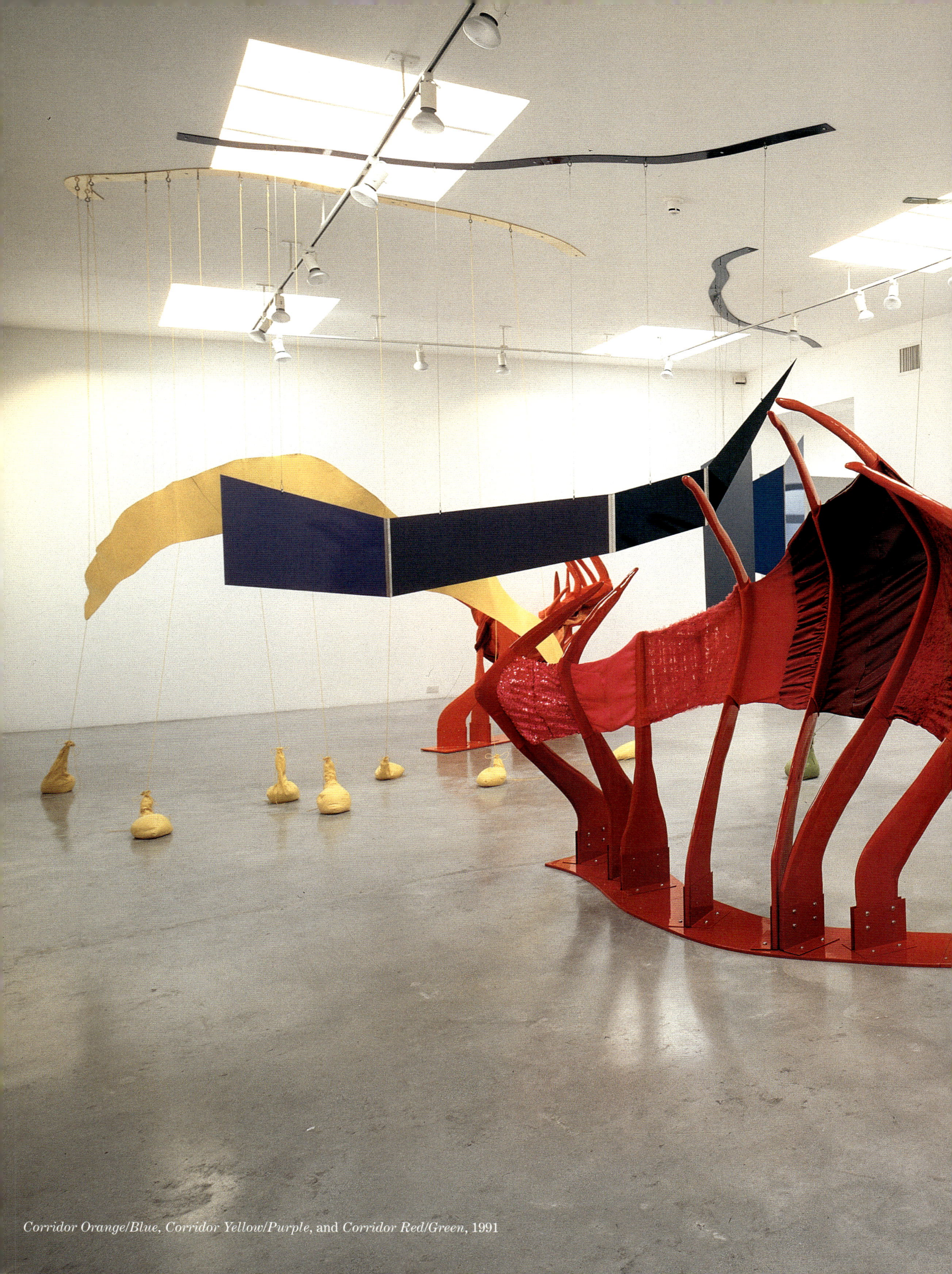

Corridor Orange/Blue, Corridor Yellow/Purple, and Corridor Red/Green, 1991

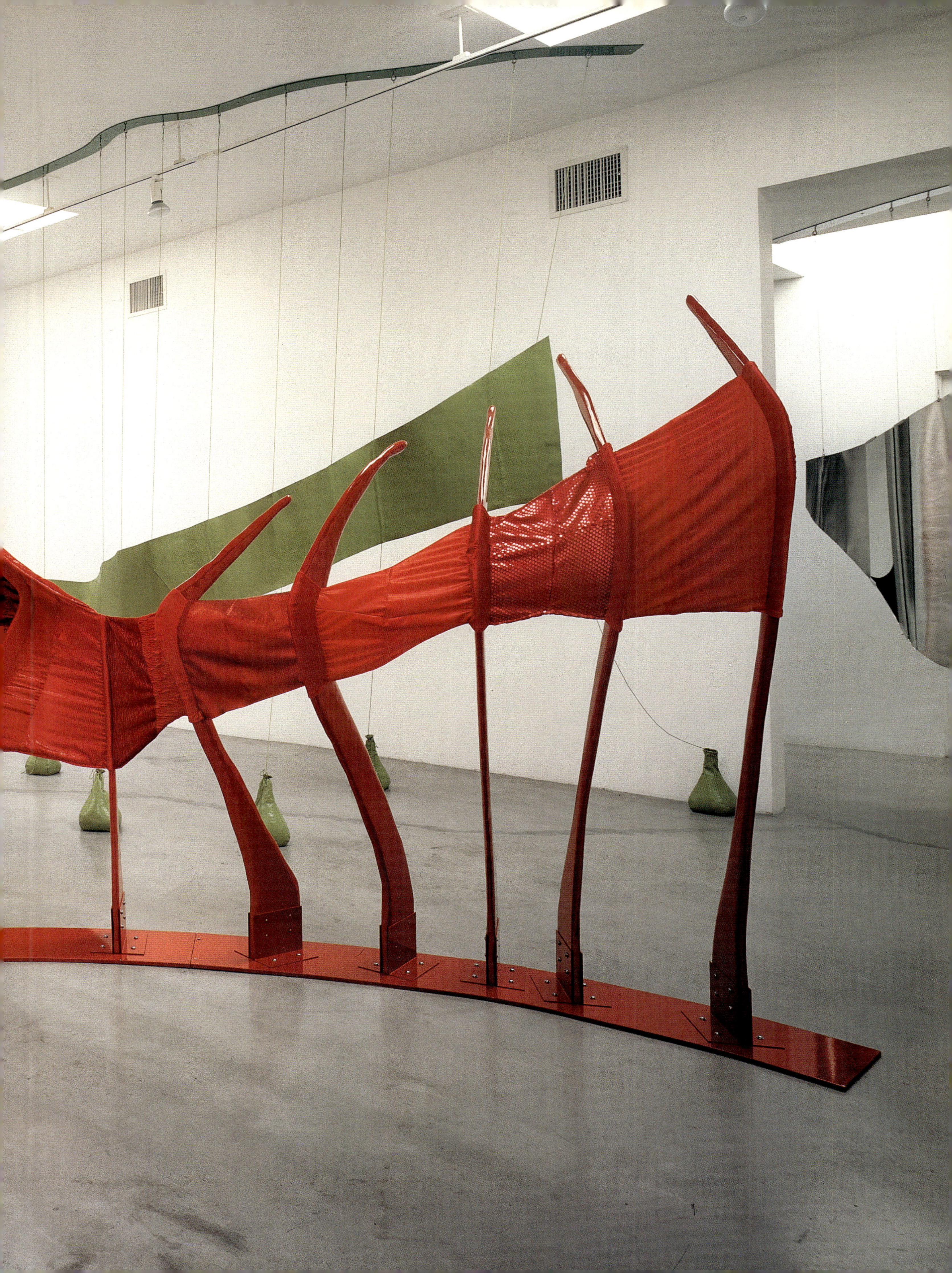

appears to be a deep, as it were natural affinity between applied color and planarity–between single colors and single planes. It is as if, under conditions of sculptural abstraction, a single plane emerges as the strongest, most direct, most convincing bearer or vehicle of a single applied color; or as if a single applied color turns out to declare a plane more strongly, directly, and convincingly than it is able to declare anything else. (As if indeed applied colors can't be said to "declare" other things so much as merely help distinguish them from yet other things or kinds of things.)[13]

The danger of treating color in sculpture in this way is the danger of pictorialism. As Rosalind Krauss wrote of Caro's work, "the color serves the aspect of the work that functions as image."[14] The suggestion that color can at best help to articulate and distinguish form, especially pictorial form, is one that Larner rejects. Even where planes of color appear in her work, as in her corridor pieces, they are severely undercut by flowing, clashing elements that mix soft and hard, biomorphic and geometric. For her, color in sculpture is not a kind of underlining or highlighting of a more fundamental structure, nor is it a move in the direction of the pictorial, which would be essentially two-dimensional. Larner is interested in color as a three-dimensional factor, an element with a value potentially equal to form itself. This is particularly evident in recent works such as *Devex Yellow* (1997), *2 as 3 and Some Too* (1997–98), *Ignis (Fake)* (1998–99), and *Surprisingly Nameless* (2000), although color has undeniably been important throughout her career. In pieces as otherwise varied as *Reticule* (1999) and *Untitled (wall)* (2000–01), Larner uses changing color to introduce an alternative structure to the works' apparent form. This other structure forms itself and collapses again in direct relationship to the

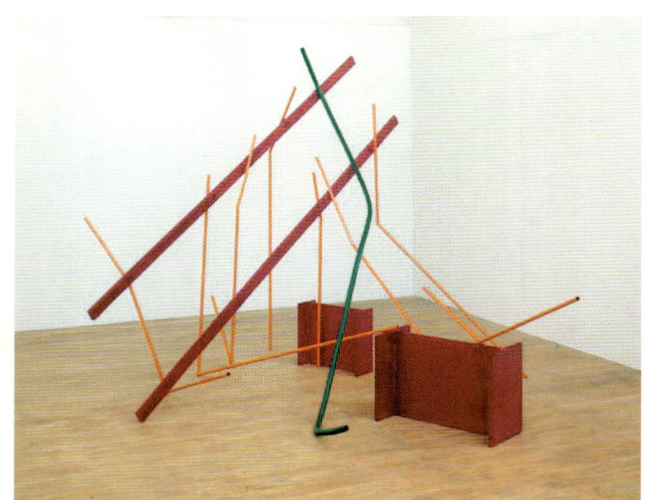

Anthony Caro, *Month of May*, 1963

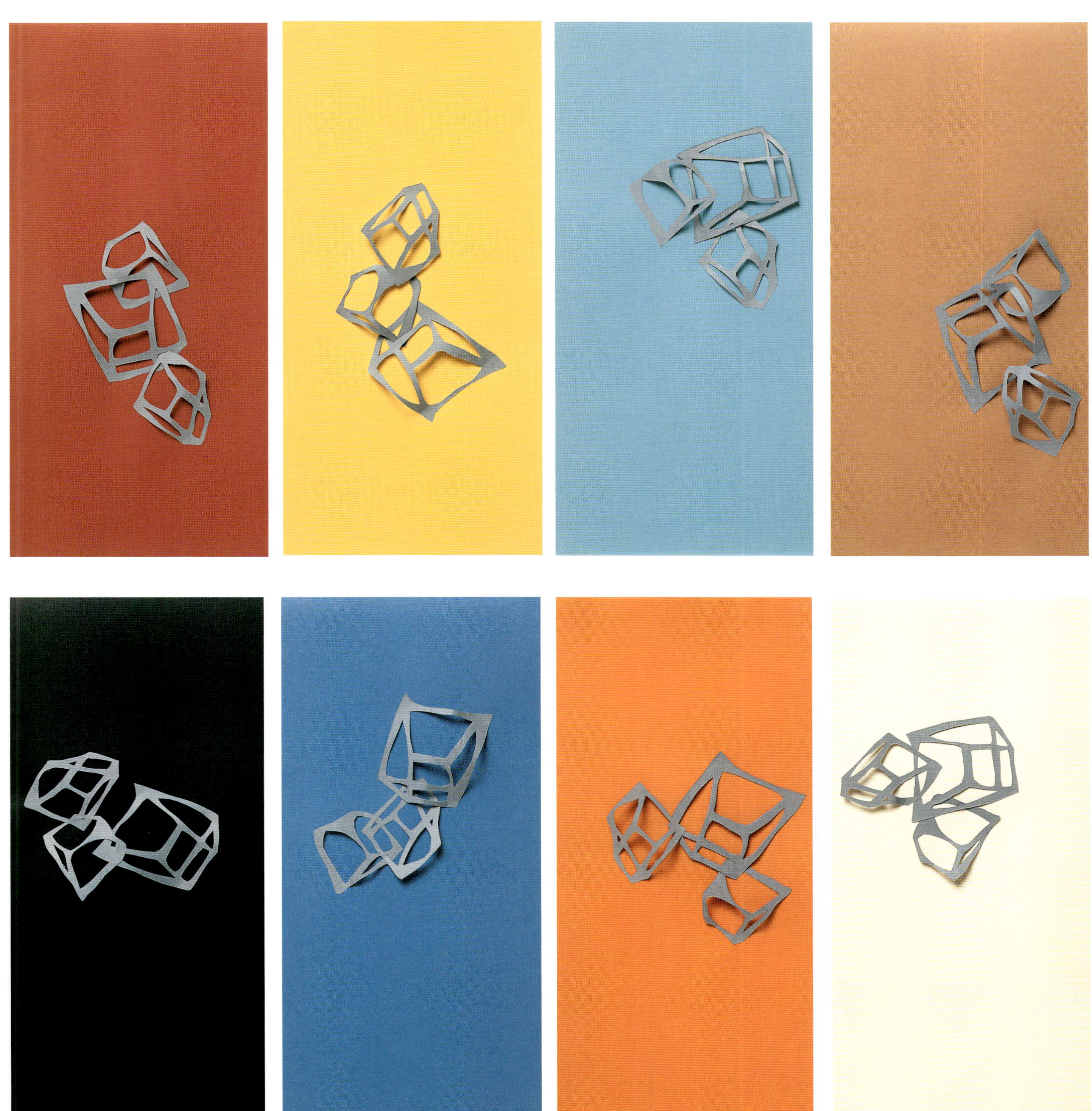

all: *Untitled (Study for 2 as 3 and Some)*, 1997

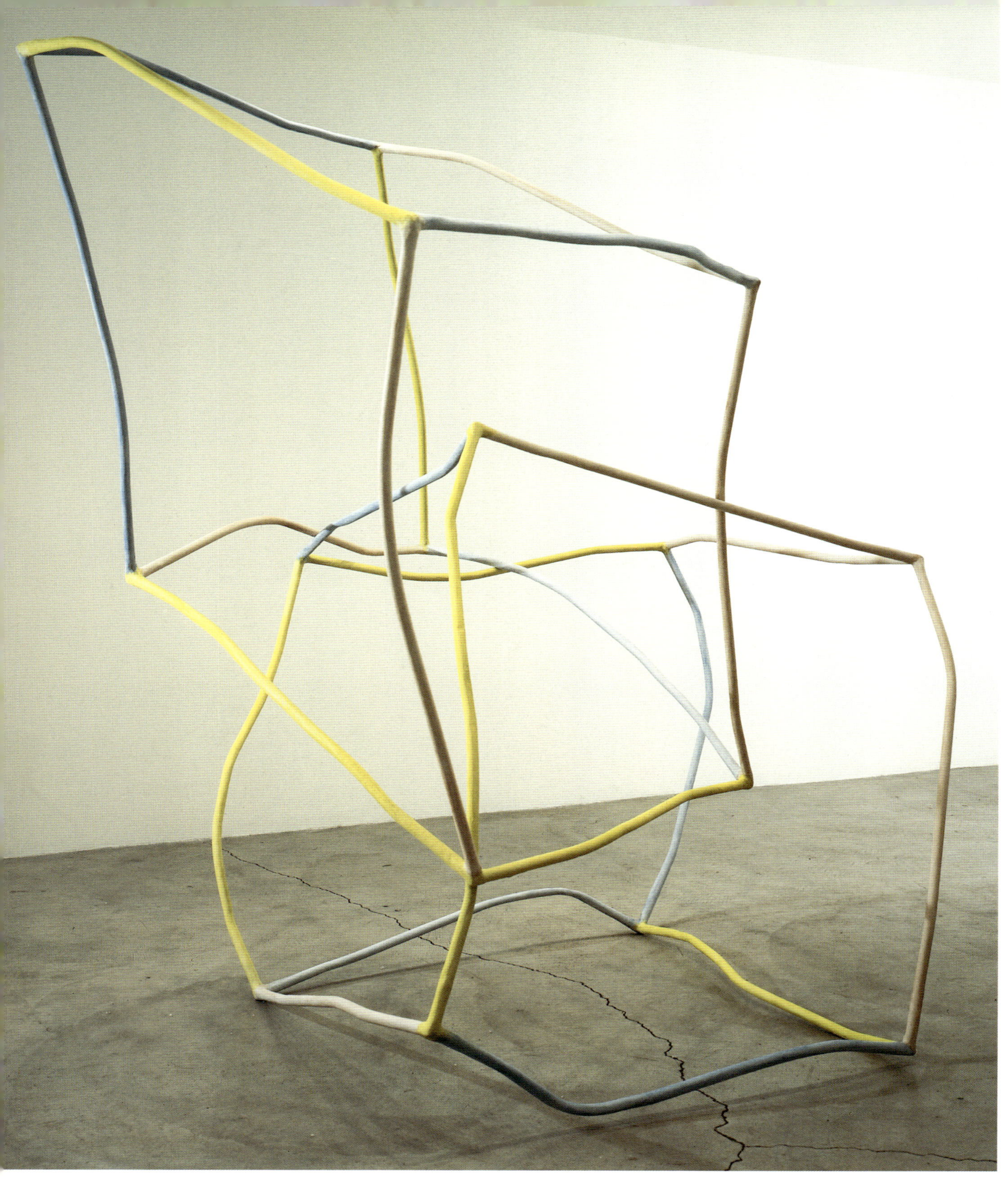

2 as 3 and Some Too, 1997–98

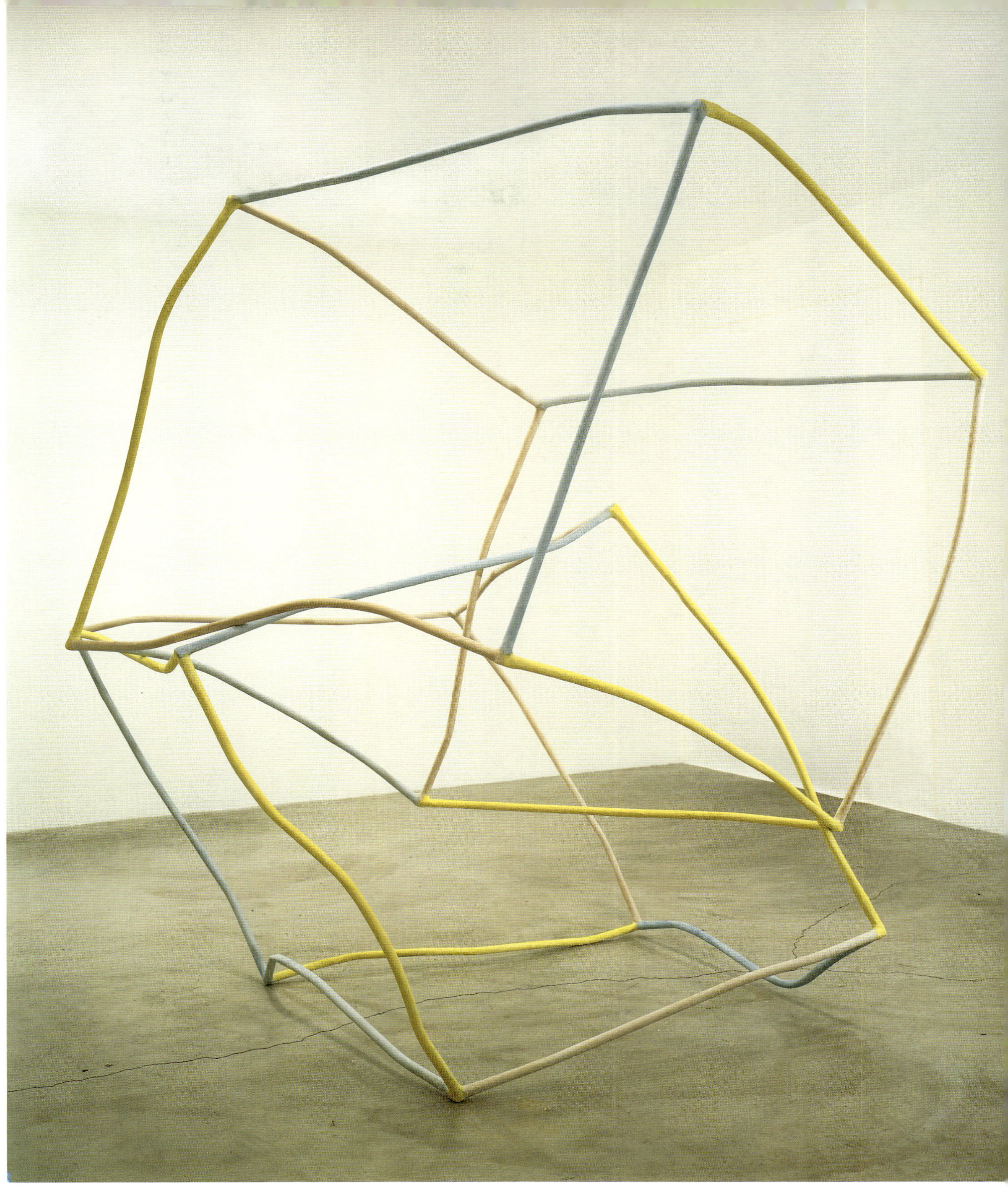

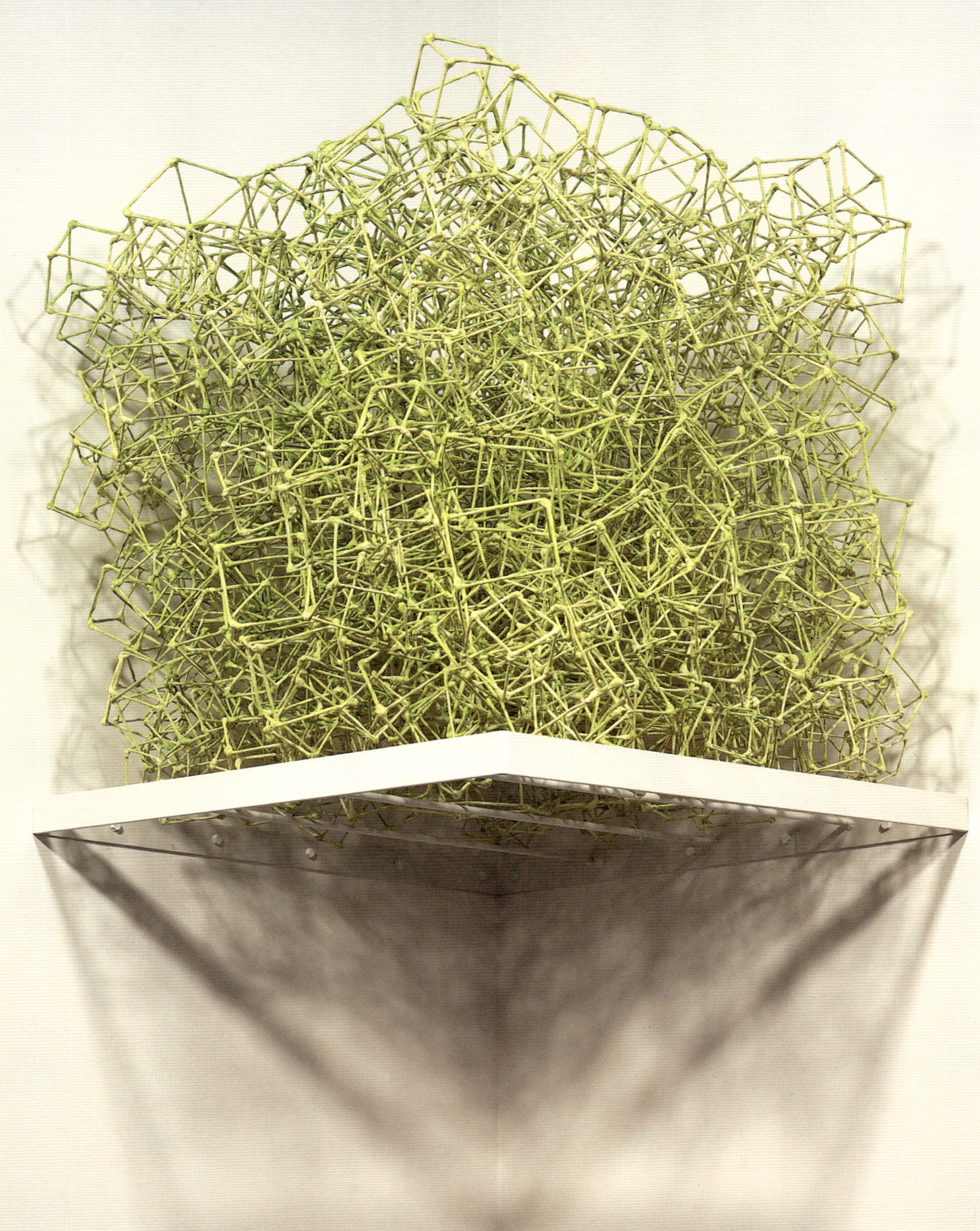

Ignis (Fake), 1998–99

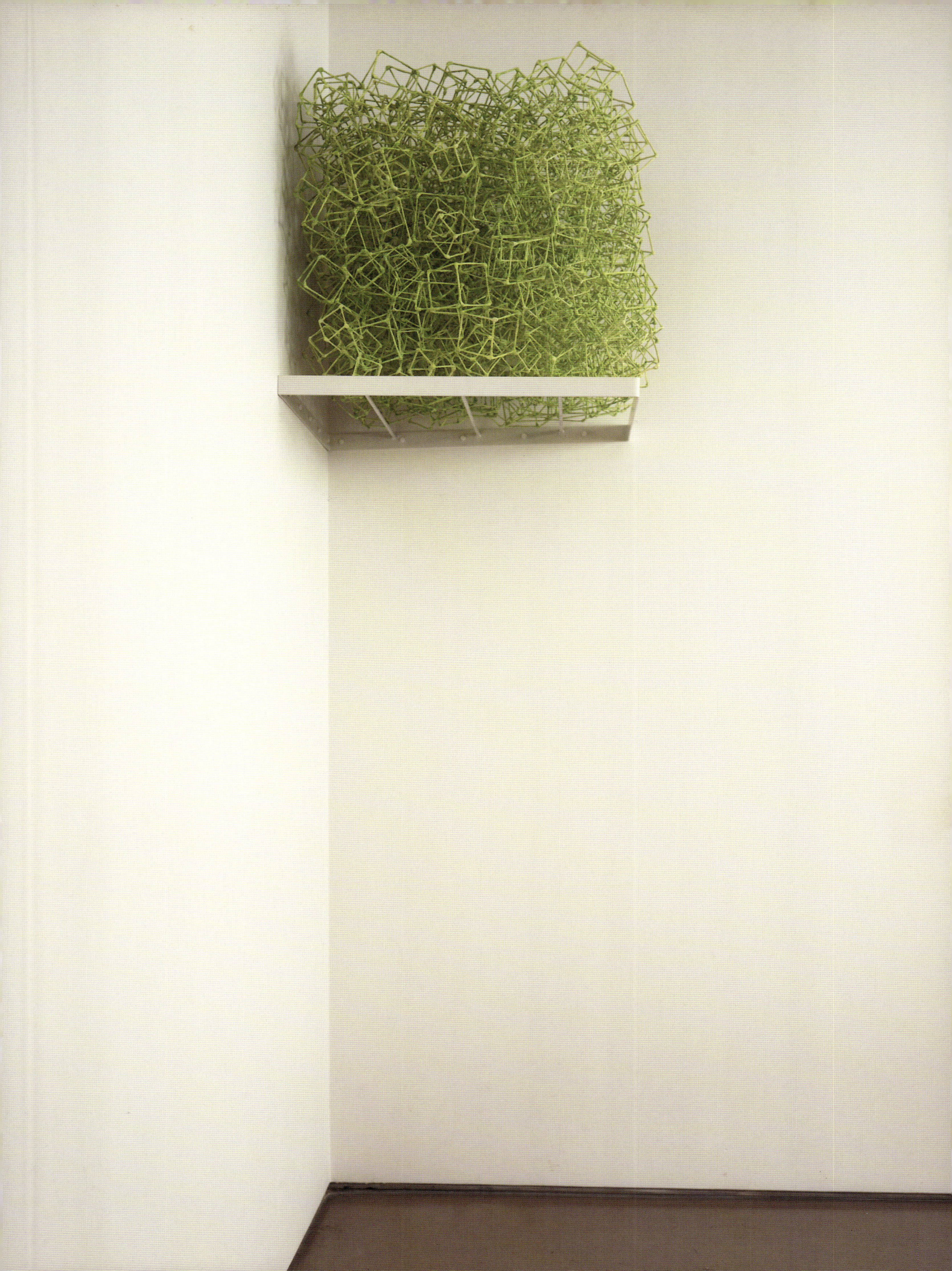

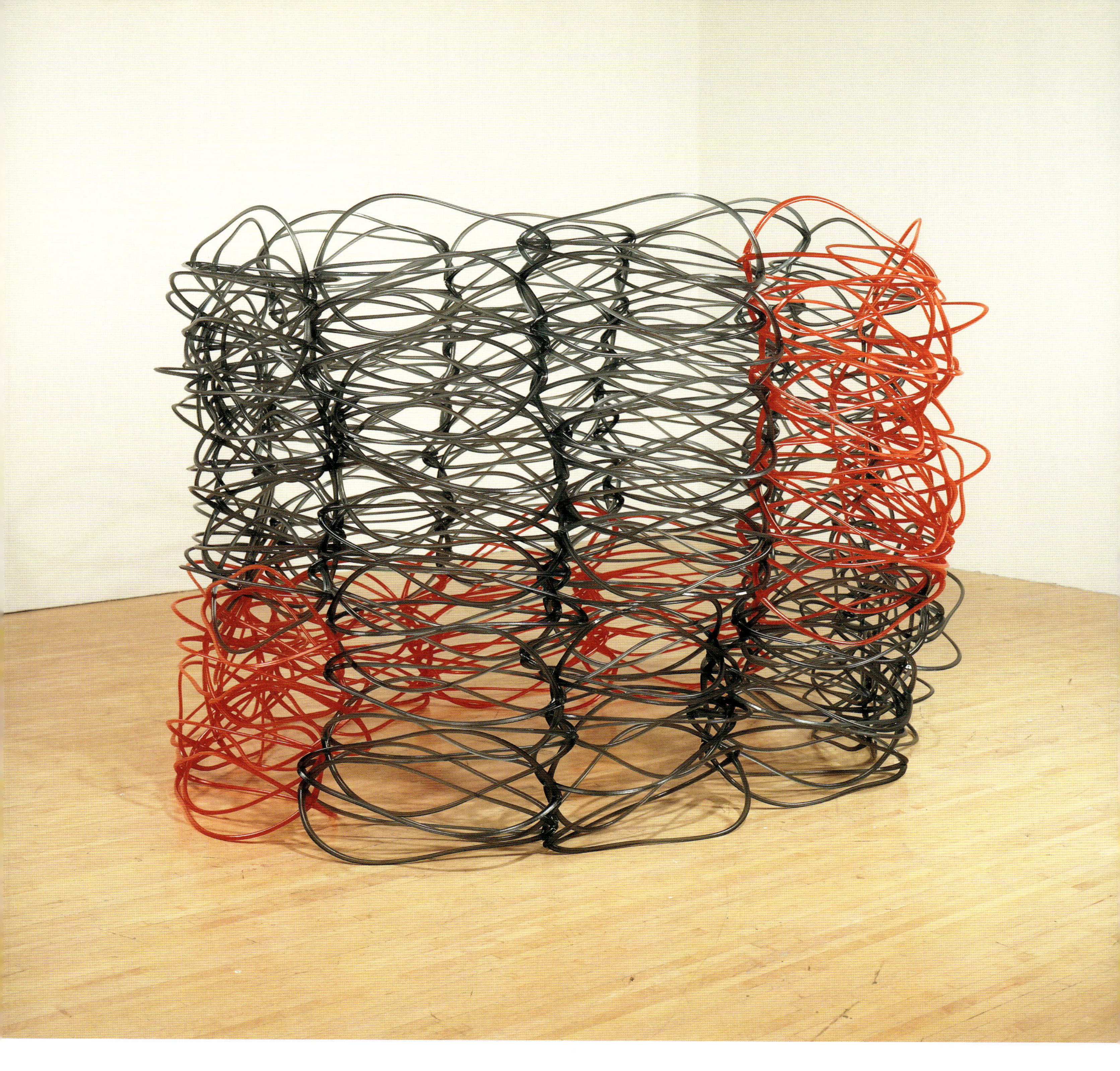

Reticule, 1999

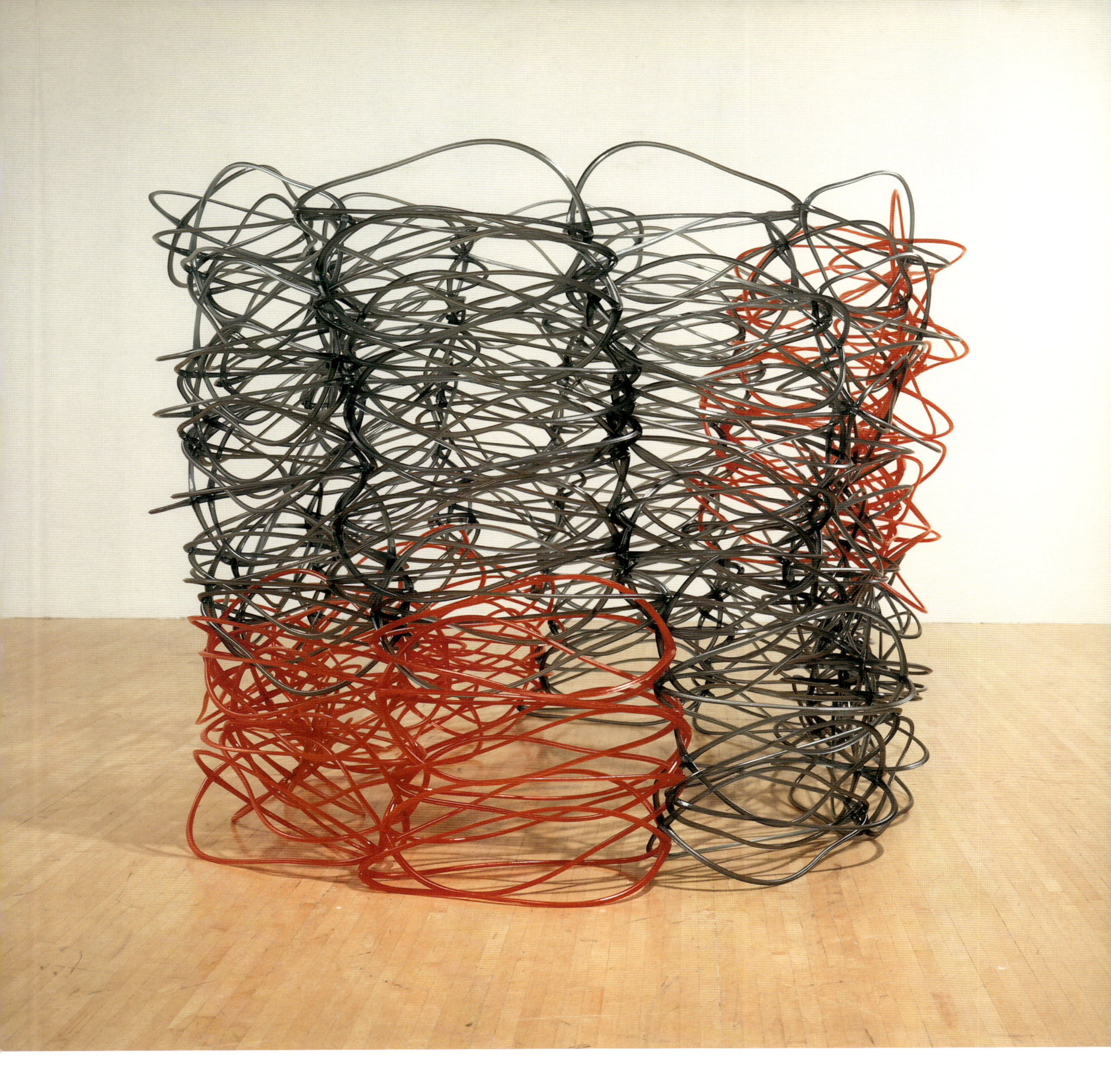

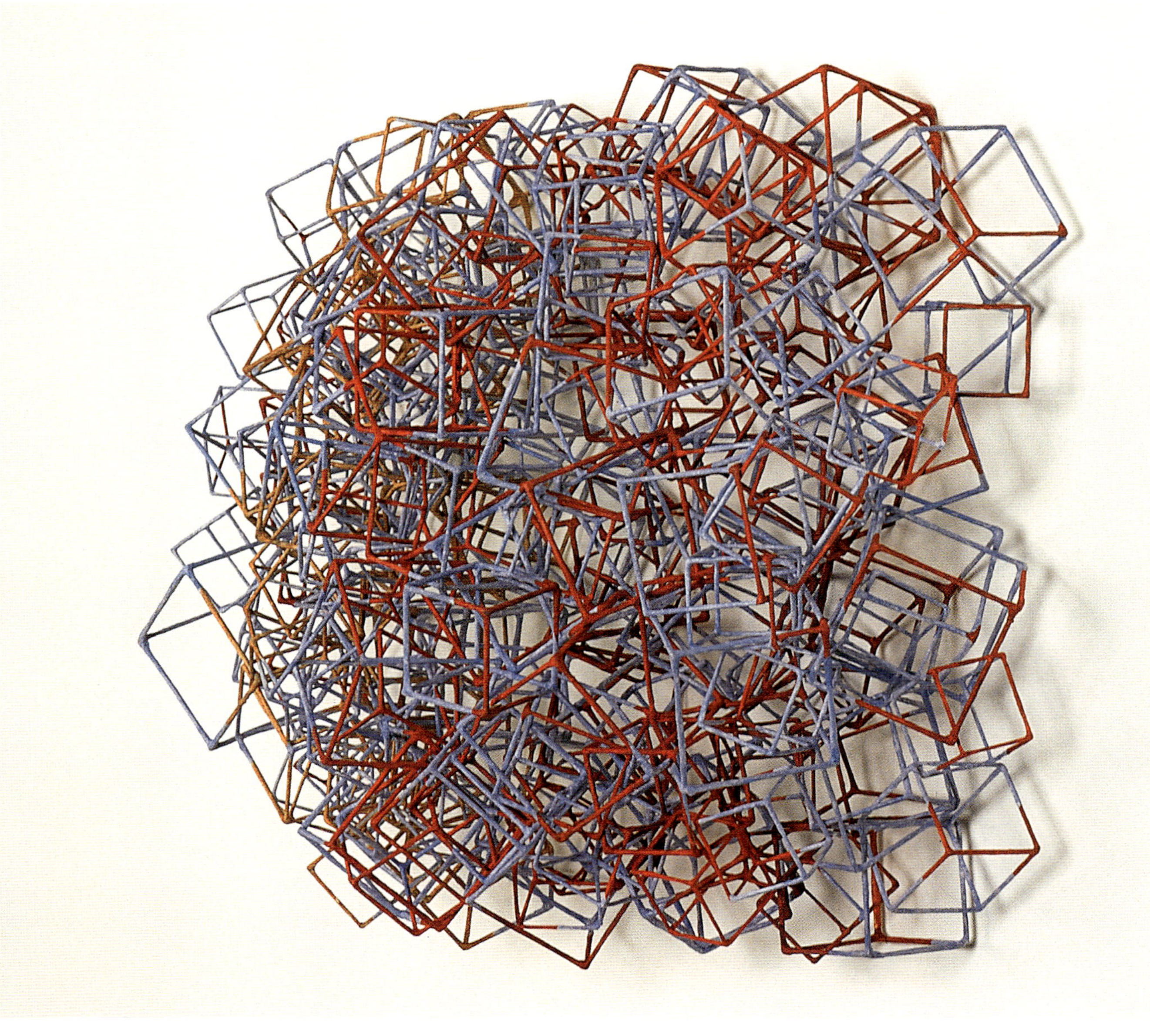

Untitled (side view), 2000

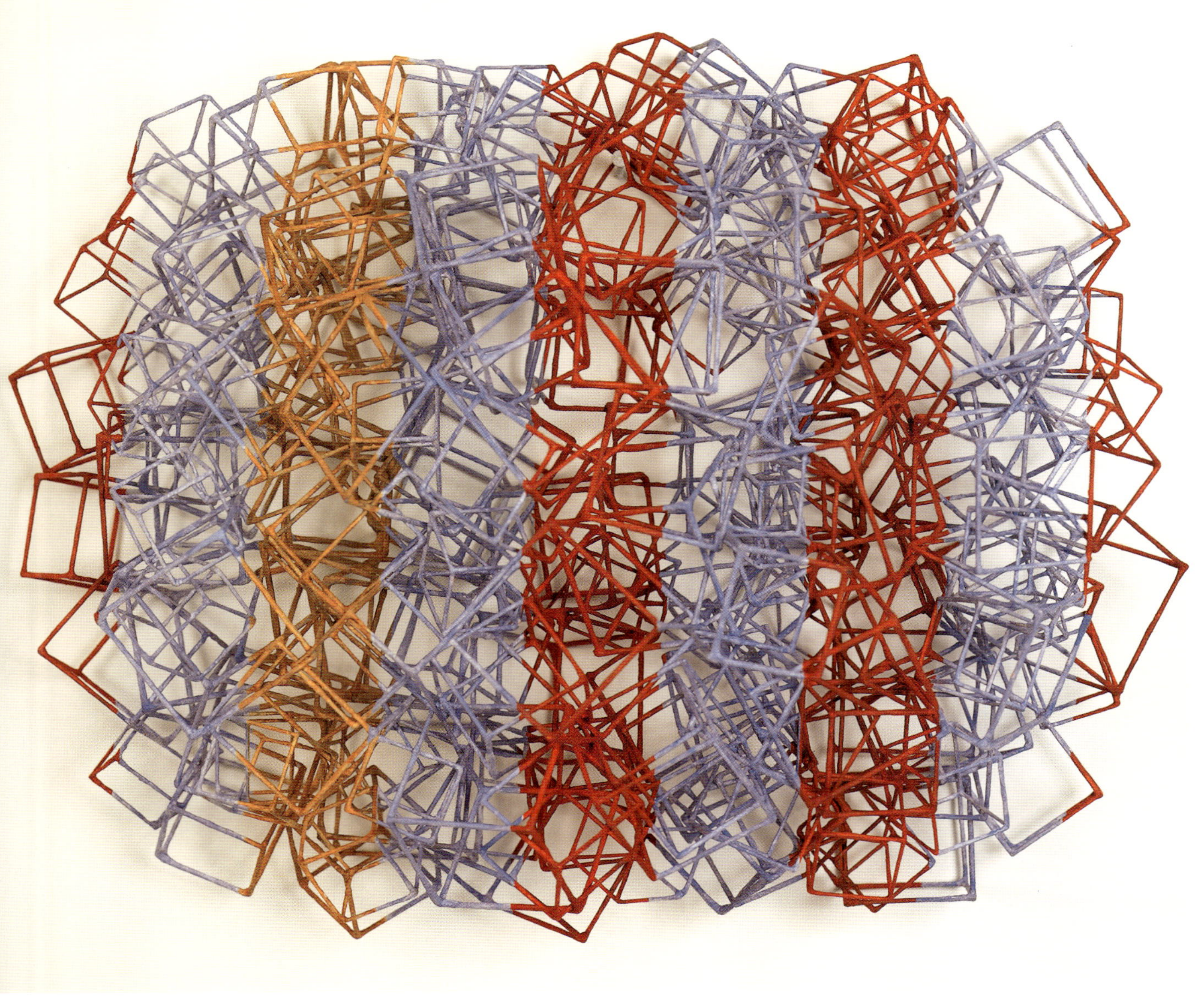

Untitled (front view), 2000

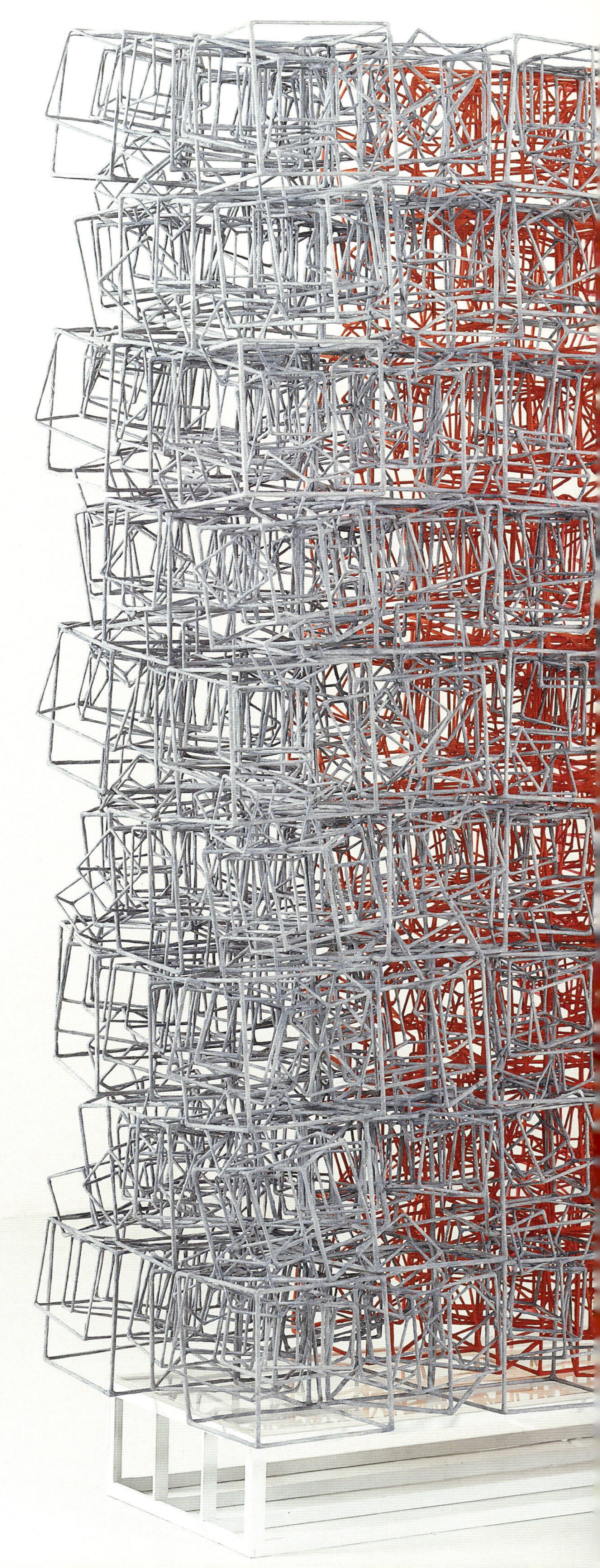

Untitled (wall), 2000–01

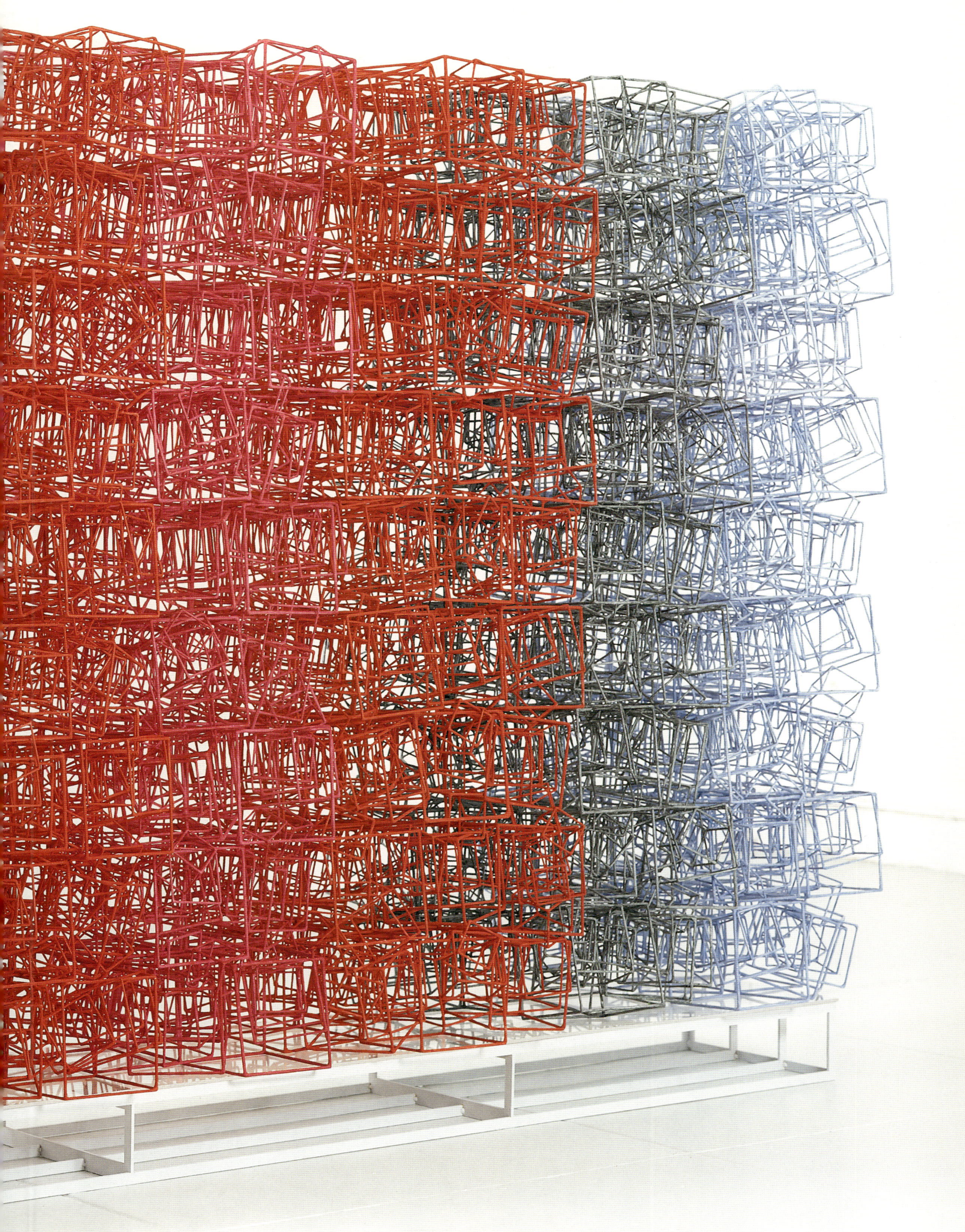

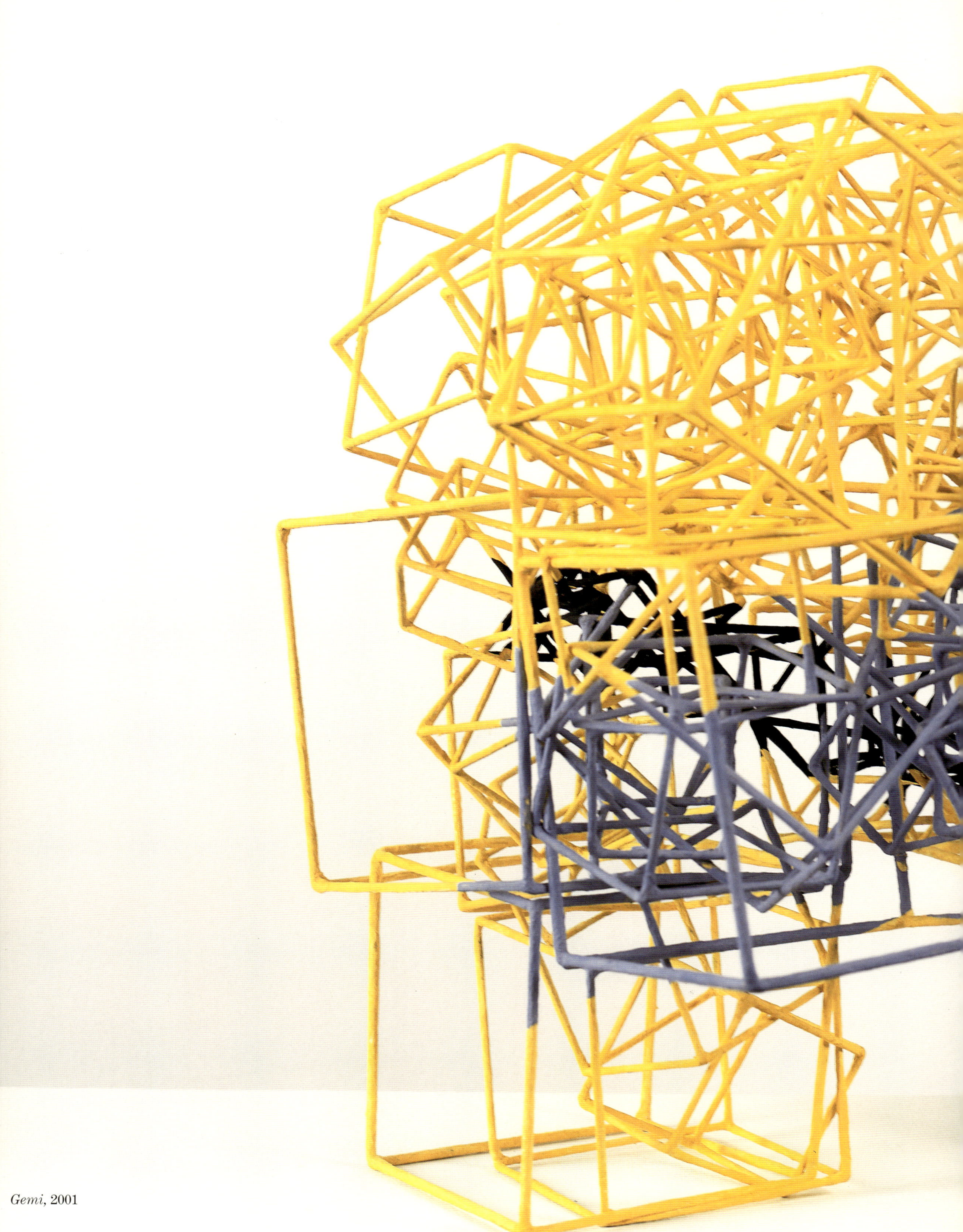

Gemi, 2001

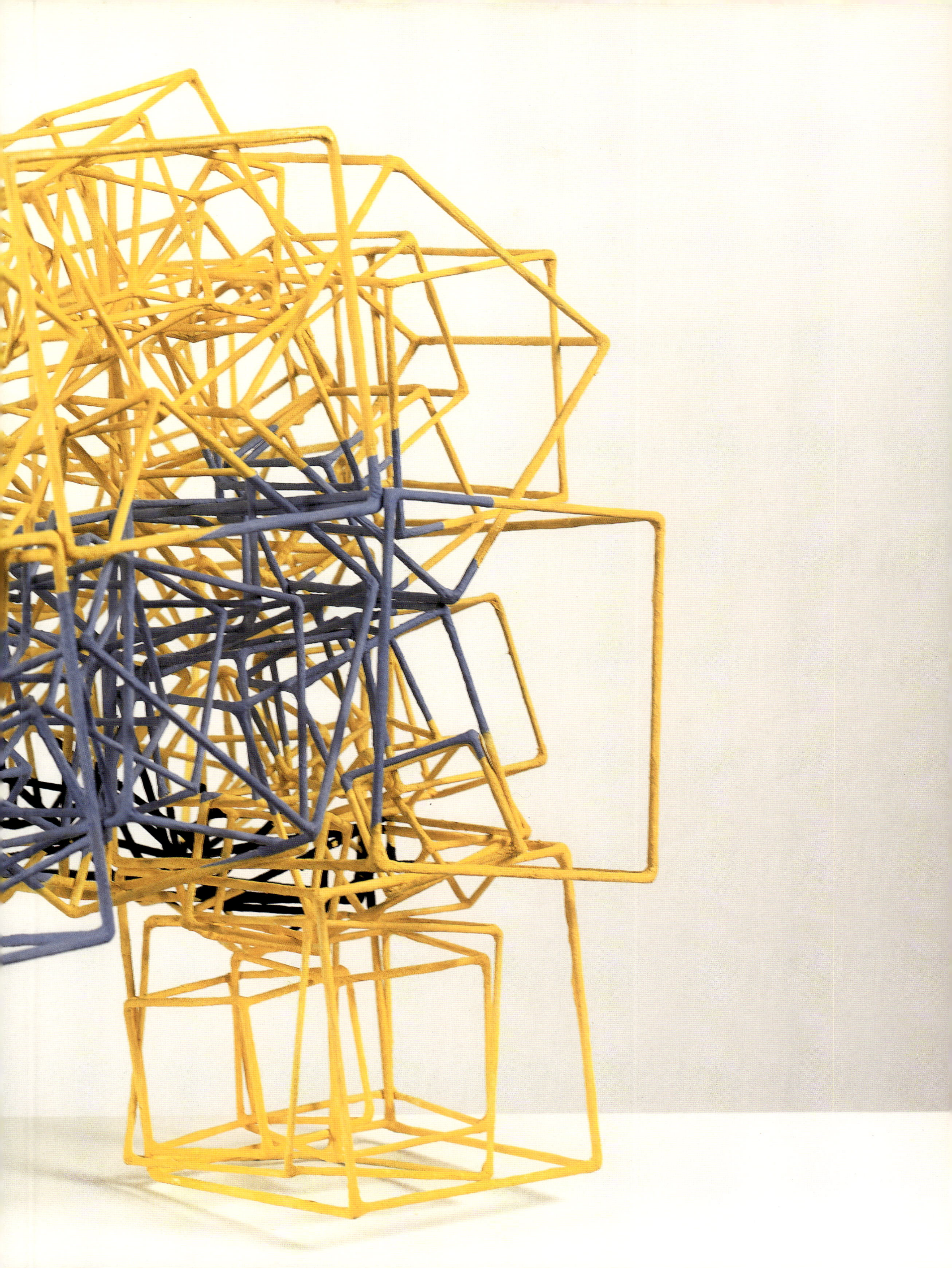

viewer's passage around the sculpture. "In my most recent work," Larner says, "I use color in a way that doesn't reiterate the form of the sculpture, but interrupts it and reinvents it as something else. At the same time the color doesn't erase or hide what the sculpture is structurally."[15] This disruptive power of color is useful to Larner in the same way that linearity is: as part of a larger effort to engage with spatiality without falling back on sheer mass to do it.

Perhaps some sense of Larner's ongoing approach to highly specific issues of spatiality can be gleaned from an examination of her approach over a number of years to the question of the corner. "I wanted to bring things to the corners because it seems like a sort of dead space within our viewing context," she says, "People have dealt with the wall, or the floor, but where two walls meet is a really beautiful, poetic space. Where two axes arrive and touch each other should not be a dead space; it should be one of the most powerful spaces. I like moving things into the corners and sometimes trying to change the shape of the corner."[16]

One of her earliest attempts to do just that was the notorious *Corner Basher* (1988), a ball and chain attached to a pole on wheels. When *Corner Basher*'s motor is activated (visitors turn it on and off) it flails away at the walls on either side of the corner, doing real damage to them while sending plaster and other debris flying. "*Corner Basher* rips a hole in the corner and carves it out into another form," Larner says, "so it's like sweeping into those forces of the two walls." *Corner Basher* makes literal the violence otherwise only implied in pieces such as *Used to Do the Job*. Despite appearances, Larner does not see *Corner Basher* as an assault on the space of the gallery per se. Her work is never so programmatic. Rather it is intended as a way

Corner Basher, 1988

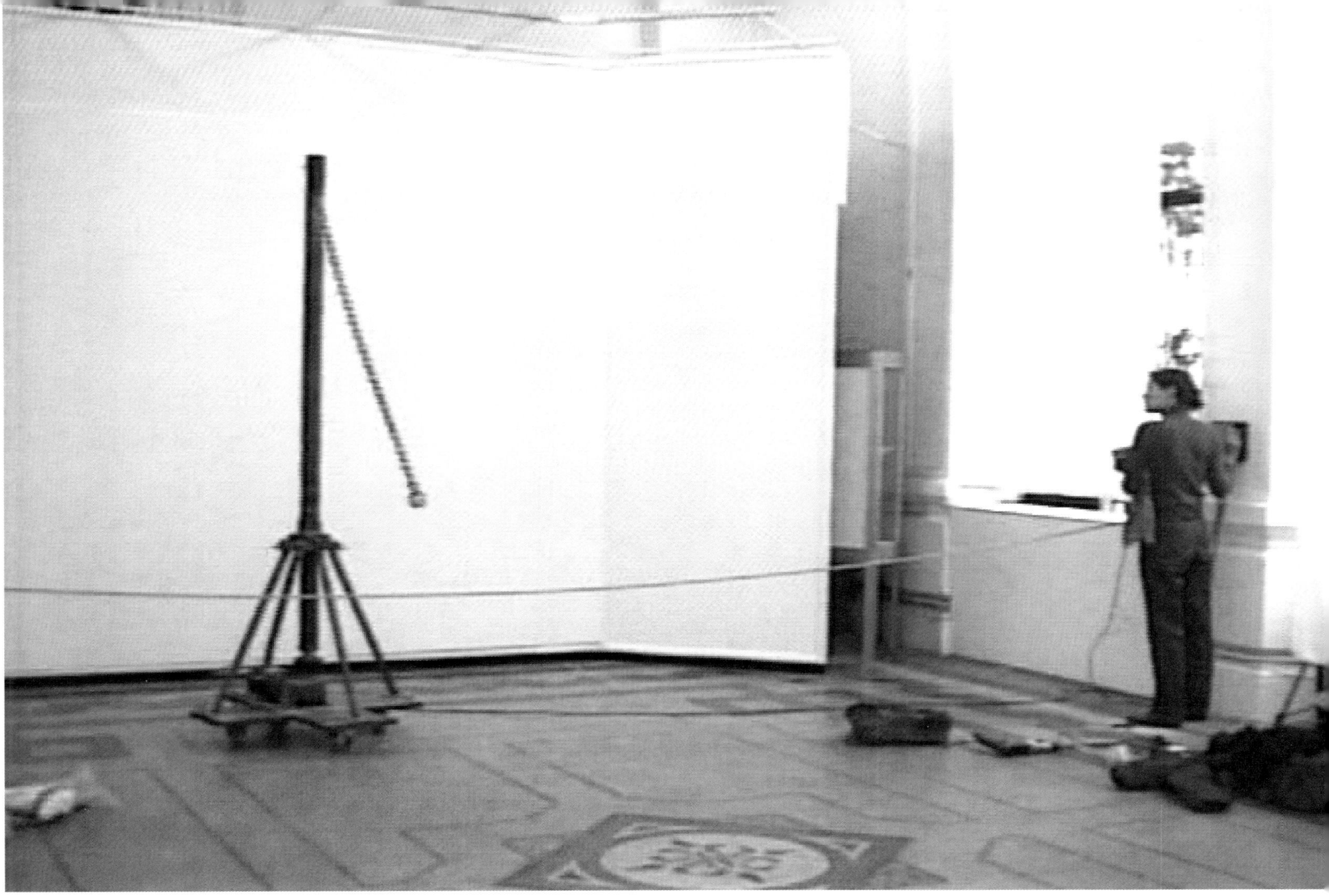

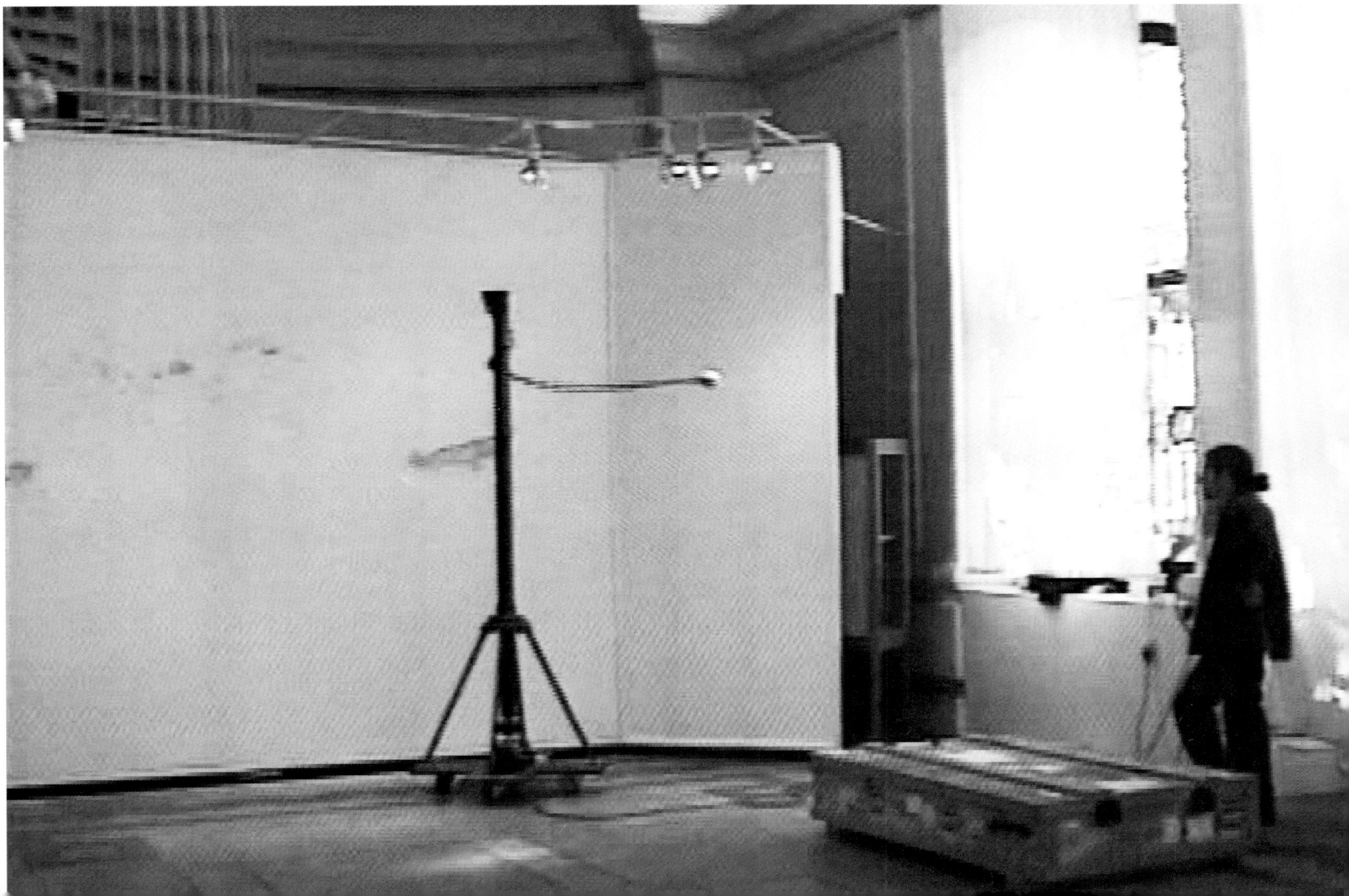

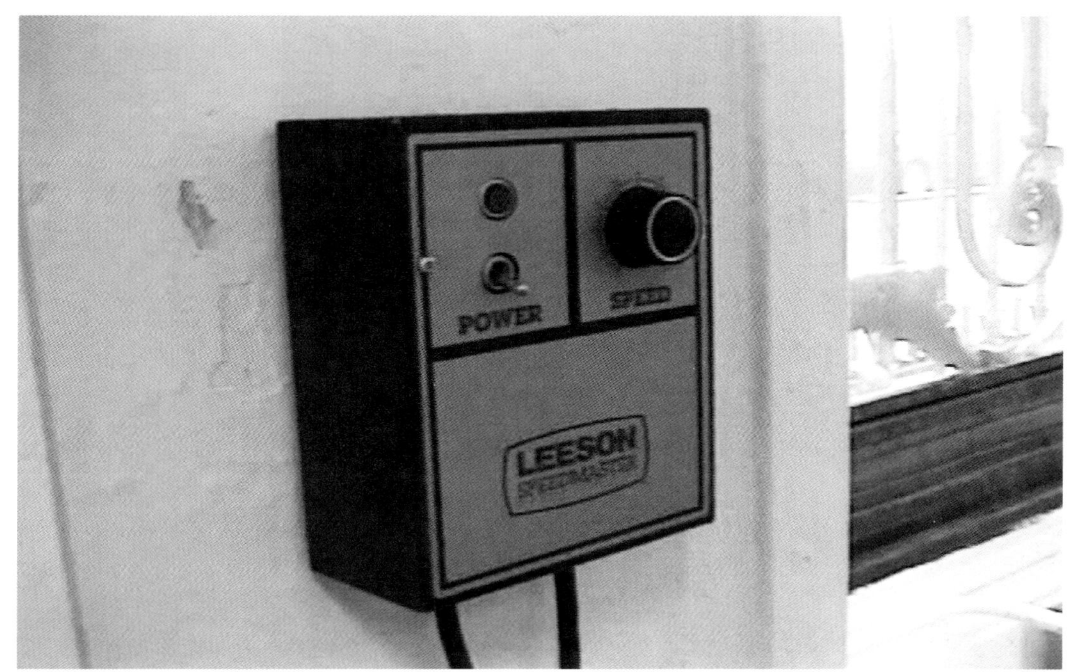

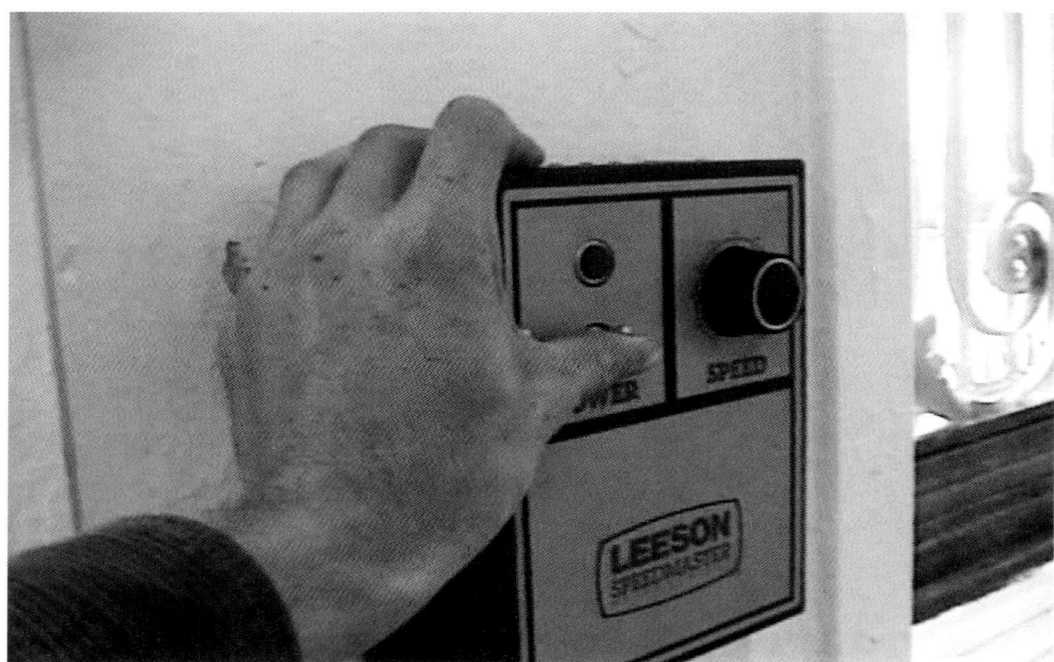

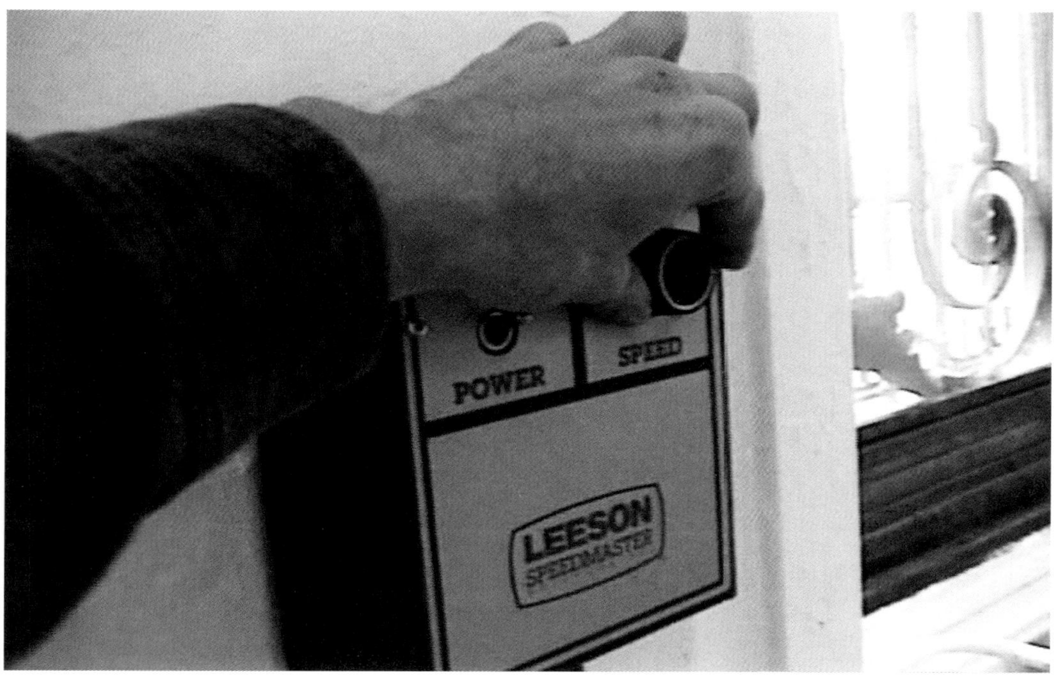

Corner Basher, 1988
Details of on/off speed control

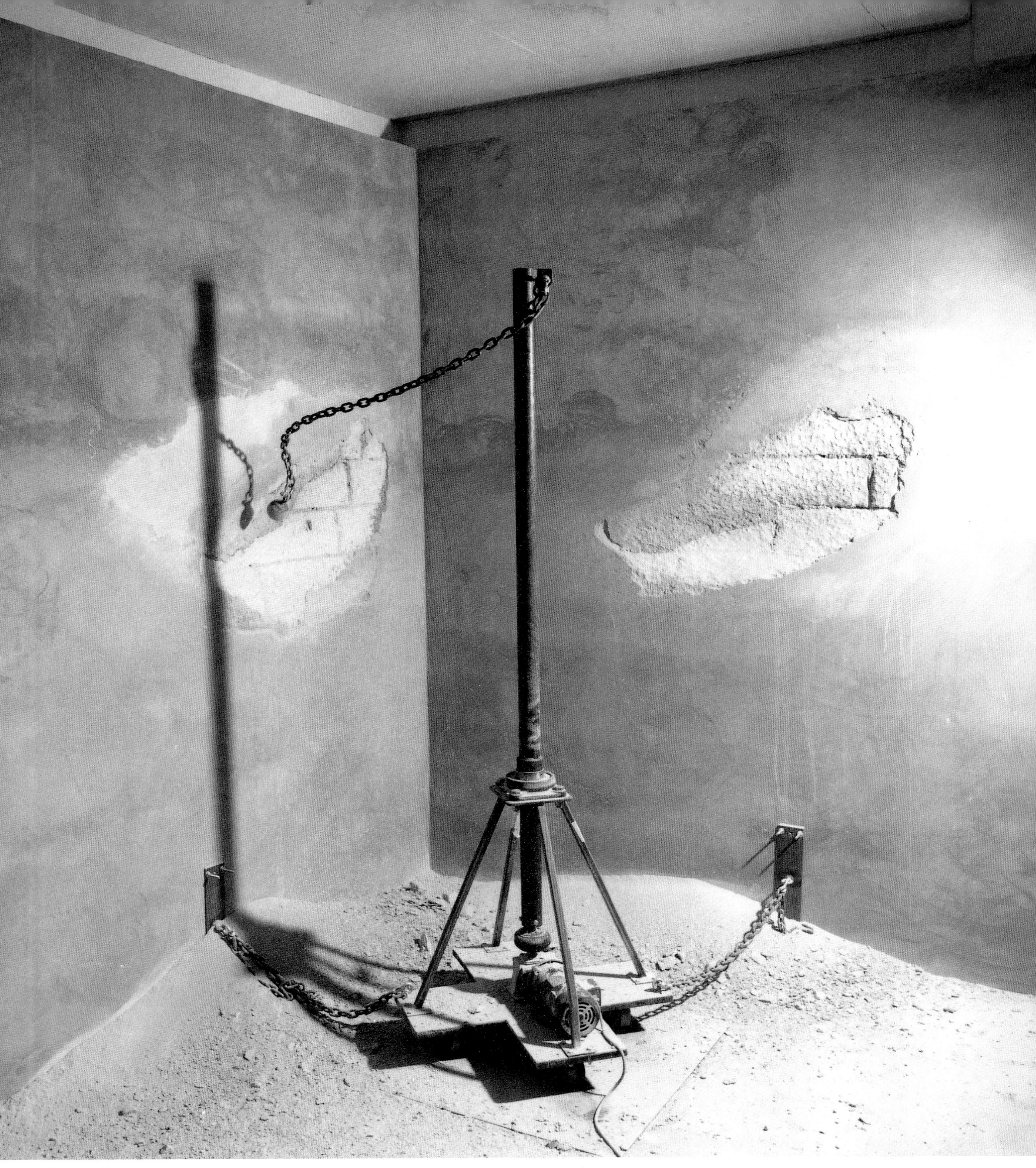

Corner Basher, 1988

of putting responsibility into the hands of the viewer, to offer them an experience of direct cause and effect, a strategy that in practice has had mixed results. *Corner Basher*'s mobile violence, however, remains inescapable, making it difficult to register other elements of its structure. It is difficult, in fact, even to compare it with other works of sculpture. A more relevant point of comparison might be Bruce Nauman's videotape *Bouncing in the Corner, No. 1* (1968), in which the artist repeatedly jumps up from the corner of his studio towards the camera before crashing back against the angle of the walls. Nauman's early practice in general, his videotaped performances and sculpture in particular, can be seen in many ways as a precursor and parallel to the kind of intensive investigation of space in which Larner is engaged, despite the lack of visual similarity in their work. It is notable, for example, that both artists have made corridor pieces, quite different in appearance but nevertheless addressing overlapping issues

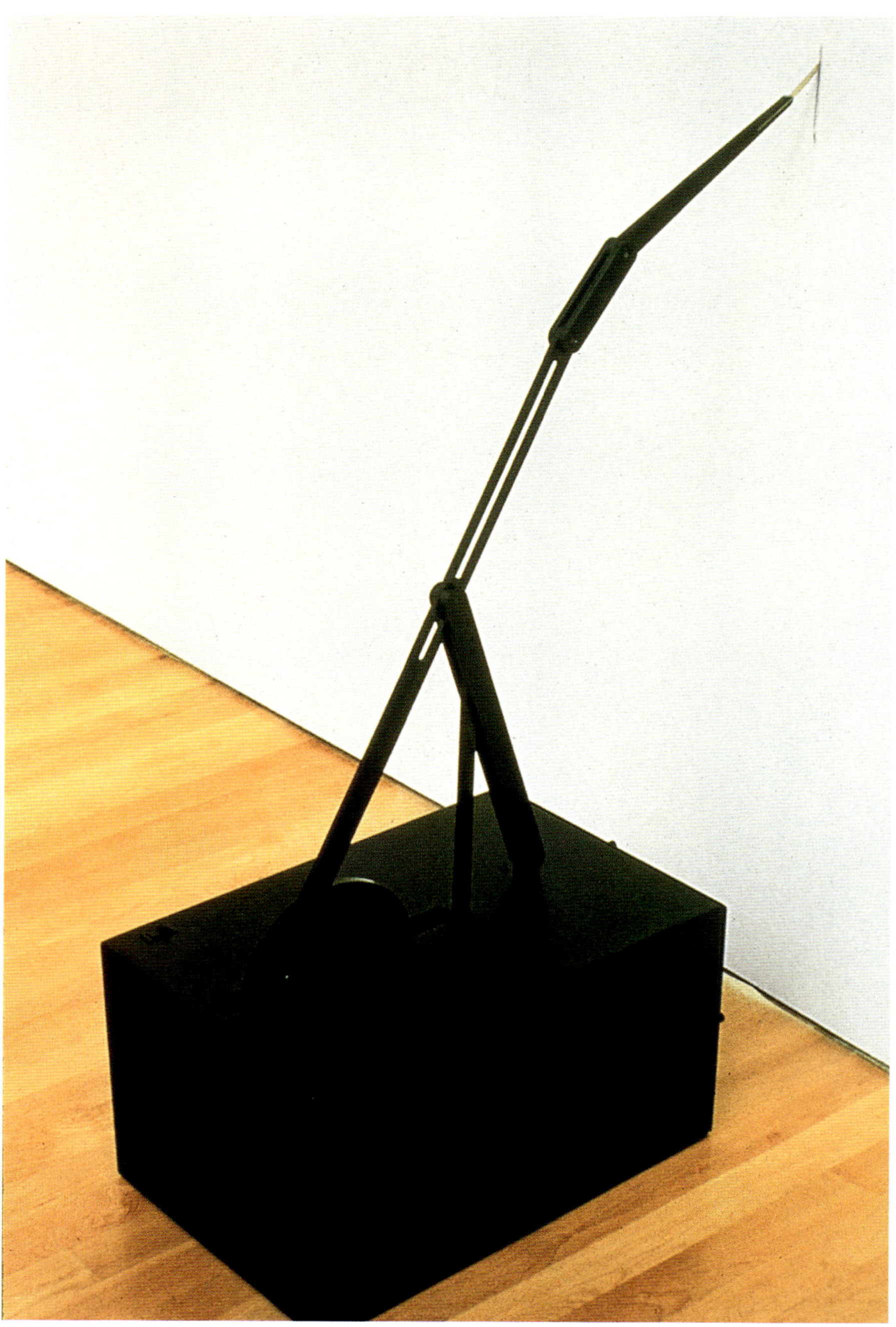

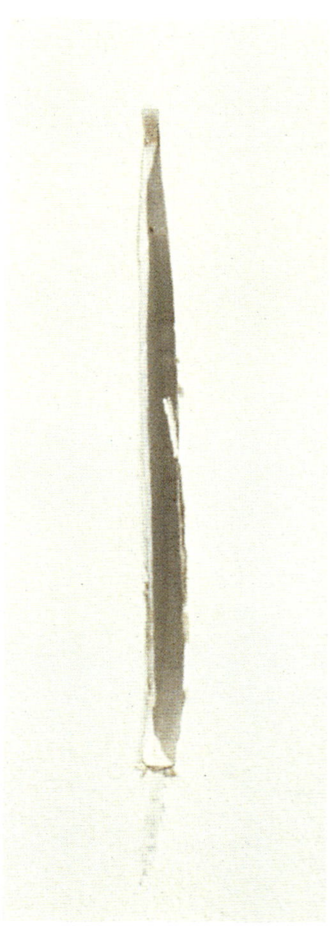

Wall Scratcher, 1988

of enclosure, openness, and control. For both artists, a direct relationship between the work and the viewer is essential.

Wrapped Corner (1991) addresses the corner by embracing a convex corner in a clasp of high-tension steel chain. While *Wrapped Corner* literally occupies almost no space, tightly bound as it is to the wall, the tension of the chain does not merely grip the corner, but is the fundamental basis for the form of the piece itself. Without the tension, the chain would lose its structure and flop loosely to the floor. The psychological and physical pressures implied by the taut chain become the essential elements in its composition. The action of the piece is simultaneously to articulate and to remove the section of the corner on which it exists.

The tension is loosened in *Devex Yellow*, a heap of yellow loops resting on a hoop mounted in a corner. "The piece is as familiar as an armload of laundry, as strange as a swarm of wasps,

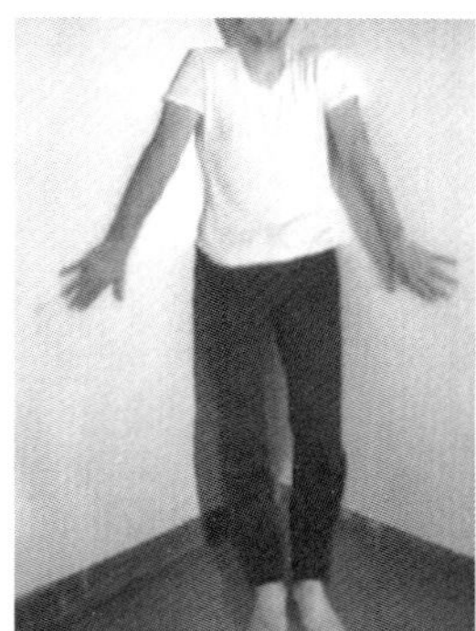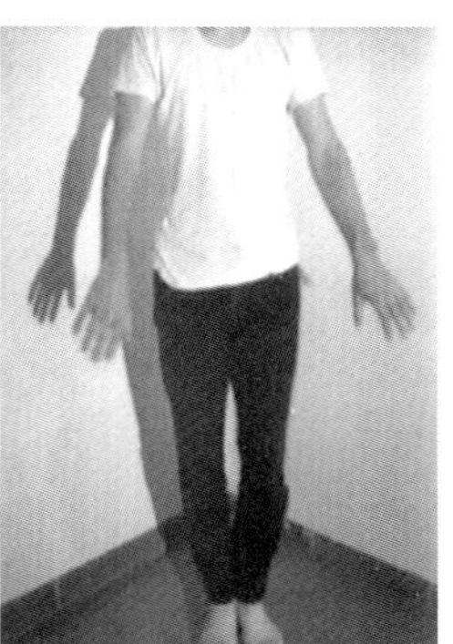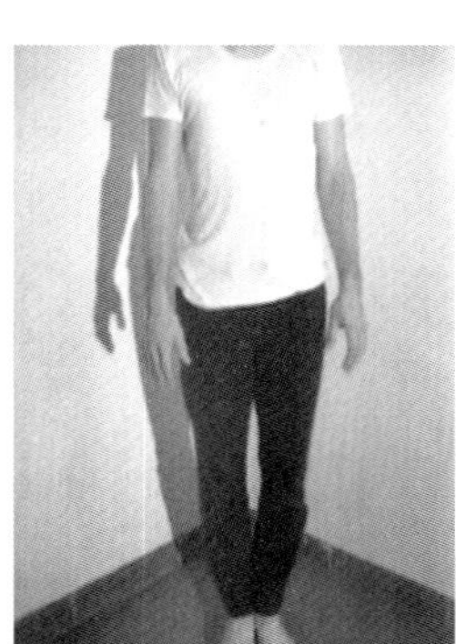

Bruce Nauman, *Bouncing in the Corner, No. 1,* 1968

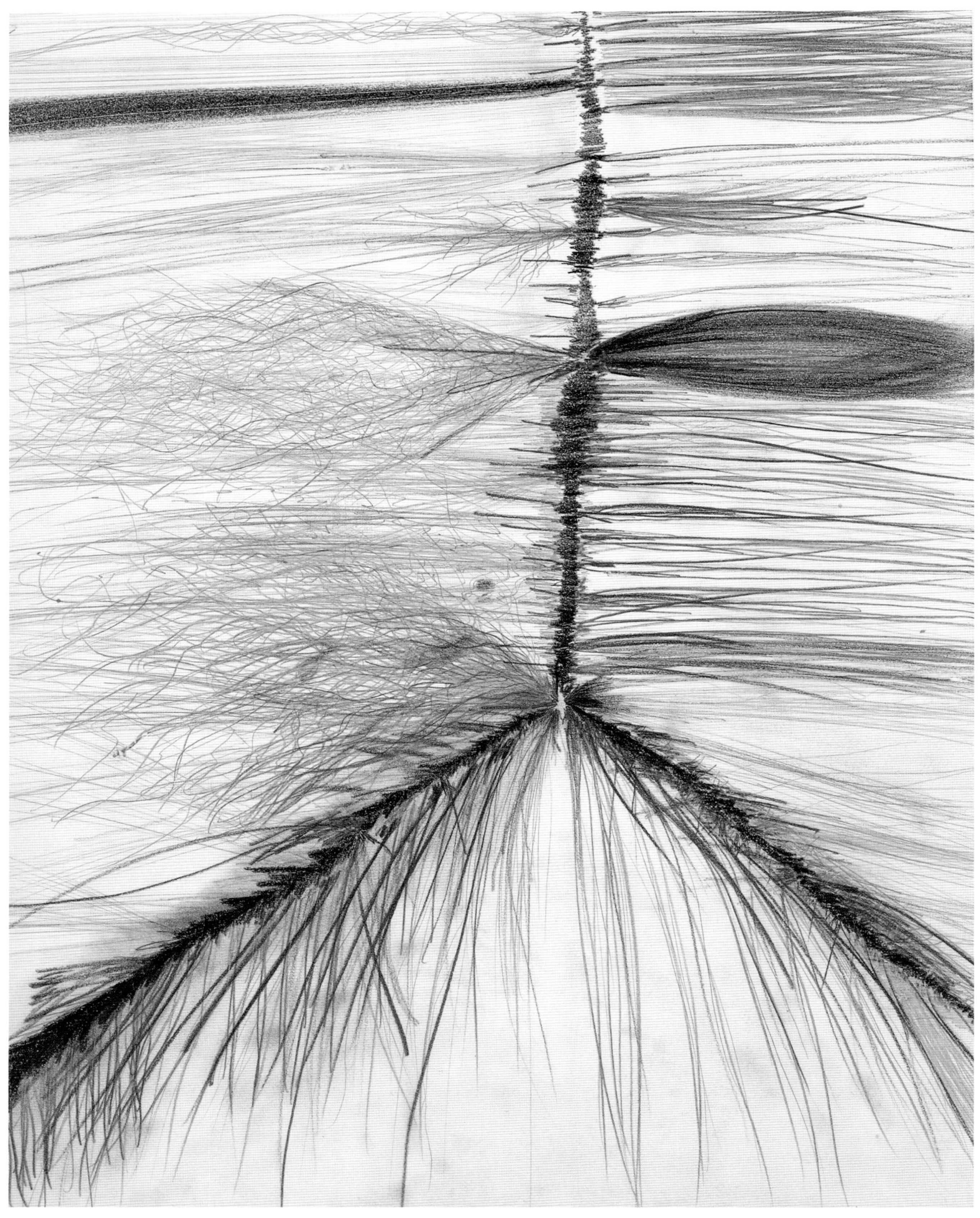

Corner, 1986

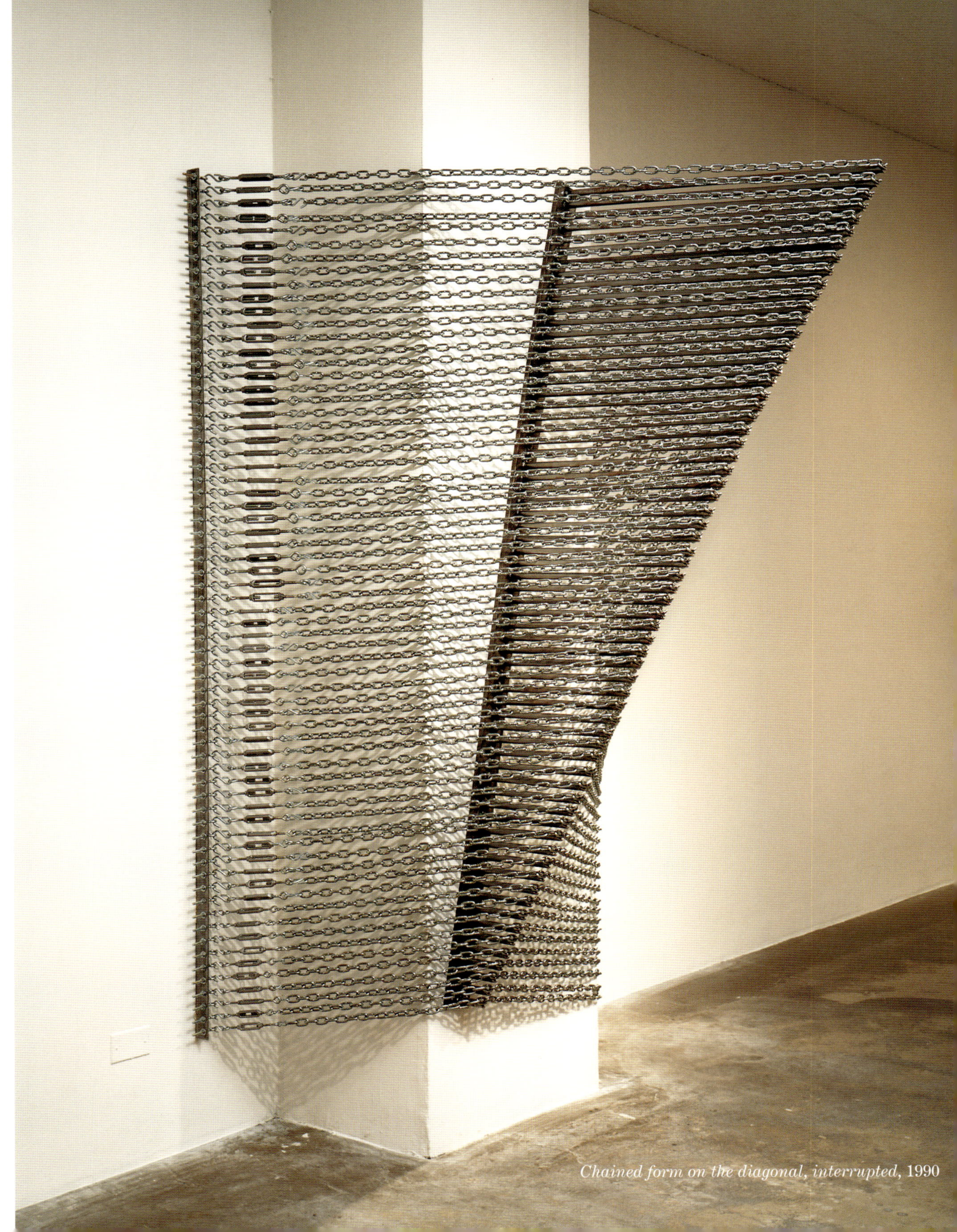

Chained form on the diagonal, interrupted, 1990

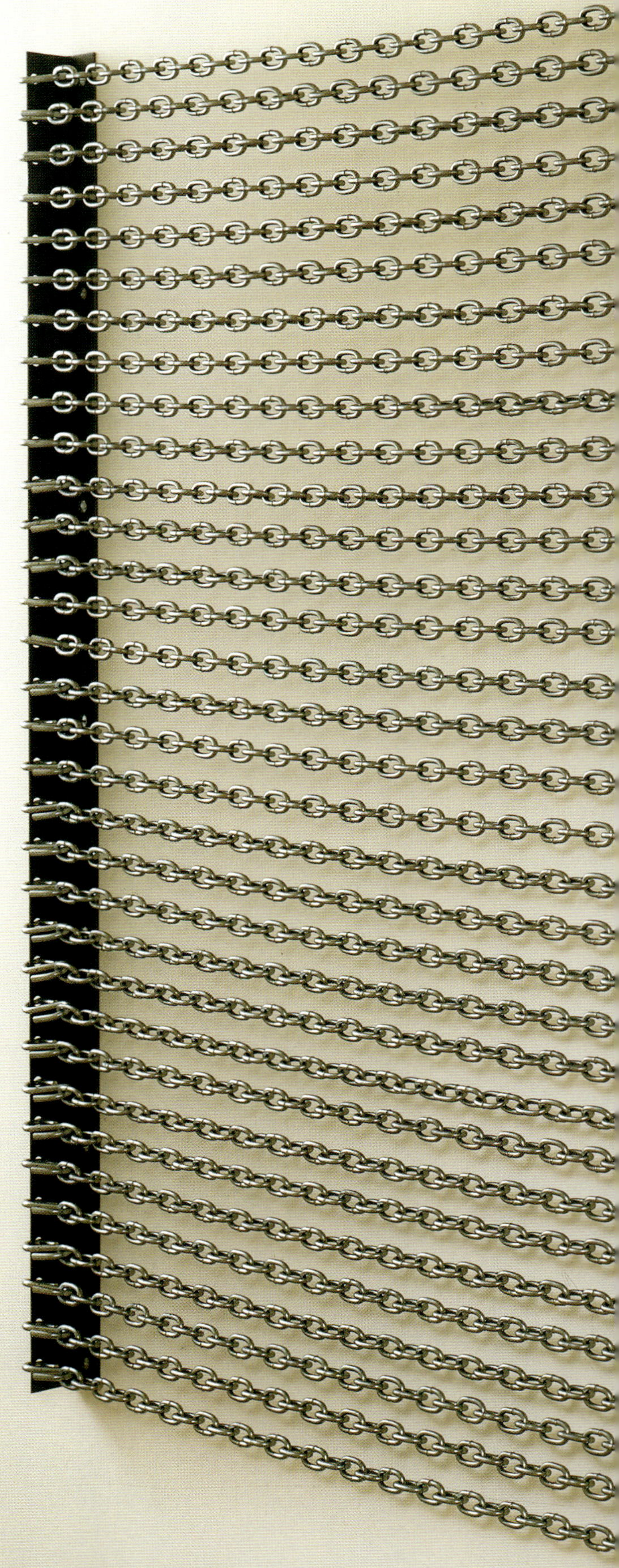

Wrapped Corner, 1991

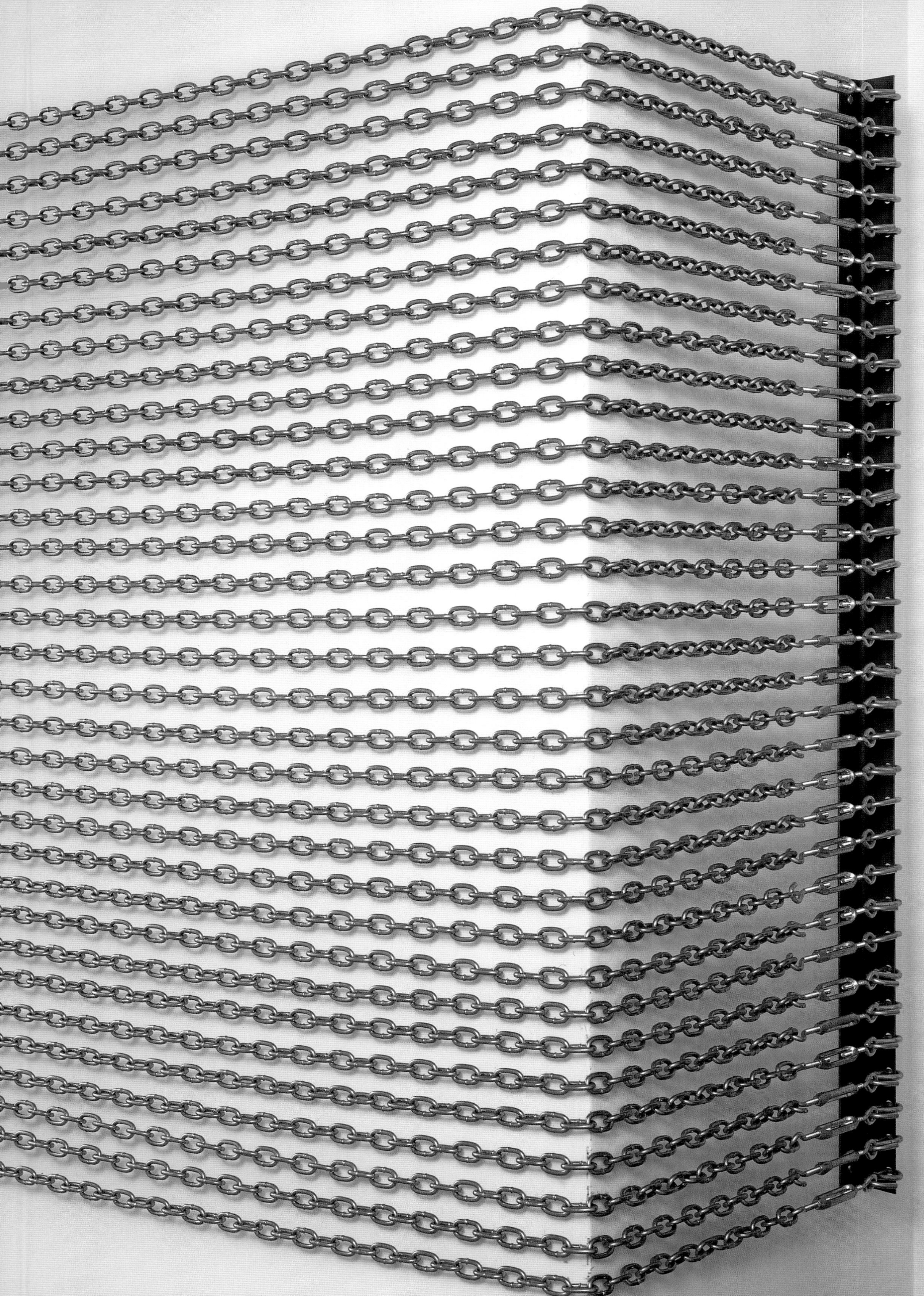

and as comfortable and banal as a dust bunny," Lisa Anne Auerbach observed.[17] The relationship of this work to the corner is, if not totally comfortable, at least less of an overt struggle than in previous works. The sculpture seems to have found a certain *modus vivendi* with its host. As Larner puts it, "*Devex Yellow* creates this little bubble in the corner. It's attached to the walls, but it gets into this interstitial space. It's attached to the wall, but it's hanging out into space. Its convexity describes a concavity." Coming after a series of assaults on the problematic space of the corner, *Devex Yellow* addresses itself equally to the corner, to the remaining space in the room, and to the viewer.

My discussion of Larner's treatment of the corner in three sculptures spanning ten years suggests, I hope, the way in which she will return again and again to a sculptural question that engages her. However, since the example I chose—the corner—might also be thought of as a problem of (or for) architecture, it is important to distinguish between these two different sets of concerns. Although Larner has recently designed a genuine work of architecture— a pedestrian bridge for Walt Disney Studios—she makes a clear distinction between architecture and sculpture. While works such as *Rubber Divider* (1989), *Reticule*, and *Untitled (wall)* make use in part of an architectural vocabulary, they turn away from architectural issues per se. Although *Untitled (wall)* makes explicit reference to a wall it is a very fragile one, fugitive almost, despite its size and presence. Her sculpture is about negotiating a space through a physical presence within it, and the relationship of that presence to the spectator. It is not about the construction or organization of the space itself. As she puts it, "Sculpture lets you see space. It's not a representation of space, and it's not a total, surrounding environment

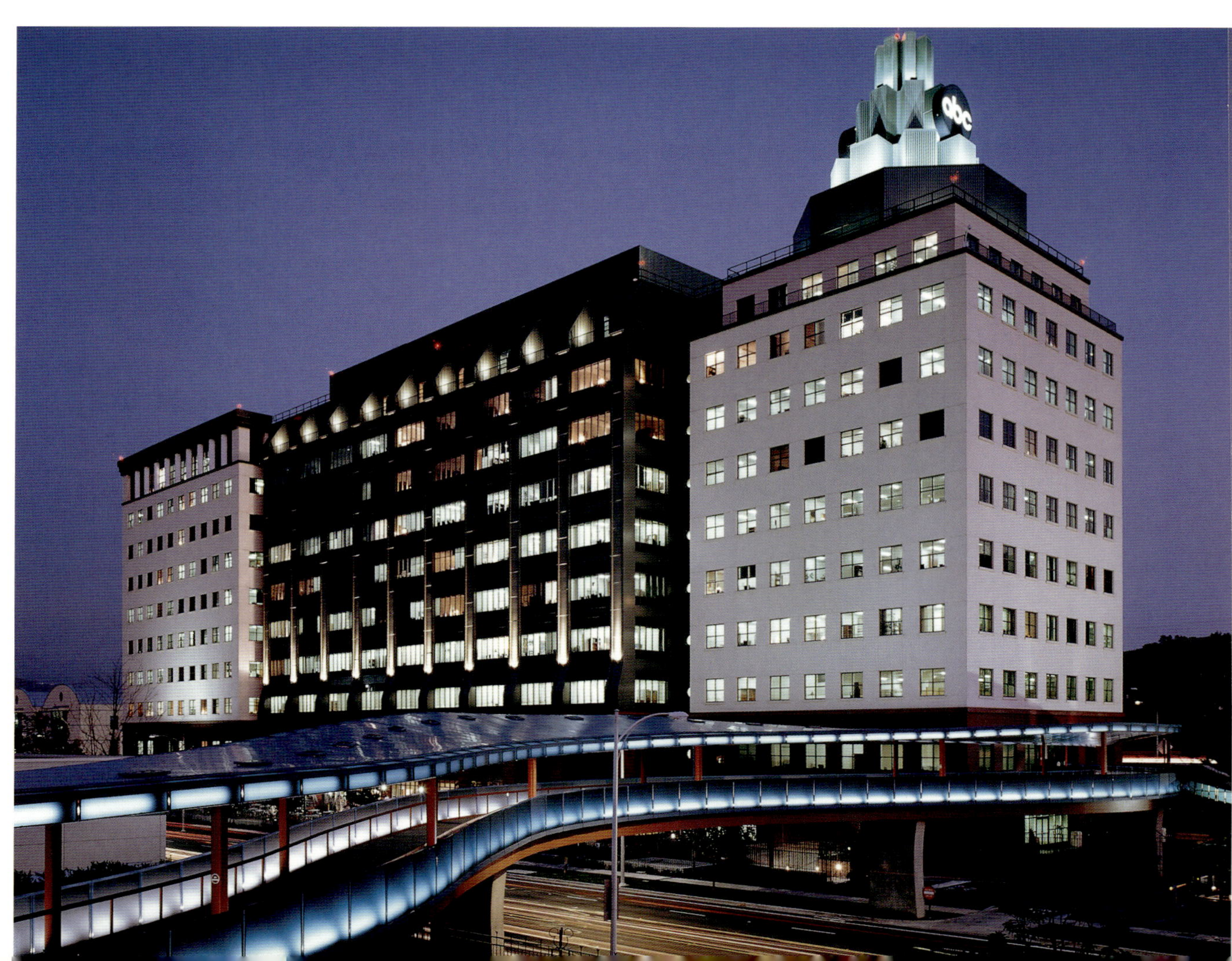

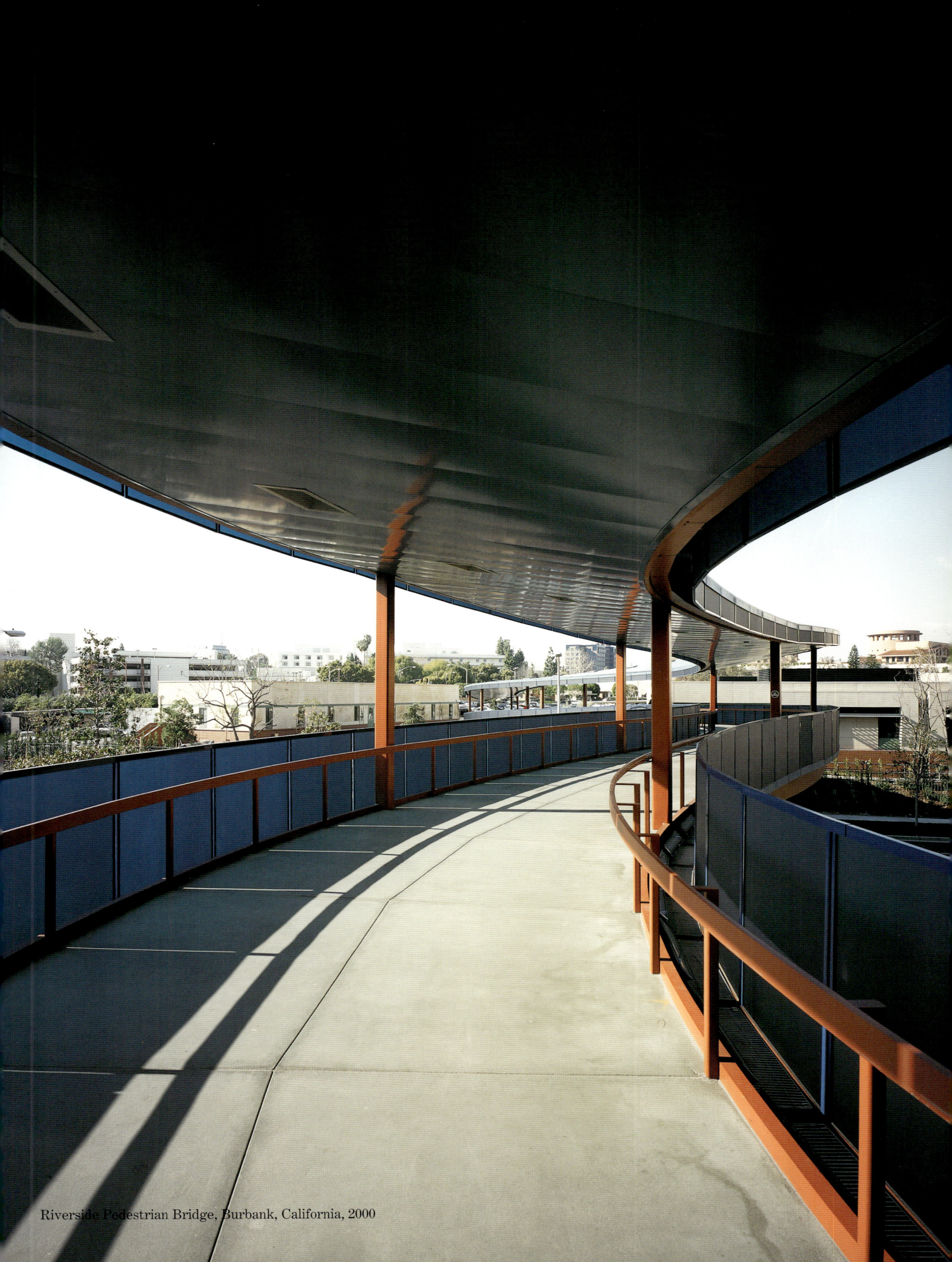

Riverside Pedestrian Bridge, Burbank, California, 2000

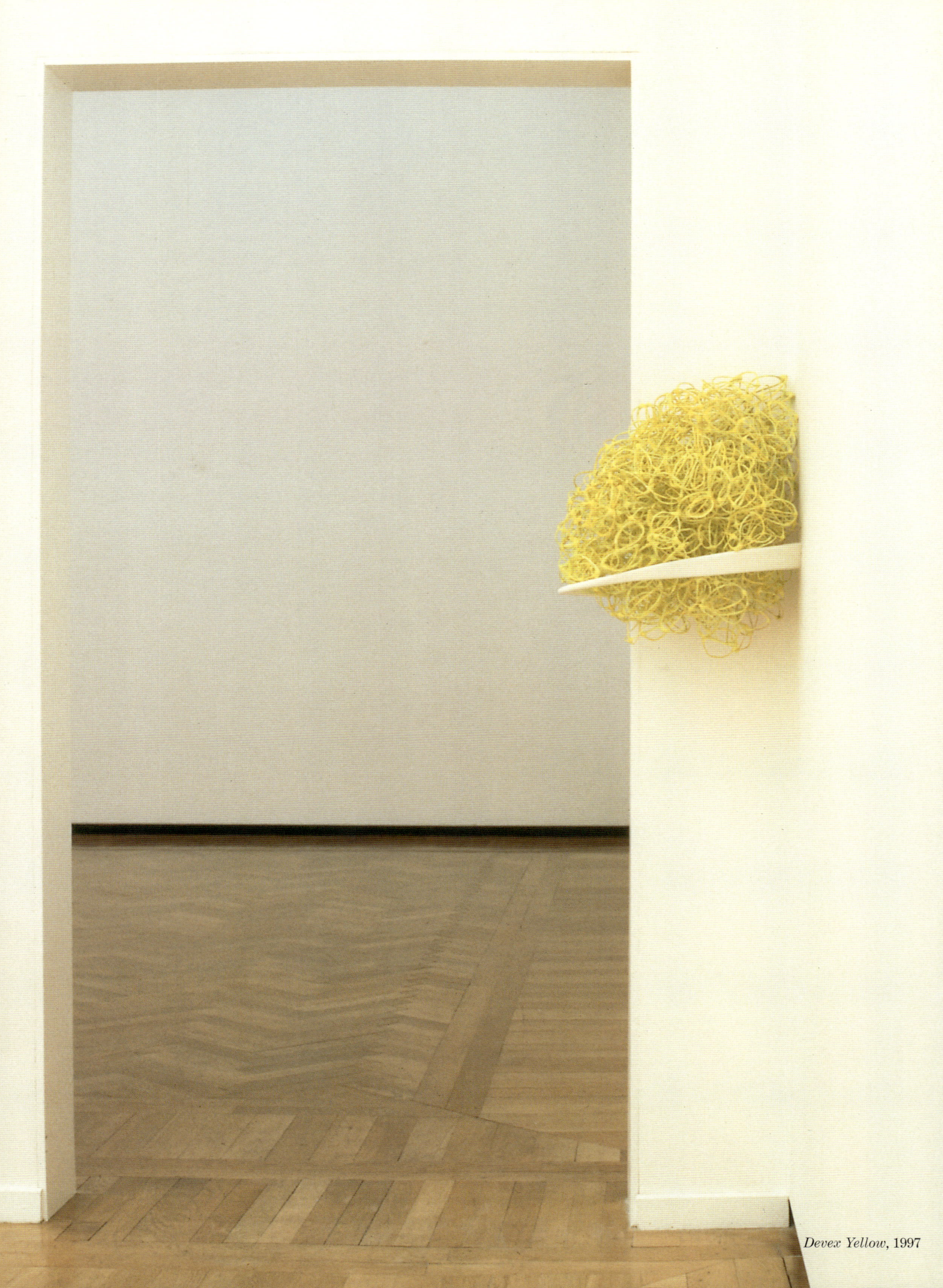

Devex Yellow, 1997

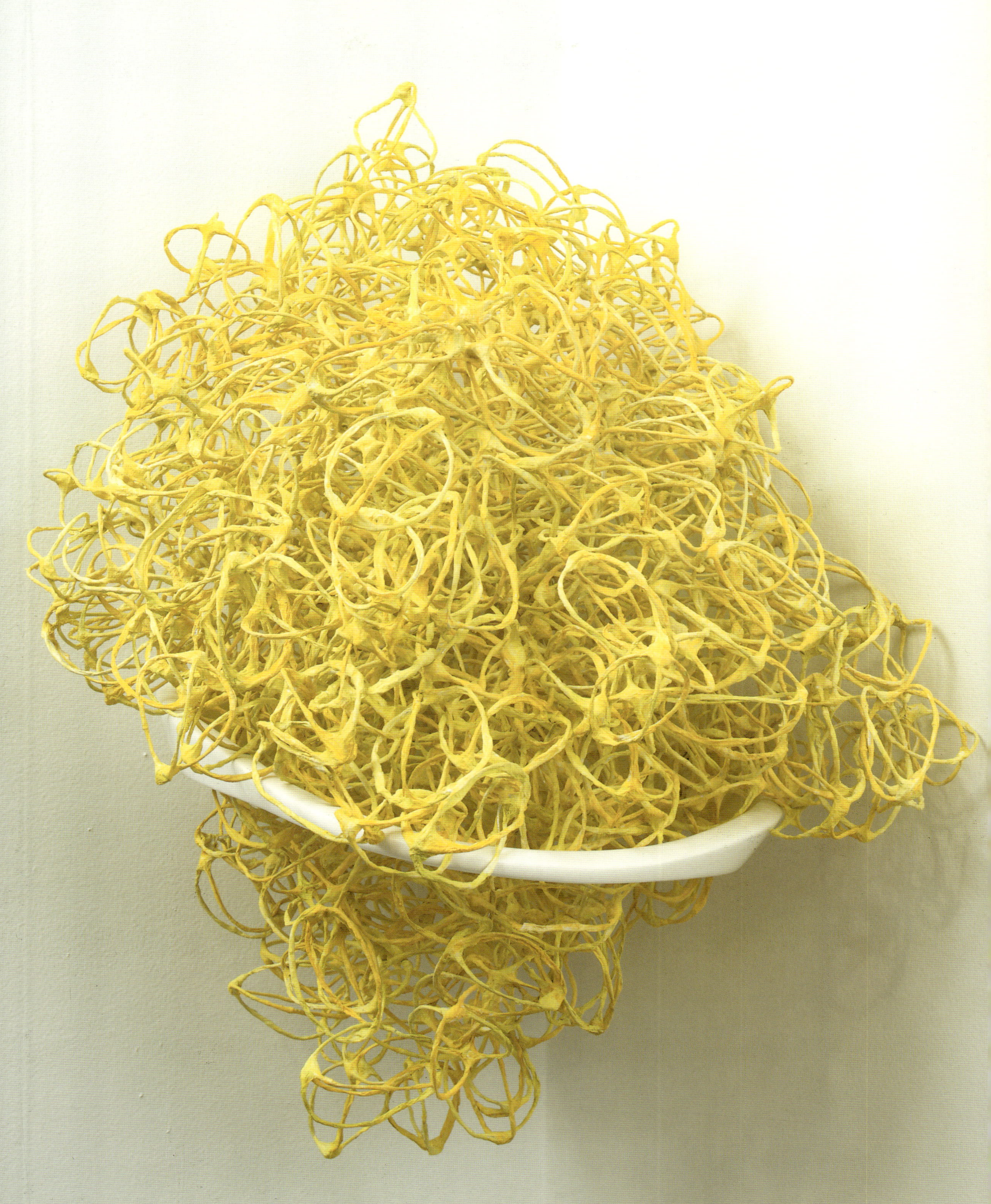

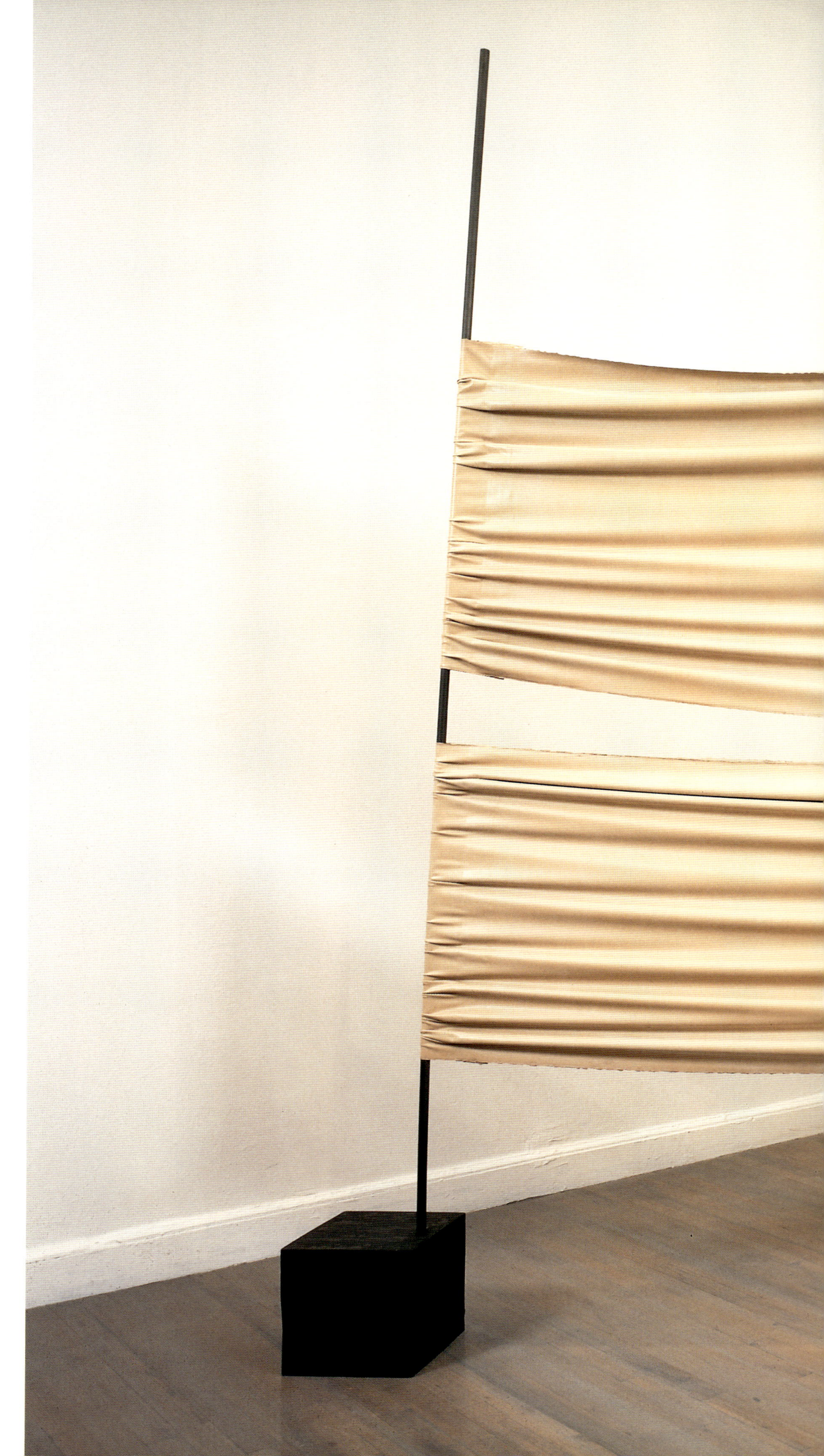

Rubber Divider, 1989

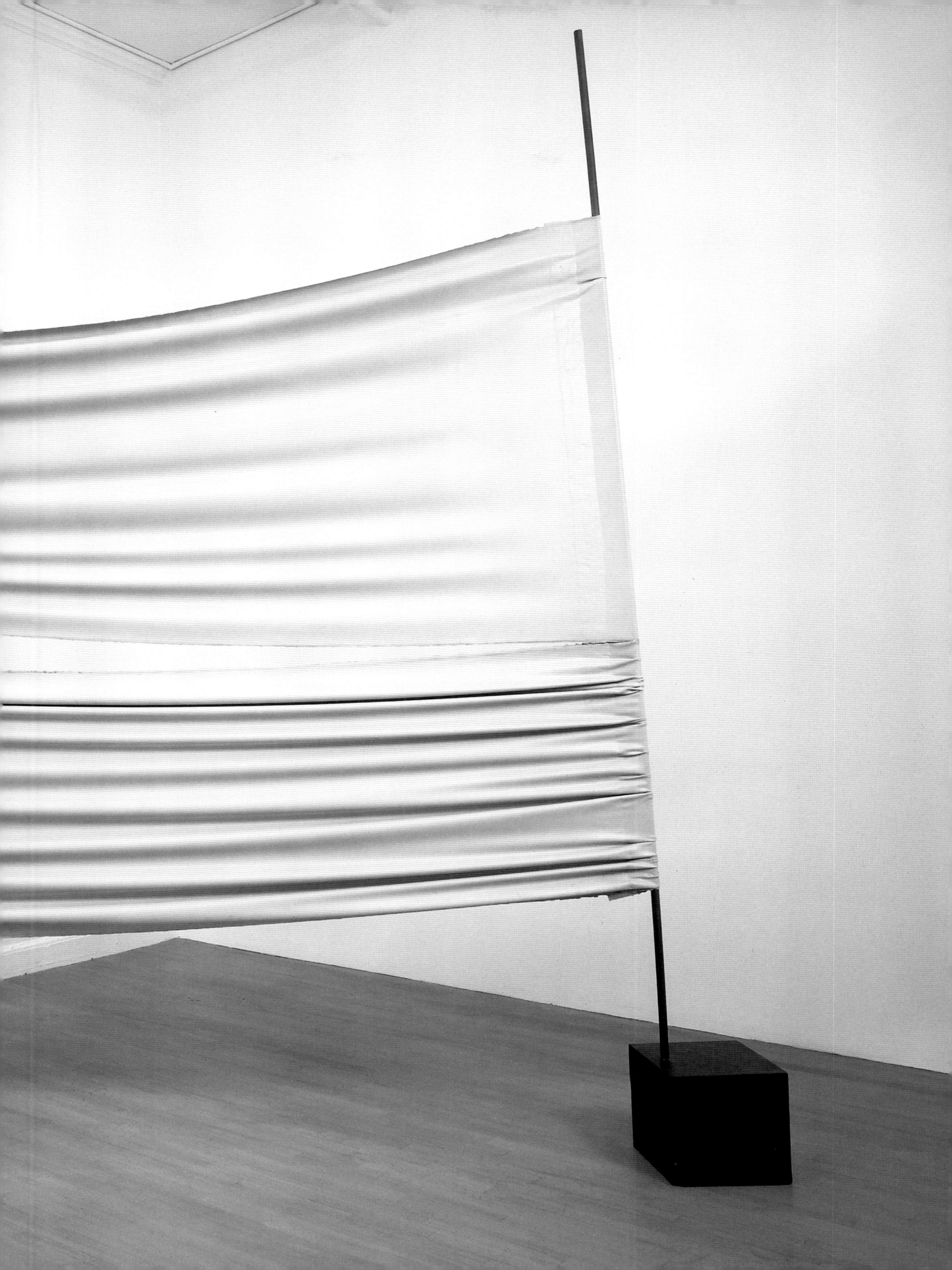

either. It takes up the same space the viewer does, so it's halfway between architecture and a human subject." The viewer experiences the space as articulated by the sculpture, and the sculpture as positioned in the space.

For Larner, the mid-1990s were a period of introspection and transition. At one point her studio burned down. Although she continued to work, she became somewhat dissatisfied with what she was doing. For a few years her work became distinctly less visible. "I did some work I didn't like, so I didn't show it," she says simply.[18] It was during this time that Larner became an increasingly influential teacher at Art Center College of Design in Pasadena, a position she continues to hold. A number of Larner's students are now recognized artists in their own right, and her importance as a teacher is widely acknowledged. The sculptors Jason Meadows and Evan Holloway have worked as studio assistants for Larner, and her emphasis on the physicality

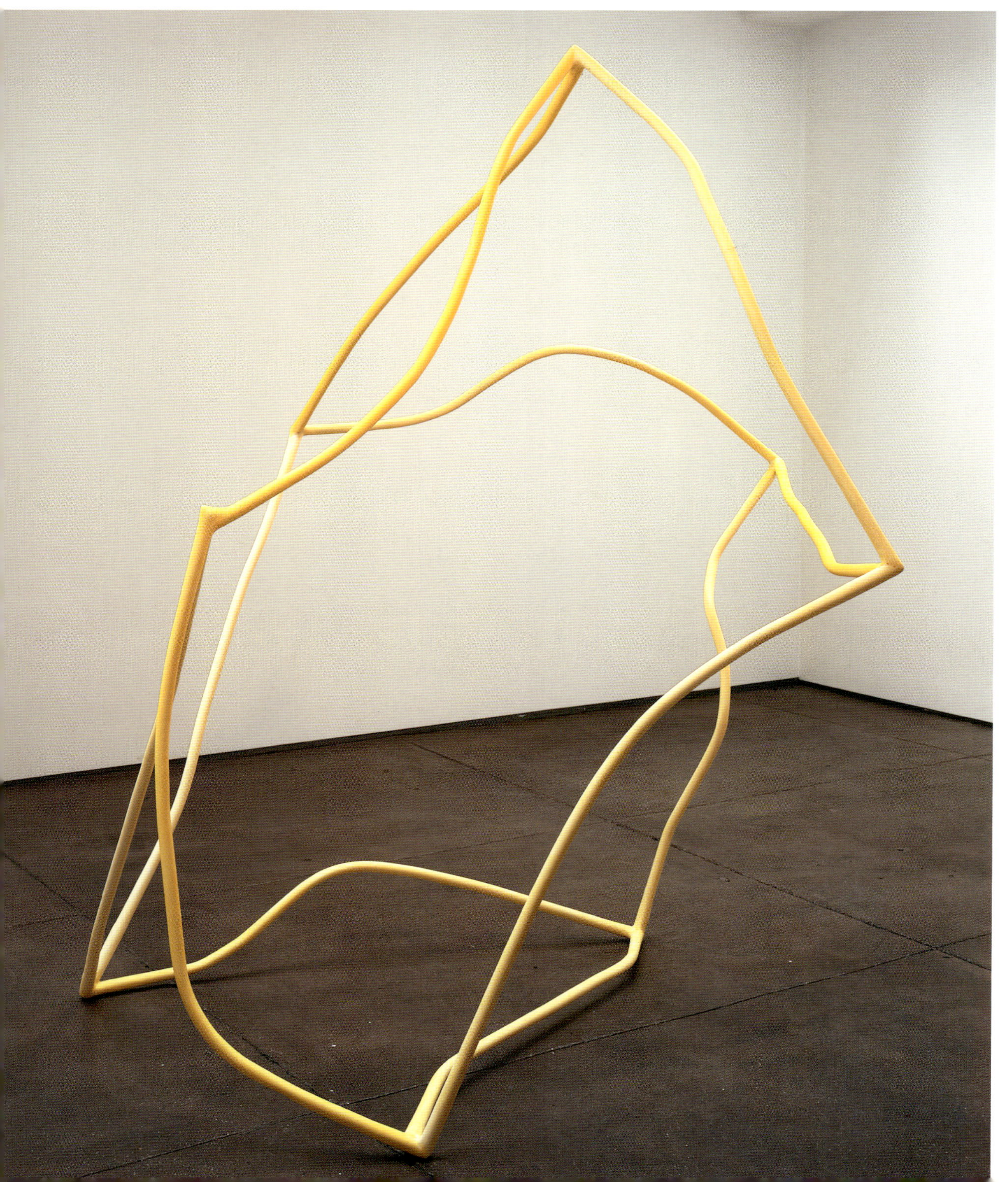

and unique presence of the object are evident in their work.

This period of transition came to an end in 1997. The tension of the chain pieces was replaced by a much more relaxed, looping linearity. Her use of color, too, became much more loose and intuitive, reflecting a confidence gained from years of studio experimentation. *Devex Yellow* was quickly followed by *2 as 3 and Some Too*, which represented a decisive move away both from the raw viscerality of her earlier work with live cultures, and from the motifs of control that characterized the series of chain works. The new sculpture has a calmness about it, and a sense of balance. It is not dependent on high tension to hold itself together. There is something of an implied claim to autonomy in these works. *2 as 3 and Some Too* and the related sculpture *Two or Three or Something* (1998–99) reflect a broader move away from Larner's fascination with the potential breakdown of form towards a renewed interest in the potential of geometric

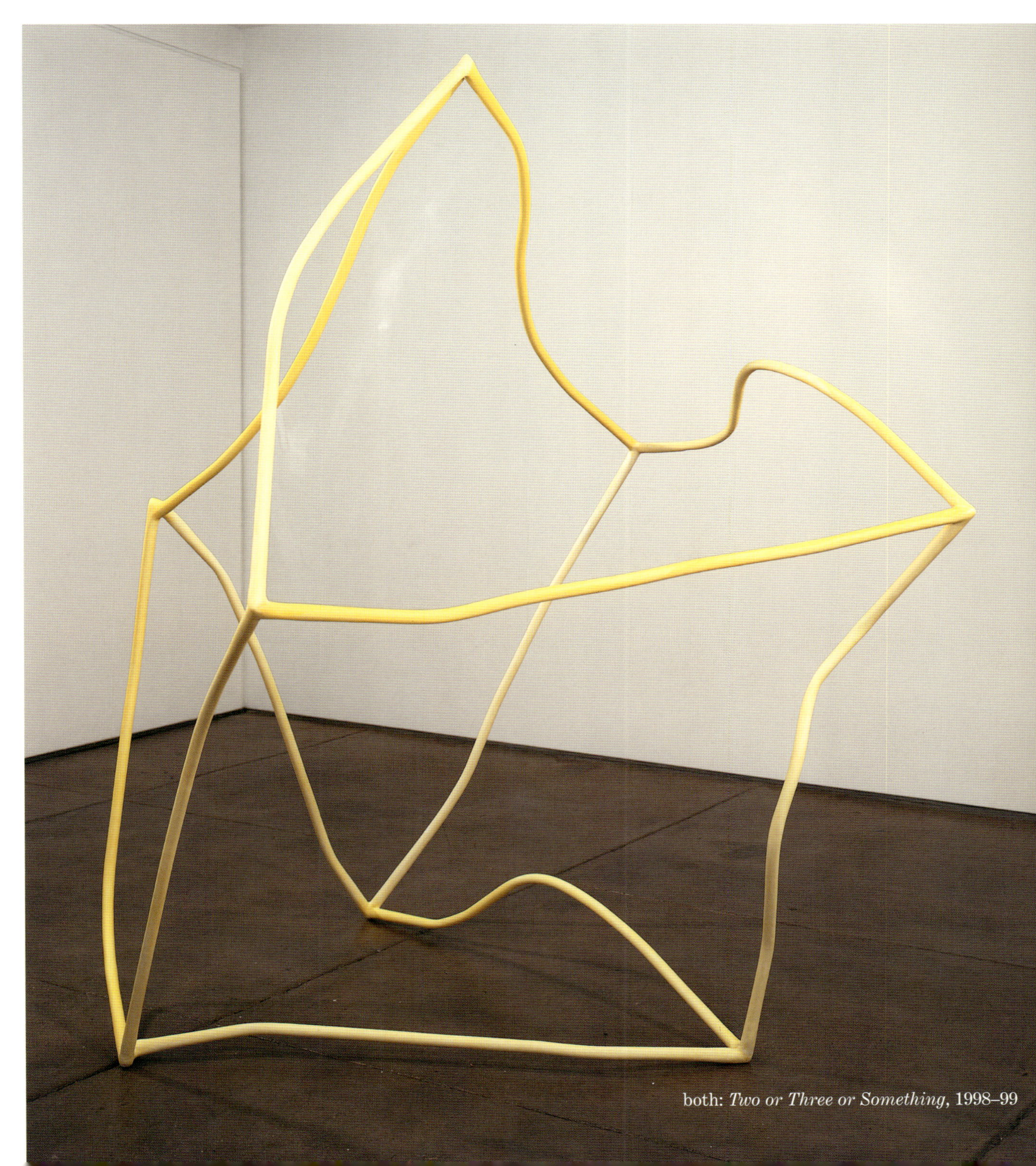

both: *Two or Three or Something*, 1998–99

structures. On one level geometry offers a more neutral vocabulary to work with, one without the viscerality of the culture pieces or the implications of restraint and captivity that come with the chain works. On the other hand, geometry is widely perceived as sculpture's most elevated vocabulary. Geometrically based sculpture has an implied claim to an almost absolute level of rigor and, indeed, purity. To enter this terrain is to leave the periphery for the center of post-war sculptural tradition.

The new sculptures are linear, but do refer to specific geometric forms. Their precursors can be found in *Used To Do the Job*, with its lethal power neatly contained within a cube; in *Copper cube, woven* (1988), where a traditionally female practice was applied to the form; and in *Grid Cube* (1989), where a perfect gunmetal-steel cube is tightly clenched by an equally perfect grid of neoprene cord. *Grid Cube* expresses a rigidity the excess of which pushes geometry to

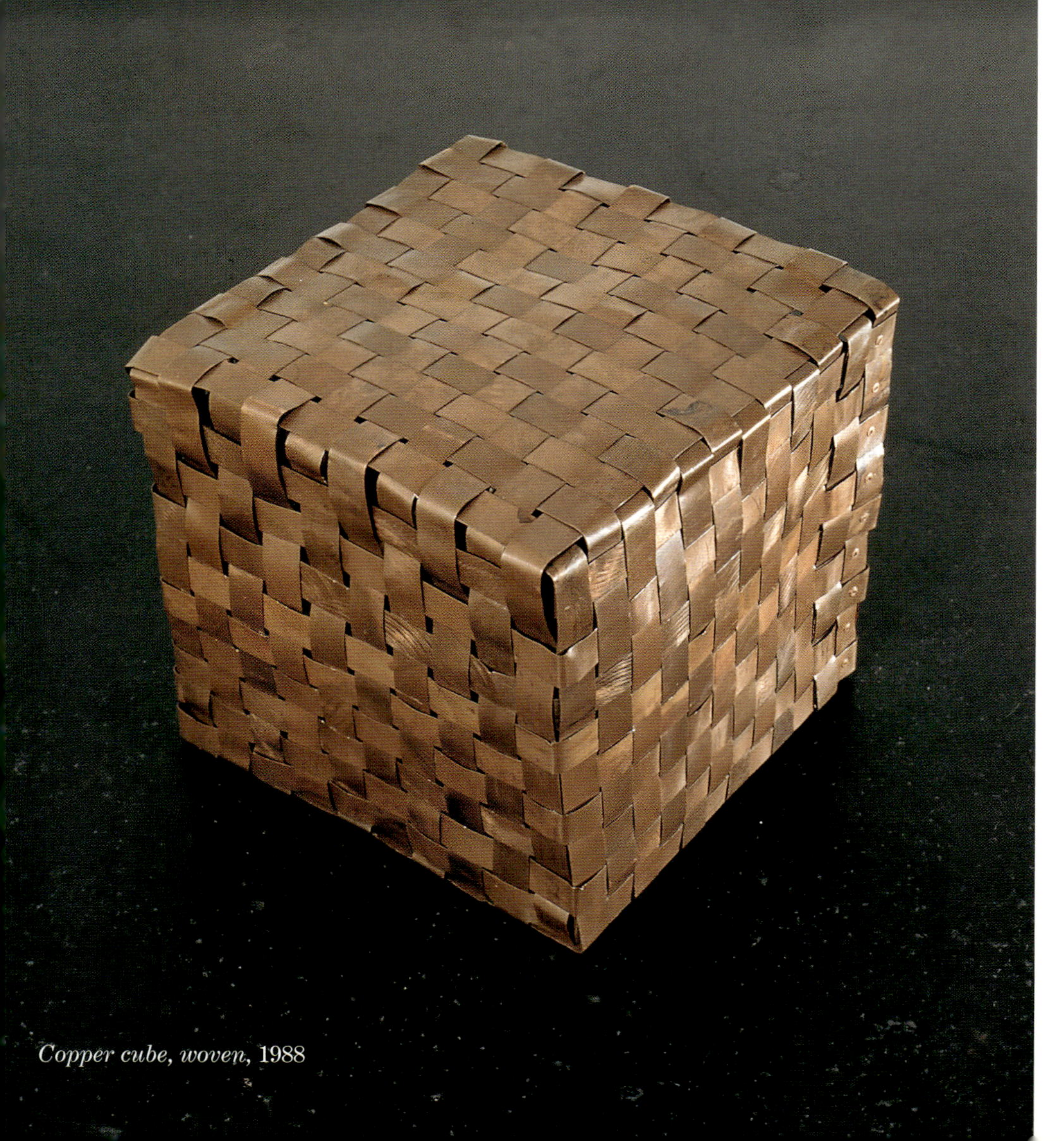

Copper cube, woven, 1988

Grid Cube, 1989

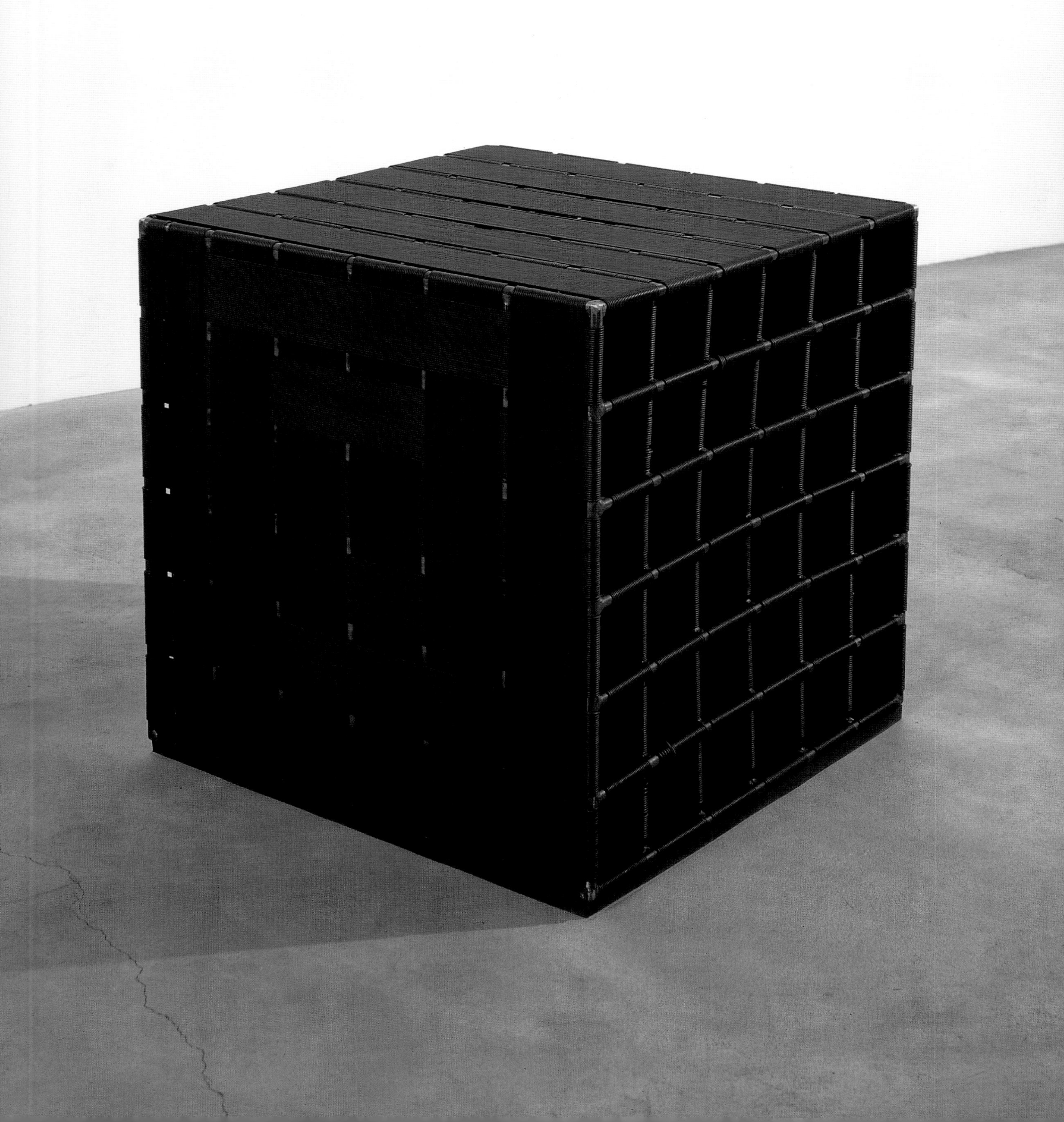

the limit. The cord grips the steel of the cube with such power that it actually buckles slightly. But her new cubes wobble and bend by themselves, calling into question the limits of the terms that define the forms. The surfaces are mottled with pale, shifting color, resistant to their own potential status as definitive boundaries. We can easily read them as cubes, but then aren't cubes supposed to have right angles and straight edges? Again, Larner is testing categories and stretching definitions. In *Surprisingly Nameless* (2000), a tangle of cubes challenges the whole idea of geometry as symbolic of order and regularity.

For viewers moving around it, *2 as 3 and Some Too* can seem almost mobile, offering up a kaleidoscopic array of changing configurations. And it is essential to move around it, because looking from a fixed point is fundamentally different from the haptic experience of a viewer with a shifting viewpoint. The sculpture plays off overlapping parts of its own structure and the

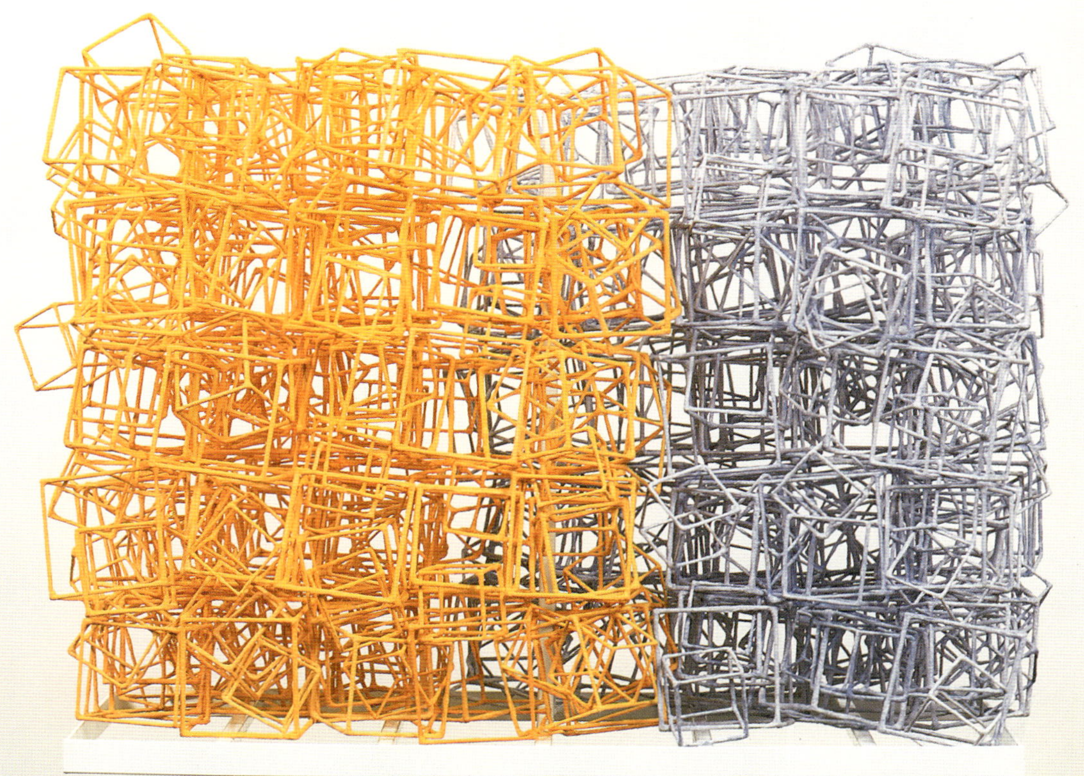

Surprisingly Nameless, 2000

otherwise empty spaces it frames and occupies. The basic structure of two cubes, juxtaposed, creates not only a third space but also multiple other spaces, depending in part on the position of the viewer. The titles of the works indicate a confusion in the distinctions between the two- and the three-dimensional, setting up an extraordinarily sophisticated relationship between the two. Her insistent questioning of sculptural norms over the last fifteen years has brought her now to a place in which the pleasures of form do not have to be challenged so relentlessly. Having thoroughly tested everything that might possibly be taken for granted, she has achieved in the end an evident confidence in her own capacity as a sculptor.

In 1997, Jeremy Gilbert-Rolfe wrote that, "In Larner's most recent works one may no longer be talking about making space visible, but about making visible that upon which visibility depends."[19] The work that she is making now, most notably *Untitled* (2001), pushes even more directly than before into fundamental issues of form and visibility. How exactly does a sphere relate to a cube? How does rotation affect perception? How does movement relate to stasis, and to sculpture in general? Taking advantage of new technology, she is now addressing these questions. The linearity of animation is spun into one object in one space. There is no "forced perspective" here, but rather a relaxed and flexible rhythm of visual and spatial possibilities.

[1] Liz Larner, unpublished written statement, May 2000.

[2] Liz Larner, interview with the author, 29 June 2001. All subsequent quotations of Larner are from this interview unless otherwise specified.

[3] Mel Bochner, in Elayne Varian, "Interview with Mel Bochner" (1969), *Documents*, no. 20 (Spring 2001): 7.

[4] Donald Judd, "Specific Objects" (1965), in Charles Harrison and Paul Wood, eds., *Art in Theory, 1900–1990: An Anthology of Changing Ideas* (Oxford: Blackwell, 1992), 810.

[5] Martin Prinzhorn, "Form and Vice Versa: The Sculptures of Liz Larner," in *Liz Larner* (Basel: Kunsthalle, 1997), n.p.

[6] Douglas Huebler, in *January 5–31, 1969* (New York: Seth Siegelaub, 1969).

[7] Liz Larner, to Catherine Liu, "Liz Larner: Embodied Tension," *Flash Art* 24, no. 156 (January–February 1991): 104.

[8] Georges Bataille, *Visions of Excess: Selected Writings, 1927–1939*, ed. and trans. Allan Stoekl (Minneapolis: University of Minnesota Press, 1985), 31. The subject is dealt with in depth by Yve-Alain Bois and Rosalind E. Krauss in *Formless: A User's Guide* (New York: Zone, 1997).

[9] Liz Larner, in Peter Noever, "Wonderful Pussycat: Interview with Liz Larner," in *Liz Larner: I thought I saw a Pussycat* (Vienna: MAK, 1998).

[10] Kirby Gookin, "Liz Larner," *Artforum* 29, no. 2 (October 1990): 165.

[11] David Batchelor, *Chromophobia* (London: Reaktion, 2000), 22–23.

[12] Liz Larner, interview with Richard Armstrong, in his *Mind Over Matter: Concept and Object* (New York: Whitney Museum of American Art, 1990), 118.

[13] Michael Fried, "Problems of Polychromy: New Sculptures by Michael Bolus," (1971) in Fried, *Art and Objecthood: Essays and Reviews* (Chicago: The University of Chicago Press, 1998), 193–94.

[14] Rosalind Krauss, *Passages in Modern Sculpture* (Cambridge, Mass.: The MIT Press, 1977), 192.

[15] Liz Larner, unpublished statement.

[16] See also Catherine Liu, "Cornering the Set-Up," in *Liz Larner*.

[17] Lisa Anne Auerbach, "Liz Larner at Regen Projects," *L.A. Weekly*, 17–23 July 1998, 61.

[18] Liz Larner, in Hunter Drohojowska-Philp, "She's Back. But She's Never Been Away…," *Los Angeles Times*, 28 June 1998, 55.

[19] Jeremy Gilbert-Rolfe, "Visible Space, Elusive Object," in *Liz Larner*, n.p.

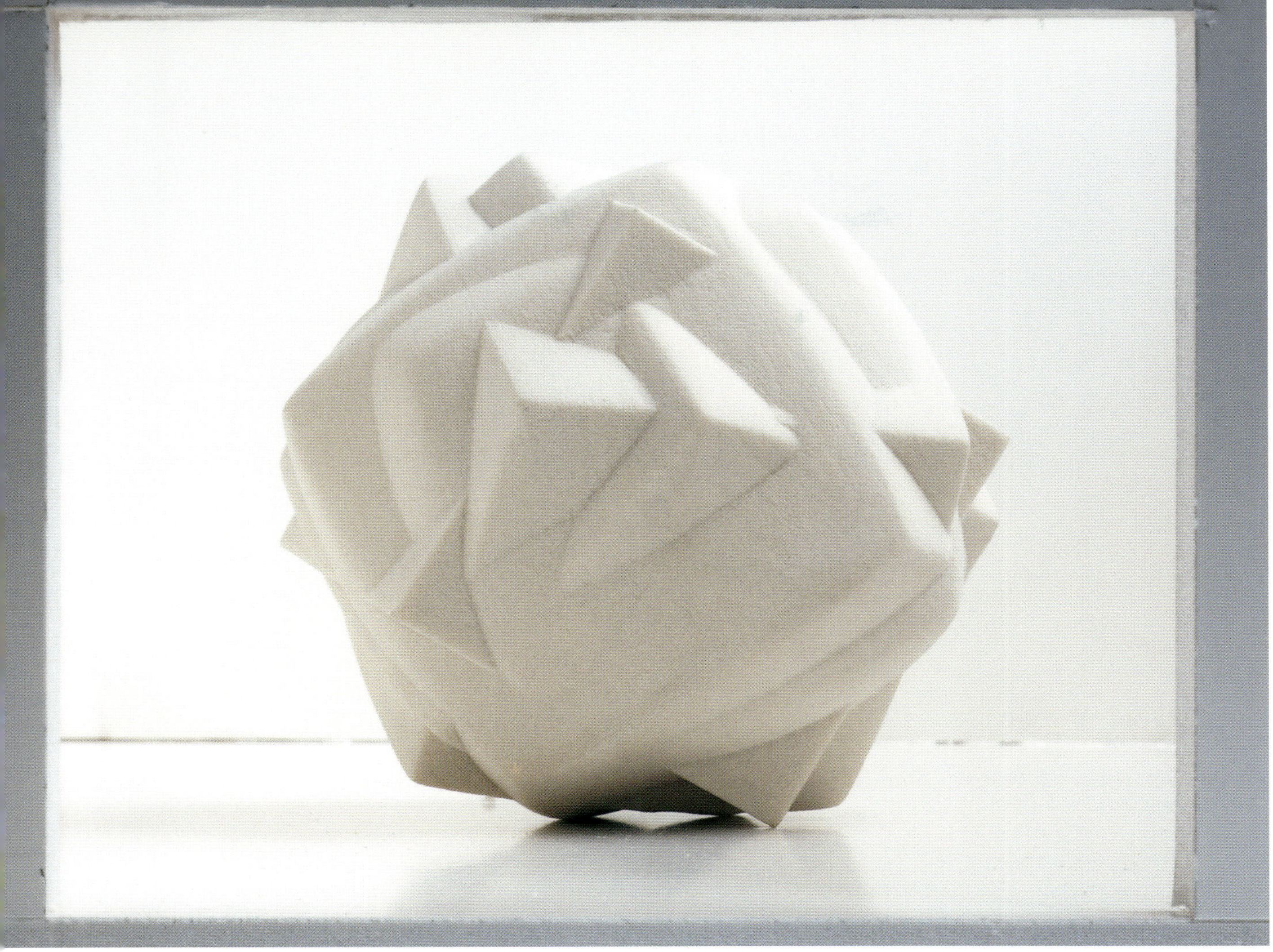

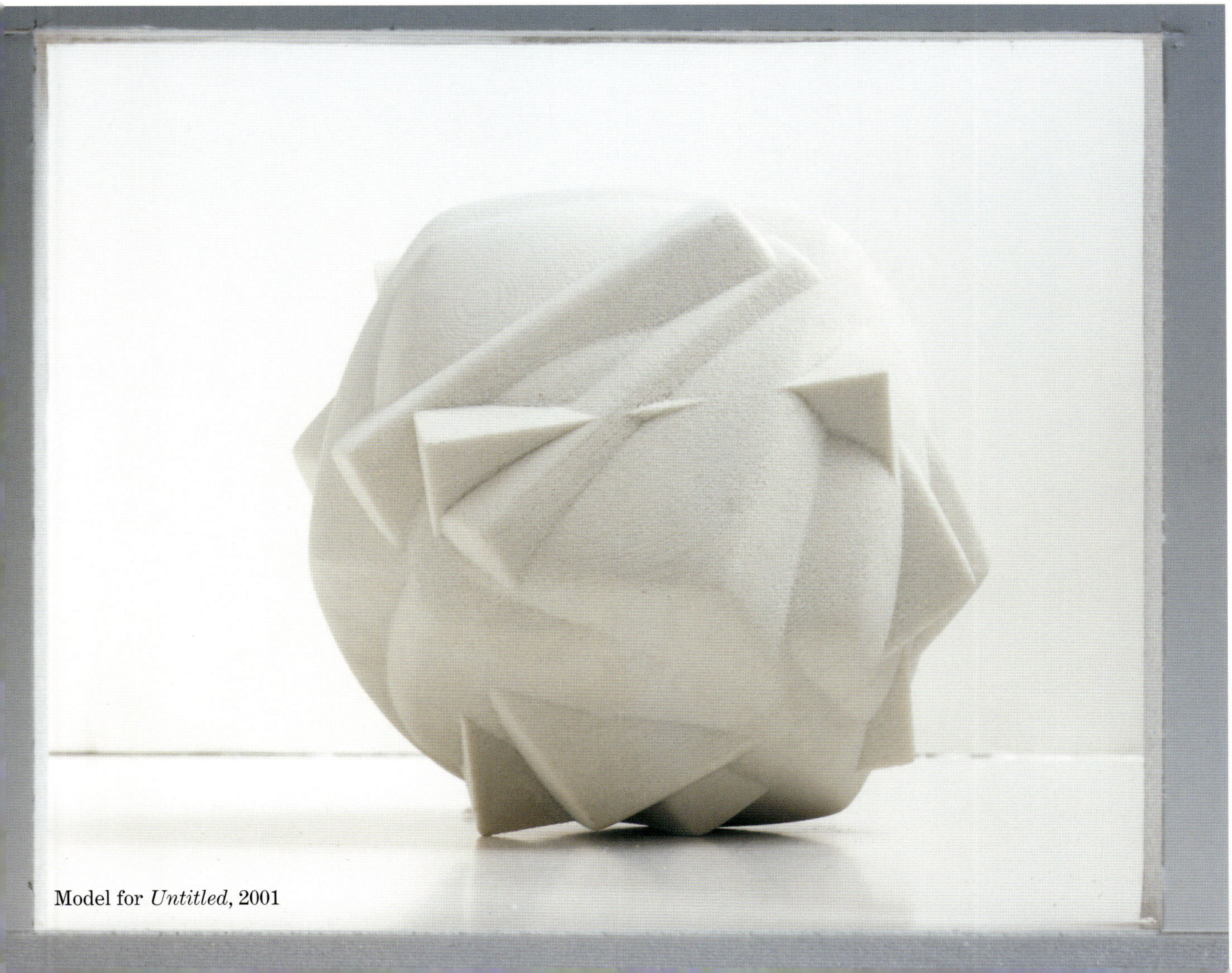

Model for *Untitled*, 2001

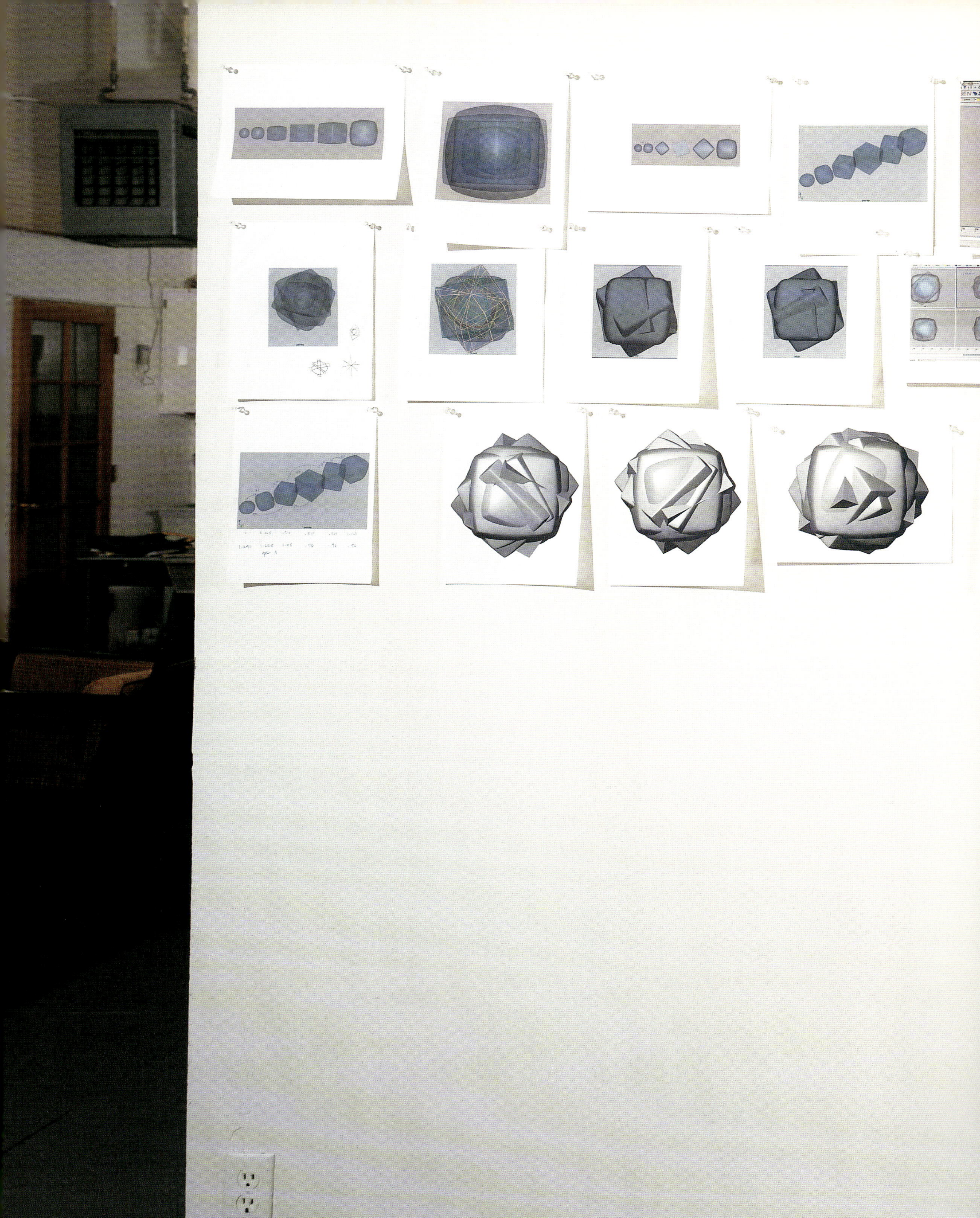

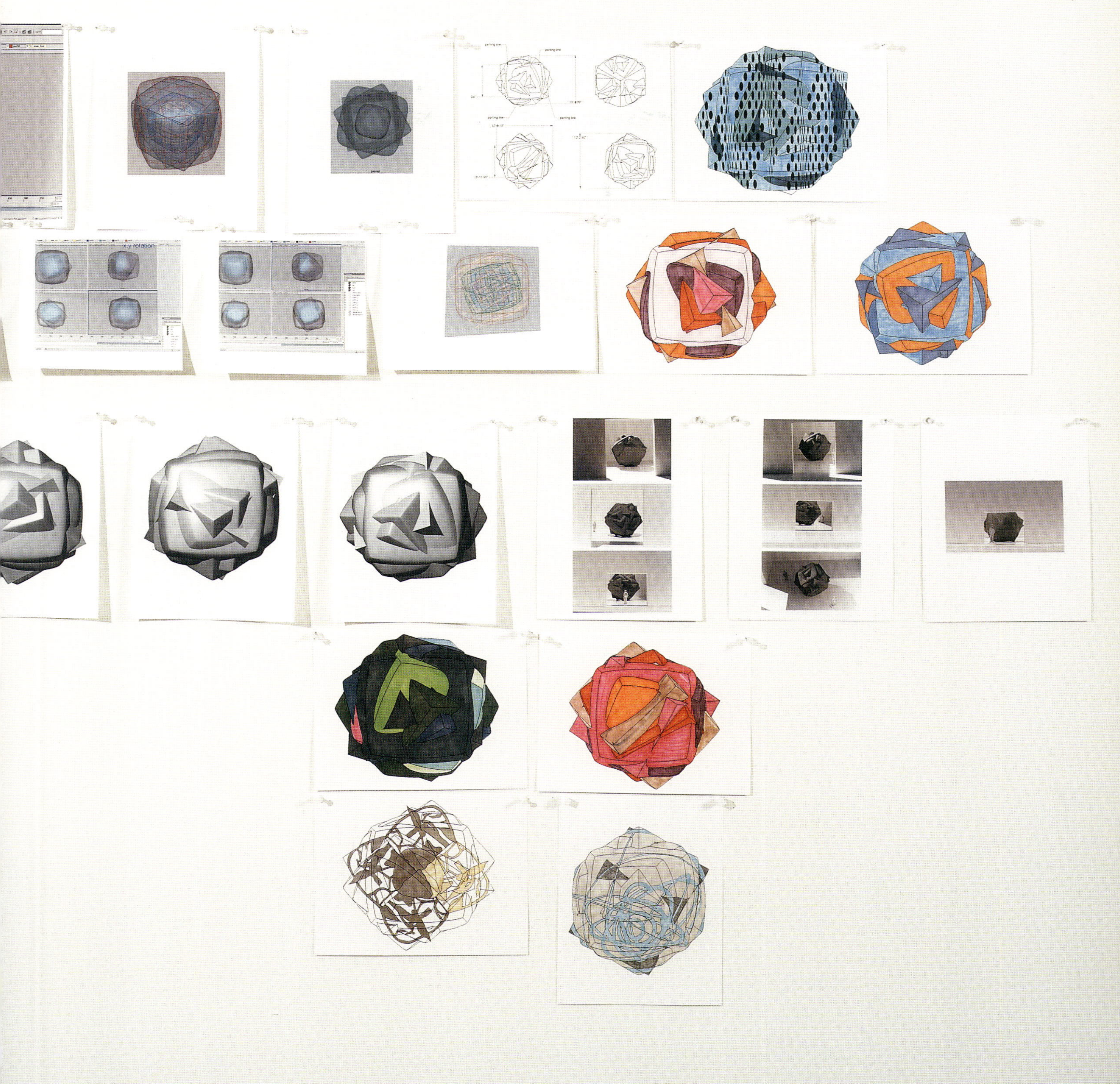

Illustrations

39. *Primary, Secondary: Culture of Empire State Building and
Twin Towers*, 1988. Bacteria, nutrient agar, food coloring,
glass, and aluminum. 42 x 12 x 14 1/2 inches. Courtesy
303 Gallery, New York, and Regen Projects, Los Angeles.
Photo courtesy 303 Gallery, New York

40–41, 42–43. *Bird in Space*, 1989. Installation at the Los Angeles
Municipal Art Gallery, 1989. Nylon cord sewn with silk,
weighted with stainless steel blocks. Dimensions variable.
Courtesy 303 Gallery, New York, and Regen Projects,
Los Angeles. Photos courtesy 303 Gallery, New York

41. Constantin Brancusi, *Bird in Space*, 1928. Bronze. 54 x 8 1/2 x 6 1/2
inches. The Museum of Modern Art, New York. Given
anonymously. © 2001 Artists Rights Society (ARS),
New York/ADAGP, Paris. Photo © 2001 The Museum
of Modern Art, New York

44. *Come Together* (detail), 1990. Mixed media. 31 1/2 x 16 x 12 feet.
Courtesy of Galerie Jennifer Flay, Paris. Photo courtesy
of the artist

45, 48, 49. *Head, Torso, Foot*, 1989. Mixed media. Dimensions variable.
Private collection, Basel, Switzerland. Photos courtesy
303 Gallery, New York

46, 47. *Head, Torso, Foot*, 1989. Installation at the Whitney Museum
of American Art, New York, 1990

50, 51. *DDEEFIIINNTU*, 1999. Flexall, sign enamel, nylon cord,
aluminum. Four pieces: 126 4/5 x 246 x 5 inches each.
Private collection, Basel, Switzerland. Photos courtesy
Galerie Peter Pakesch

52. *Chain*, 1988. Carnuba and microcrystalline wax, plaster, bronze,
steel, and stainless steel cable. 154 x 2 x 2 inches.
Whitney Museum of American Art, New York /
Purchase, with funds from the Painting and Sculpture
Committee. Photos courtesy of the artist and Regen
Projects, Los Angeles. Photo: Joshua White

53. *Untitled (Study for Chain)*, 1987. Charcoal, pastel, and graphite
on paper. 16 13/16 x 14 1/16 inches. Collection of the artist.
Photo: Brian Forrest

54, 55. *Lash Mat*, 1989. False eyelashes made from human hair, and
leather. 112 1/2 x 11 3/8 inches. The Dakis Joannou
Collection, Athens. Photos courtesy 303 Gallery, New York

57, 58–59. *Out of Touch*, 1987. Installation at St. Agnes Monastery,
Prague, 1994. Sixteen miles of surgical gauze. 48 x 48 x 48
inches. Private collection, Basel, Switzerland.
Photos courtesy Jirí Sevcík

61, 62–63, 64. *I thought I saw a pussycat*, 1997–98. Installation at
MAK—Austrian Museum of Applied Arts, Vienna, 1998.
Cast polyurethane and stainless steel. 72 1/2 x 108 x 144
inches. Photos courtesy Regen Projects, Los Angeles

65. Brice Marden, *Study for the Muses (Eaglesmere Version)*,
1991–94/1997–99. Oil on linen. 82 1/2 x 134 1/2 inches.
Photo courtesy Matthew Marks Gallery, New York

66. *Untitled*, 1998. Graphite and ink on cotton vellum. 26 1/2 x
20 1/2 inches. Collection of Laurence A. Rickels,
Los Angeles. Photo courtesy Regen Projects,
Los Angeles. Photo: Joshua White

67 top. *Untitled*, 1999. Pencil, graphite, ink, and marker on vellum.
20 x 23 1/2 inches. Collection of A.D. S. Fine Arts, Ltd.,
USA. Photo courtesy 303 Gallery, New York

67 bottom. *Untitled*, 1999. Pencil, graphite, ink, and marker on vellum.
20 x 23 1/2 inches. Collection of A.D. S. Fine Arts, Ltd.,
USA. Photo courtesy 303 Gallery, New York

68. *Forced Perspective (reversed, reflected, extended)*, 1992.
Floor plan for installation in "Helter Skelter: L.A. Art
in the 1990s" at The Museum of Contemporary Art,
Los Angeles, 1992. Photo courtesy of the artist

69 top. *Chain Perspective Reflected*, 1990. Installation at 303 Gallery,
New York, 1990. Steel chain, mirrors, and hardware.
Dimensions variable. Courtesy of the artist; 303
Gallery, New York; and Regen Projects, Los Angeles

69 bottom, 70, 71. *Forced Perspective (reversed, reflected, extended)*,
1992. Installation at The Museum of Contemporary Art,
Los Angeles, 1992. Steel chain, mirrors, and hardware.
Dimensions variable. Courtesy of the artist; 303 Gallery,
New York; and Regen Projects, Los Angeles.
Photos courtesy Regen Projects, Los Angeles.
Photo: Joshua White

72 left. *Untitled (Study for Corridors)*, 1990–91. Ink on vellum.
30 x 18 inches. Collection of the artist.
Photo: Brian Forrest

72 right. *Untitled (Study for Corridors)*, 1990–91. Ink on vellum.
30 x 18 inches. Collection of the artist.
Photo: Brian Forrest

73. *Mother (Tattoo Flash)*, 1992. Ink on vellum. 11 x 14 inches.
Collection of the artist. Photo: Brian Forrest

74. *Corridor Yellow/Purple*, 1991, and *Corridor Red/Green*, 1991.
Installation at Stuart Regen Gallery, Los Angeles, 1991.
Photo courtesy Regen Projects, Los Angeles.
Photo: Susan Einstein

75 left. *Corridor Red/Green*, 1991. Leather, rock, lead, metal,
car paint, fabric, stainless steel, and wood. Dimensions
variable. The Museum of Contemporary Art, Los Angeles.
Gift of Manfred Simchowitz. Photo: Brian Forrest

75 right. *Corridor Orange/Blue*, 1991. Lead, metal, car paint, fabric,
stainless steel, steel, and wood. Dimensions variable.
Courtesy Regen Projects, Los Angeles, and 303 Gallery,
New York

76–77. *Corridor Orange/Blue*, 1991; *Corridor Yellow/Purple*, 1991;
Corridor Red/Green, 1991. Installation at Stuart Regen
Gallery, Los Angeles, 1991. Photo courtesy 303 Gallery,
New York.

78. Anthony Caro, *Month of May*, 1963. Steel and aluminum,
painted magenta, orange, and green. 110 x 120 x 141
inches. Private collection, London. Photo courtesy
of Anthony Caro. Photo: John Riddy

79 all. *Untitled (Study for 2 as 3 and Some)*, 1997. Construction
paper and glue. 12 5/8 x 6 1/4 inches. Collection of the
artist. Photos: Brian Forrest

80, 81. *2 as 3 and Some Too*, 1997–98. Watercolor, paper, and steel.
112 x 137 x 95 inches. The Museum of Contemporary Art,
Los Angeles. Purchased in memory of Stuart Regen with
funds provided by Thea Westreich and Ethan Wagner,
Pam and Dick Kramlich, Norman and Norah Stone,
and Chara Schreyer

82, 83. *Ignis (Fake)*, 1998–99. Installation at 303 Gallery, New
York, 1999. Watercolor, paper, aluminum, and powder-
coated steel base. 32 x 32 x 34 inches. Collection
of Michael and Susan Hort, New York. Photos courtesy
303 Gallery, New York

84, 85. *Reticule*, 1999. Cast polyurethane. 74 x 112 x 80 inches.
Courtesy 303 Gallery, New York. Photo: Brian Forrest

86, 87. *Untitled*, 2000. Watercolor, paper, and stainless steel. 30 x
25 x 13 inches. Collection of Deedie and Edward Rose,
Dallas / Courtesy Thea Westreich Art Advisory Services.
Photos courtesy Regen Projects, Los Angeles.
Photo: Joshua White

88–89. *Untitled (wall)*, 2000–01. Watercolor, gouache, paper,
water-based primer, and stainless steel; base is paint
and steel. 66 x 80 x 10 inches. Courtesy of the artist
and Regen Projects, Los Angeles. Photo courtesy
Regen Projects, Los Angeles. Photo: Joshua White

90–91. *Gemi*, 2001. Watercolor, paper, water-based primer, and
stainless steel. 18 1/2 x 18 1/2 x 13 inches. Courtesy
of the artist and 303 Gallery, New York

93 top. *Corner Basher*, 1988. Steel, stainless steel, electric motor,
and speed control. 10 feet high. Collection of Michael
Janssen, Cologne. Photo courtesy of the artist

93 bottom. *Corner Basher*, 1988. Installation at L'Éspace d'art moderne
et contemporain de Toulouse et Midi-Pyrénées,
Toulouse. Photo courtesy of the artist

94 all. *Corner Basher*, 1988. Details of on/off speed control. Photo courtesy of the artist

95. *Corner Basher*, 1988. Installation at Louisiana Museum of Modern Art, Humlebaek, Denmark, 1993. Photo courtesy of the Louisiana Museum of Modern Art, Humlebaek, Denmark

96. *Wall Scratcher*, 1988. Anodized aluminum, 12-volt gear motor and battery, and spring steel. 47 x 18 1/2 x 12 1/4 inches. Collection of Lori and Ira Young, Vancouver, Canada. Photo courtesy of Regen Projects, Los Angeles. Photo: Joshua White

97. Bruce Nauman, *Bouncing in the Corner, No. 1*, 1968. Black-and-white videotape with sound. Dimensions variable. Photo courtesy Electronic Arts Intermix

98. *Corner*, 1986. Graphite on paper. 11 x 14 1/16 inches. Collection of the artist. Photo: Brian Forrest

99. *Chained form on the diagonal, interrupted*, 1990. Steel and stainless steel. 84 x 66 x 42 inches. Private collection. Photo courtesy of Regen Projects, Los Angeles. Photo: Joshua White

100–101. *Wrapped Corner*, 1991. Stainless steel chain and hardware. 49 x 90 inches. Collection of Norah and Norman Stone, San Francisco / Courtesy Thea Westreich Art Advisory Services

102, 103. Riverside Pedestrian Bridge, 2000. Steel, glass, and concrete. 304 feet 5 inches x 15 feet x 30 feet 3 inches. Photo courtesy Regen Projects, Los Angeles. Photo: Joshua White

104, 105. *Devex Yellow*, 1997. Installation at Kunsthalle Basel, Basel, Switzerland, 1997. Aluminum, paper, watercolor, maple, and casein paint. 40 x 34 x 27 inches. Collection of Chara Schreyer, Tiburon, California. Photo courtesy Regen Projects, Los Angeles. Photo: Joshua White

106–107. *Rubber Divider*, 1989. Torch-cut steel and pure gum rubber sheeting. Dimensions variable. Collection of Gabi and Wilhelm Schürmann, Germany. Photo courtesy Regen Projects, Los Angeles. Photo: Joshua White

108, 109. *Two or Three or Something*, 1998–99. Watercolor, paper, water-based primer, and steel. 100 x 80 x 68 inches. Collection of the Whitney Museum of American Art, New York / Purchase, with funds from the Contemporary Committee. Photo courtesy Regen Projects, Los Angeles. Photo: Joshua White

110. *Copper cube, woven*, 1988. Copper. 12 3/4 x 12 3/4 x 12 3/4 inches. Private collection, Basel, Switzerland. Photo courtesy Regen Projects, Los Angeles. Photo: Joshua White

111. *Grid Cube*, 1989. Steel with gunmetal bluing and neoprene rubber cord. 24 x 24 x 24 inches. Private collection, Stockholm. Photo courtesy 303 Gallery, New York

113. *Surprisingly Nameless*, 2000. Watercolor, paper, water-based primer, stainless steel; base is powder-coated steel. 123 x 28 1/4 x 52 inches. Collection of Rebecca and Alexander Stewart, Seattle. Photos courtesy Regen Projects, Los Angeles. Photo: Joshua White

115. Model for *Untitled*, 2001. Plaster. Photos courtesy of the artist. Photos: Joshua White

116–117. Storyboard for *Untitled*, 2001. Studio view. Photo courtesy of the artist

123. *Untitled*, 1999. Watercolor, ink, and graphite on cotton vellum. 19 1/6 x 25 inches. Collection of the artist. Photo: Brian Forrest

126. *Untitled*, 1986. Ink on paper. 4 7/8 x 7 7/16 inches. Collection of the artist. Photo: Brian Forrest

Checklist

Untitled, 1985
Silver-gelatin print
Triptych: 24 x 20 inches each
Courtesy 303 Gallery, New York, and Regen Projects, Los Angeles

Corner, 1986
Graphite on paper
11 x 14 1/16 inches
Collection of the artist

Untitled, 1986
Ink on paper
4 7/8 x 7 7/16 inches
Collection of the artist

Orchid, Buttermilk, Penny, 1987
Cibachrome print
15 1/2 x 19 1/2 inches
Courtesy of the artist; 303 Gallery, New York; and Regen Projects, Los Angeles

Orchid, Buttermilk, Penny (3 weeks), 1987
Cibachrome print
15 1/2 x 19 1/2 inches
Courtesy of the artist; 303 Gallery, New York; and Regen Projects, Los Angeles

Out of Touch, 1987
Sixteen miles of surgical gauze
48 x 48 x 48 inches
Private collection, Basel, Switzerland

Ten Different Brown Liquors at the Tropicana Motel, LA, 1987
Cibachrome print
12 3/4 x 19 1/4 inches
Courtesy of the artist; 303 Gallery, New York; and Regen Projects, Los Angeles

Tropicana Pool Water, Guitar Strings, and Mercury, 1987
Cibachrome print
12 3/4 x 19 1/4 inches
Courtesy of the artist; 303 Gallery, New York; and Regen Projects, Los Angeles

Untitled (Study for Chain), 1987
Charcoal, pastel, and graphite on paper
16 13/16 x 14 1/16 inches
Collection of the artist

Used to Do the Job, 1987
Steel, aluminum, coal, copper, iron, zinc, copper carbonate, brass, bronze, saltpeter, bursera gummfera, glass, iron oxide, santalum album, bluestone, sulfur, tar, rubber, volcanic ash, lodestones, trinitrotoluene (TNT), ammonium nitrate, and other natural and artificial ingredients suspended in microcrystalline wax and paraffin on sheet-metal base
48 1/2 x 25 3/4 x 24 3/4 inches
Collection of Alan Dinsfriend, Boston

Chain, 1988
Carnuba and microcrystalline wax, plaster, bronze, steel, and stainless steel cable
154 x 2 x 2 inches
Whitney Museum of American Art, New York / Purchase, with funds from the Painting and Sculpture Committee

Gold, Collagen, and Water-Soluble Fluorescent Dye, 1988
Gold, collagen, water-soluble fluorescent dye, glass, stainless steel, and deirin
10 x 12 x 5 inches
Fogg Art Museum, Harvard University Art Museums; Gift of Leroy and Dorothy Levine

More Congeries, 1988
Xerox and watercolor on rag
23 7/8 x 17 15/16 inches
Collection of the artist

Bird in Space, 1989
Nylon cord sewn with silk, weighted with stainless steel blocks
Dimensions variable
Courtesy 303 Gallery, New York, and Regen Projects, Los Angeles

Lash Mat, 1989
False eyelashes made from human hair, and leather
112 1/2 x 11 3/8 inches
The Dakis Joannou Collection, Athens

Something I Got Out of the Museum Here in L.A., 1989
Glass vial found in the third pit during Chris Burden's *Exposing the Foundation of the Museum* installation at MOCA; glass vial on wooden stand, contents of vial unknown
9 x 3 x 3 inches
Collection of Kirby Gookin and Robin Kahn, New York

No M, No D, Only S & B, 1990
Leather, sand, brass zipper, and waxed cotton thread
36 x 48 x 60 inches
Private collection

Untitled (Study for Corridors), 1990–91
Ink on vellum
30 x 18 inches
Collection of the artist

Untitled (Study for Corridors), 1990–91
Ink on vellum
30 x 18 inches
Collection of the artist

Untitled (Study for Corridors), 1990–91
Ink on vellum
30 x 18 inches
Collection of the artist

Corridor Orange/Blue, 1991
Lead, metal, car paint, fabric, stainless steel, steel, and wood
Dimensions variable
Courtesy Regen Projects, Los Angeles, and 303 Gallery, New York

Corridor Red/Green, 1991
Leather, rock, lead, metal, car paint, fabric, stainless steel, and wood
Dimensions variable
The Museum of Contemporary Art, Los Angeles. Gift of Manfred Simchowitz

Wrapped Corner, 1991
Stainless steel chain and hardware
49 x 90 inches
Collection of Norah and Norman Stone, San Francisco / Courtesy Thea Westreich Art Advisory Services

Between Loves Me and Not, 1992
Graphite on drafting film
28 3/4 x 29 inches
Collection of Sally Willcox and Daniel Ross, Los Angeles

Between Loves Me and Not, 1992
Twenty-one pieces of mirror, each 6 mm. thick
Dimensions variable
Courtesy of Galerie Jennifer Flay, Paris

Park, 1996
Agave Americana, concrete, and plant material
40 feet long
Courtesy of the artist; 303 Gallery, New York; and Regen Projects, Los Angeles

Devex Yellow, 1997
Aluminum, paper, watercolor, maple, and casein paint
40 x 34 x 27 inches
Collection of Chara Schreyer, Tiburon, California

2 as 3 and Some Too, 1997–98
Watercolor, paper, and steel
112 x 137 x 95 inches
The Museum of Contemporary Art, Los Angeles. Purchased in memory of Stuart Regen with funds provided by Thea Westreich and Ethan Wagner, Pam and Dick Kramlich, Norman and Norah Stone, and Chara Schreyer

Untitled (Color Study, Orange/Blue), 1997
Acrylic and watercolor on paper
15 x 20 inches
Collection of the artist

Untitled (Study for 2 as 3 and Some), 1997
Construction paper and glue
12 5/8 x 6 1/4 inches
Collection of the artist

Untitled (Study for 2 as 3 and Some), 1997
Construction paper and glue
12 5/8 x 6 1/4 inches
Collection of the artist

Untitled (Study for 2 as 3 and Some), 1997
Construction paper and glue
12 5/8 x 6 1/4 inches
Collection of the artist

Untitled (Study for 2 as 3 and Some), 1997
Construction paper and glue
12 5/8 x 6 1/4 inches
Collection of the artist

Ignis (Fake), 1998–99
Watercolor, paper, aluminum, and powder-coated steel base
32 x 32 x 34 inches
Collection of Michael and Susan Hort, New York

Two or Three or Something, 1998–99
Watercolor, paper, water-based primer, and steel
100 x 80 x 68 inches
Collection of the Whitney Museum of American Art, New York / Purchase, with funds from the Contemporary Committee

Untitled, 1998
Graphite and ink on cotton vellum
26 1/2 x 20 1/2 inches
Collection of Laurence A. Rickels, Los Angeles

Reticule, 1999
Cast polyurethane
74 x 112 x 80 inches
Courtesy 303 Gallery, New York

Untitled, 1999
Watercolor, ink, and graphite on cotton vellum
19 1/16 x 25 inches
Collection of the artist

Surprisingly Nameless, 2000
Watercolor, paper, water-based primer, stainless steel; base is powder-coated steel
123 x 28 1/4 x 52 inches
Collection of Rebecca and Alexander Stewart, Seattle

Untitled, 2000
Watercolor, paper, and stainless steel
30 x 25 x 13 inches
Collection of Deedie and Edward Rose, Dallas / Courtesy Thea Westreich Art Advisory Services

Untitled (wall), 2000–01
Watercolor, gouache, paper, water-based primer, and stainless steel; base is paint and steel
66 x 80 x 10 inches
Courtesy of the artist and Regen Projects, Los Angeles

Untitled, 2001
Fiberglass, paint, and steel
144 x 144 x 144 inches
Courtesy of the artist

Biography

Lives and works in Los Angeles

Education
1985   B.F.A., California Institute of the Arts,
            Valencia, California

Solo Exhibitions
2001   The Museum of Contemporary Art, Los Angeles
1999   303 Gallery, New York
1998   MAK—Austrian Museum of Applied Arts, Vienna
            Regen Projects, Los Angeles
1997   303 Gallery, New York
            Kunsthalle Basel, Basel, Switzerland
1994   303 Gallery, New York
1993   Galerie Jennifer Flay, Paris
1992   Galerie Peter Pakesch, Vienna
1991   Stuart Regen Gallery, Los Angeles
            303 Gallery, New York
1990   Galleri Nordanstad-Skarstedt, Stockholm
            303 Gallery, New York
1989   Galerie Peter Pakesch, Vienna
            303 Gallery, New York
1988   Margo Leavin Gallery, Los Angeles

Selected Group Exhibitions
2001   "A Room of Their Own," The Museum of Contemporary
            Art, Los Angeles

2000   "00: Drawings 2000 at Barbara Gladstone Gallery,"
            Barbara Gladstone Gallery, New York
            "Raumkörper—Netze und andere Gebilde," Kunsthalle
            Basel, Basel, Switzerland

1999   "Description Without Place," AC Project Room,
            New York
            "Life Is Elsewhere," Th.E.—Theoretical Events,
            Naples, Italy
            "Proliferation," The Museum of Contemporary Art,
            Los Angeles

1997   "Elusive Paradise: Los Angeles Art from the Permanent
            Collection," The Museum of Contemporary Art,
            Los Angeles
            "Maxwell's Demon," Margo Leavin Gallery, Los Angeles
            "Painting Machines/Machines Painting," Boston University
            Art Gallery, Boston

1996   "Everything That's Interesting Is New," Deste Foundation,
            Athens
            "Final Projects: The House," MAK Center for Art and
            Architecture, Schindler House, Los Angeles
            "The Garage Project," MAK Center for Art and
            Architecture, Mackey Apartments, Los Angeles
            "Just Past: The Contemporary in the Permanent Collection,
            1975–96," The Museum of Contemporary Art,
            Los Angeles

1995   "Ambient," Olivier Antoine, Nice, France
            "The Big Night," Art Center College of Design, Pasadena
            "Plane/Structures," White Columns, New York
            "Saturday Night Fever," Thomas Solomon's Garage,
            Los Angeles

1994   "Plane/Structures," Otis Gallery, Los Angeles
            "Un papillon sur la roue," L'Éspace d'art moderne et
            contemporain de Toulouse et Midi-Pyrénées, Toulouse,
            France

1993   "At the Edge of Chaos—New Images of the World,"
            Louisiana Museum of Modern Art, Humlebaek, Denmark
            "Co-Conspirators," James Corcoran Gallery, Santa Monica,
            California
            "Informationsdienst," Art Acker, Berlin
            "Just What Is It That Makes Today's Homes So Different,
            So Appealing?," Galerie Jennifer Flay, Paris
            "Sonsbeek 93," Arnhem, The Netherlands

1992   "FluxAttitudes," New Museum of Contemporary Art,
            New York
            "Group Drawing Show," Stuart Regen Gallery, Los Angeles
            "Helter Skelter: L.A. Art in the 1990s," The Museum of
            Contemporary Art, Los Angeles
            Galerie Max Hetzler, Cologne
            "How It Is," Tony Shafrazi Gallery, New York
            "Multiplicity," Thea Westreich Associates, New York
            "Not Quiet: Felix Gonzalez-Torres, Liz Larner,
            Christian Marclay, Matthew McCaslin," Galerie
            Jennifer Flay, Paris
            "Recent Acquisitions: Selected New Works in the
            Permanent Collection," The Museum of Contemporary
            Art, Los Angeles
            "Speaker Project," Institute of Contemporary Arts, London
            "Tattoo Collection," Galerie Jennifer Flay, Paris

1991   "American Art of the Eighties," Museo di Arte Moderna
            e Contemporanea, Trento, Italy
            "The Body," The Renaissance Society, University of
            Chicago, Chicago
            "Devices," Josh Baer Gallery, New York
            "Drawings," Luhring Augustine Hetzler, Santa Monica,
            California
            "Enclosure's," Municipal Art Gallery, Barnsdall Park,
            Los Angeles
            "FluxAttitudes," Hallwalls, Buffalo, New York
            "Gulliver's Travels," Galerie Sophia Ungers, Cologne
            "The Köln Show," various galleries, Cologne
            "Lick of the Eye," Shoshana Wayne Gallery,
            Santa Monica, California
            "Liz Larner, Karen Kilimnik, Collier Schorr, Anne Walsh,"
            Richard Kuhlenschmidt Gallery, New York
            "New Works by Gallery Artists," 303 Gallery, New York
            "nonrePRESENTation," Security Pacific Corporation
            Gallery, Los Angeles
            "Plastic Fantastic Lover (object a)," Blum Helman
            Warehouse, New York
            "Santa Monica Editions," Luhring Augustine Hetzler,
            Santa Monica, California
            "Work in Progress? Work?," Andrea Rosen Gallery,
            New York
            Luhring Augustine Gallery, New York

Untitled, 1999

1990   "Artificial Nature," Deste Foundation for Contemporary Art, The House of Cyprus, Athens
"Liz Larner, Rosemarie Trockel, Meg Webster," Stuart Regen Gallery, Los Angeles
"Mind Over Matter: Concept and Object," Whitney Museum of American Art, New York
"Signs of Life: Process and Materials, 1960–1990," Institute of Contemporary Art, University of Pennsylvania, Philadelphia
"Stendahl Syndrome: The Cure," Andrea Rosen Gallery, New York
Galerie Sophia Ungers, Cologne

1989   "Archaelogy II," Roy Boyd Gallery, Los Angeles
"David Cabrera, Larry Johnson, Liz Larner," 303 Gallery, New York
"The Desire of the Museum," Whitney Museum of American Art, Downtown at Federal Reserve Plaza, New York
"Specific Metaphysics," Sandra Gering Gallery, New York
Galerie Ryszard Varisella, Frankfurt
"Whitney Biennial 1989," Whitney Museum of American Art, New York

1988   DAG, Los Angeles
"A Drawing Show," Cable Gallery, New York
"Graz 1988," Grazer Kunstverein, Stadtmuseum Graz, Austria
"Life Like," Lorence Monk Gallery, New York
"Nayland Blake, Liz Larner, Richard Morrison, Charles Ray," 303 Gallery, New York
"Re:Placement," L.A.C.E., Los Angeles

1987   Jeffrey Linden Gallery, Los Angeles
"L.A. Hot and Cool," M.I.T. List Visual Arts Center, Cambridge, Massachusetts
"1987 Annuale," L.A.C.E., Los Angeles
"Nothing Sacred," Margo Leavin Gallery, Los Angeles
"Reworks: Recent Sculpture," New Langton Arts, San Francisco
"Room 9," Tropicana Hotel, Los Angeles

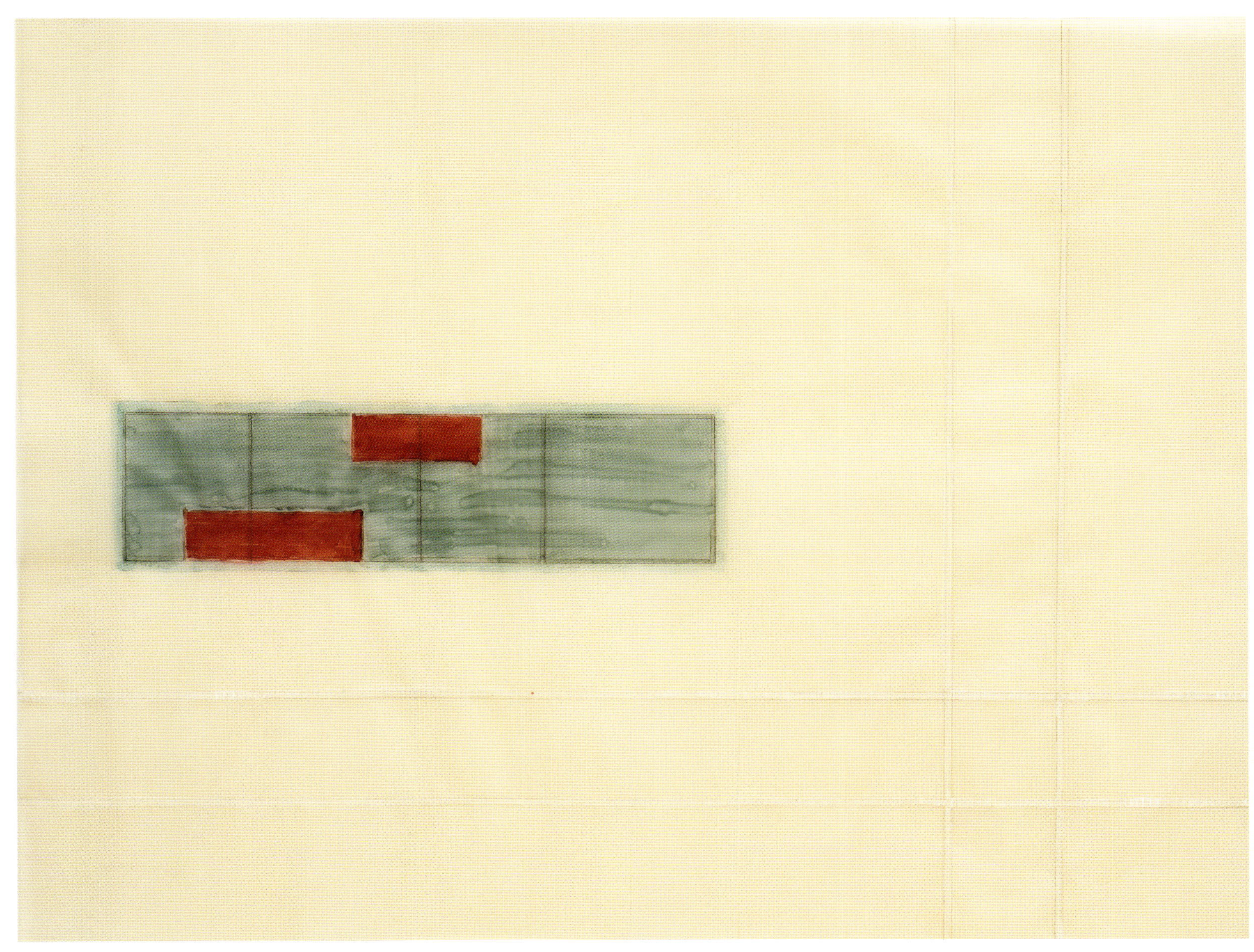

Bibliography

Artificial Nature. Exh. cat. Edited by Jeffrey Deitch and Dan Friedman. Athens: Deste Foundation for Contemporary Art, 1990.

Auerbach, Lisa Anne. "Liz Larner at Regen Projects." *L.A. Weekly*, 17 July 1998, 61.

Avgikos, Jan. "Liz Larner at 303 Gallery." *Flash Art* 23, no. 154 (October 1990): 154.

Bernard, Christian. *Galeries Magazine* (October/November 1992): 135.

Bonetti, David. "Welcome to L.A.: Art That Blows Hot and Cool." *The Boston Phoenix*, 15 January 1988, III–14.

Brenson, Michael. "In the Arena of the Mind, at the Whitney." *The New York Times*, 19 October 1990, C33.

Breslauer, Jan. "Liz Larner at Margo Leavin Gallery." *L.A. Weekly*, 30 September 1988, 45.

Brock, Hovey. "Liz Larner at Gallery 303." *Artnews* 91, no. 1 (January 1992): 130.

Calame, Ingrid. "Liz Larner at Regen Projects." *art issues*, no. 54 (September/October 1998): 46.

Cameron, Dan. "Changing Priorities in American Art." *Art International* (Spring 1990): 86–90.

Chattopadhyay, Collette. "Liz Larner at Regen Projects." *Sculpture* 17, no. 10 (December 1998): 51–52.

Conal, Robbie. "Good Times: View With A Room." *L.A. Weekly* 9, no. 18, 27 March 1987, 62.

Cotter, Holland. "A Bland Biennal." *Art in America* 77, no. 9 (September 1989): 81–87.

Curtis, Cathy. "The Galleries: La Cienega Area." *Los Angeles Times*, 2 February 1990, F22.

Darling, Michael. "Garage Project at MAK Center for Art and Architecture, Los Angeles." *frieze*, no. 31 (November–December 1996): 88.

———. "Liz Larner at Regen Projects." *dArt* (Fall 1998): 27.

Decter, Joshua. "Liz Larner at 303 Gallery." *Artscribe*, no. 83 (September–October 1990): 85–86.

———. "New York in Review." *Arts Magazine* 65, no. 7 (March 1991): 99–100.

Drohojowska-Philp, Hunter. "She's Back. But She's Never Been Away…." *Los Angeles Times*, 28 June 1998, Calendar 55–56.

Dubin, Zan. "L.A.C.E. 'Annuale' Exhibition Set to Open this Week." *Los Angeles Times*, 30 August 1987.

Everything That's Interesting Is New: The Dakis Joannou Collection. Exh. cat. Essays by Jeffrey Deitch and Stuart Morgan. Athens: Deste Foundation for Contemporary Art; and Ostfildern, Germany: Cantz Verlag, 1996.

Fama & Fortune Bulletin. Exh. cat. Vienna: Verlag Pakesch & Schlebrugge, 1996.

Fehlau, Fred. "Liz Larner at Margo Leavin, Los Angeles." *Flash Art*, no. 143 (December 1988): 122.

Gerstler, Amy. "Liz Larner at Margo Leavin." *Art Issues* 1, no. 1 (January 1989): 21.

Gilbert-Rolfe, Jeremy. "A Stroll Above the Freeway." http://www.artnet.com/Magazine/features/gilbert-rolfe/gilbert-rolfe7-23-01.asp

Gookin, Kirby. "Dimensions variable: Liz Larner." *Parkett*, no. 36 (June 1993): 118–23.

———. "Liz Larner at 303 Gallery." *Artforum* 29, no. 2 (October 1990): 165.

Grove, Nancy. "Angle of Vision. Tradition and Its Discontents." *Art & Antiques* (November 1990): 121–22.

Hayt, Elizabeth. "People Are Talking About: Arts." *Vogue* (September 1997).

Heartney, Eleanor. "FIAC 93 Galeries: Nouvelle Generation." *Artpress*, no. 184 (October 1993): 24–28.

Helter Skelter: L.A. Art in the 1990s. Exh. cat. Essays by Norman M. Klein, Lane Relyea, and Paul Schimmel. Los Angeles: The Museum of Contemporary Art, 1992.

Hofleitner, Johanna. "Bedeutung hinter Schriftzaunen." *Kultur* (Vienna), 8 December 1992.

Hultkrans, Andrew. "Surf and Turf." *Artforum* 36, no. 10 (Summer 1998): 106–13, 146.

Indiana, Gary. "Science Holiday." *The Village Voice*, 15 March 1988, 90.

Johnson, Ken. "Liz Larner at 303." *Art in America* 80, no. 2 (February 1992): 115–16.

Jones, Amelia G. "The Contingency of the Non-representational: Liz Larner's Objects." *Visions Art Quarterly*, no. 10 (Spring 1989): 8–12.

———. "Museum Bashing." *Art International*, no. 3 (Summer 1988): 59–62.

Kandel, Susan. "L.A. in Review." *Arts Magazine* 64, no. 9 (May 1990): 121–23.

Kelley, Mike. "Foul Perfection: Thoughts on Caricature." *Artforum* 27, no. 5 (January 1989): 92–99.

Knight, Christopher. "L.A., Lately." *Elle* (December 1989): 190, 192.

———. "A Provocative Frame of Reference." *Los Angeles Times*, 21 March 1991.

———. "Re: Placement Parts." *Los Angeles Herald Examiner*, 20 March 1988, E1, E10.

———. "Sixties Sculpture Relieves Summer Doldrums." *Los Angeles Herald Examiner*, 17 July 1987, 33.

———. "Whitney Biennial review." *The Los Angeles Herald Examiner*, 7 May 1989.

Krumpl, Doris. "Mit vollen Symbolik-Segeln: Liz Larners 'Sign of a Sign.'" *Der Standard* (Vienna), 1 December 1992.

Liz Larner. Exh. cat. Essays by Rosetta Brooks, Jeremy Gilbert-Rolfe, Jürg Laederach, Catherine Liu, and Martin Prinzhorn. Basel: Kunsthalle Basel, 1997.

Liz Larner: I thought I saw a pussycat. Exh. cat. Essays by
    Jeremy Gilbert-Rolfe, Giovanni Intra, Terry R. Myers,
    and Jan Tumlir. Interview with Peter Noever. Vienna:
    MAK-Galerie, 1998.

Larner, Liz. Column in "The Question of Gender in Art."
    Tema Celeste, no. 39 (Winter 1993): 57–58.

Larson, Kay. "Every Object Tells a Story." *New York*
    (29 October 1990): 64–65.

———. "The Children's Hour." *New York* (Summer 1989): 94–95.

Liu, Catherine. "Liz Larner: Embodied Tension." *Flash Art* 24,
    no. 156 (January/February 1991): 103–05.

Louisiana Revy. Humlebaek, Denmark: Louisiana Museum
    of Modern Art, 1993.

McKenna, Kristine. "Larner Gives Sculpture New Perspective."
    Los Angeles Times, 1 February 1991, F22.

Miller, John. "Liz Larner at Margo Leavin." *Artscribe*, no. 73
    (January/February 1989): 85–86.

Mind Over Matter: Concept and Object. Exh. cat. New York:
    Whitney Museum of American Art, 1990.

"Mind Over Matter: Group Show at the Whitney." *Flash Art* 23,
    no. 154 (October 1990): 170.

Morgan, Robert C. "New York In Review." *Arts Magazine* 63,
    no. 10 (Summer 1989): 99.

Muchnic, Suzanne. "'Annuale': Recognition, Not Coherence,
    Is Point." *Los Angeles Times*, 26 September 1987, VI–8.

Myers, Terry R. "Liz Larner: Kunsthalle Basel." *art/text*
    (November 1997–January 1998): 83.

The Naming of Colors. Exh. cat. Essay by Kirby Gookin.
    New York: White Columns, 1993.

nonrePRESENTation. Exh. cat. Los Angeles: Colin Gardner
    Security Pacific Corporation Gallery, 1990.

Not Quiet. Exh. cat. Paris: Galerie Jennifer Flay, 1992.

O'Brien, Glenn. "Culture." *Artforum* 31, no. 4
    (December 1992): 72–73.

Pagel, David. "Liz Larner." *Arts Magazine* 63, no. 4
    (December 1988): 93.

———. "Re:Placement." *High Performance*, no. 43 (Fall 1988): 87.

———. "Works That Move Through Space in Three Dimensions."
    Los Angeles Times, 3 July 1998, F26.

Painting Machines: Industrial Images and Process in Contemporary
    Art. Exh. cat. Essay by Caroline A. Jones. Boston:
    Boston University Art Gallery, 1997.

Plane/Structures. Exh. cat. Essays by Dave Hickey, David Pagel,
    and Joe Scanlan. Los Angeles: Otis Gallery and the Fellows
    of Contemporary Art, 1994.

Power, Tim. "Notes on Works by Liz Larner." In *Graz 1988*, 103–05.
    Exh. cat. Graz, Austria: Stadtmuseum Graz, 1988.

Raczka, Robert. "Reviews: LACE Annuale." *New Art Examiner* 15,
    no. 4 (December 1987): 58.

Rian, Jeffrey. "Past Sense, Present Sense." *Artscribe*, no. 73
    (January/February 1989): 60–65.

Rickels, Laurence A. "Already Given at the Office: On Techno
    Feminism." *Parallax*, no. 5 (September 1997).

Rugoff, Ralph. "An Impressive Group of Emerging Talents Extends
    the Limits of 'L.A. Art': The Wry Stuff." *LA Style*
    (March 1988): 78.

———. "L.A.'s Female Art Explosion." *Harper's Bazaar*
    (April 1997): 204–05, 246.

Schjeldahl, Peter. "Theory-it is." *7 Days*, 23 August 1989.

1989 Biennal Exhibition. Exh. cat. New York: Whitney Museum
    of American Art, 1989.

Signs of Life: Process and Materials, 1960–1990. Exh. cat.
    Essay by Melissa E. Feldman. Philadelphia: Institute
    of Contemporary Art, University of Pennsylvania, 1990.

Smith, Roberta. "Art That Hails From the Land of Déja Vu."
    The New York Times, 4 June 1989, II 29, 38.

———. "More Women and Unknowns in the Whitney Biennial."
    The New York Times, 28 April 1989, C32.

———. "The Whitney Interprets Museums' Dreams."
    The New York Times, 23 July 1989, II 31–32.

Sonsbeek 93. Exh. cat. Arnhem, The Netherlands: Stichting
    Sonsbeek 93, 1993.

Stals, José Lebrero. "The Köln Show: A Capital Accumulation
    of Young Galleries." *Flash Art* 23, no. 154
    (October 1990): 148–49.

Stark, Frances. "Girl in the Garage." *Los Angeles Reader*,
    17 May 1996, 21.

Stendhal Syndrome: The Cure. Exh. cat. Essays by Rhonda
    Lieberman, Catherine Liu, and Laurence Rickels.
    New York: Andrea Rosen Gallery, 1990.

"Stendahl Syndrome Examined at Andrea Rosen Gallery in
    New York." *Flash Art* 23, no. 154 (October 1990): 183.

"Szene Los Angeles: Liz Larner." *art: Das Kunstmagazin*
    (December 1997): 32.

Taylor, Robert. "'LA Hot and Cool' a Rewarding Exhibit."
    The Boston Globe, 17 January 1988.

Tumlir, Jan. "Liz Larner: Knock Knock." *art/text*, no. 65
    (May–July 1999): 56–61.

———. "On Young Art in L.A." *L.A. Muscle*
    (February/March 1997): 9.

Ubl, Ralph. "Rafiniertes, Schamloses." *Die Presse* (Vienna),
    3 December 1992.

Vincent, Steven. "Impact Players." *Art & Auction*
    (15 May 1999): 74–81.

Von Kunstadt, Theodor. "The 1989 Whitney Biennial: Triumphant
    Commingling of Hetergeneity and Blandness." *Flash Art*,
    no. 147 (Summer 1989): 139.

"Was Wann Wohin." *Profil*, no. 1, 4 (January 1993): 74–75.

Wilson, William. "Review." *Los Angeles Times*, 16 September 1988,
    VI-19.

Yau, John. "Official Policy: Toward the 1990s with the Whitney
    Biennial." *Arts Magazine* 64, no. 1 (September 1989): 50–54.

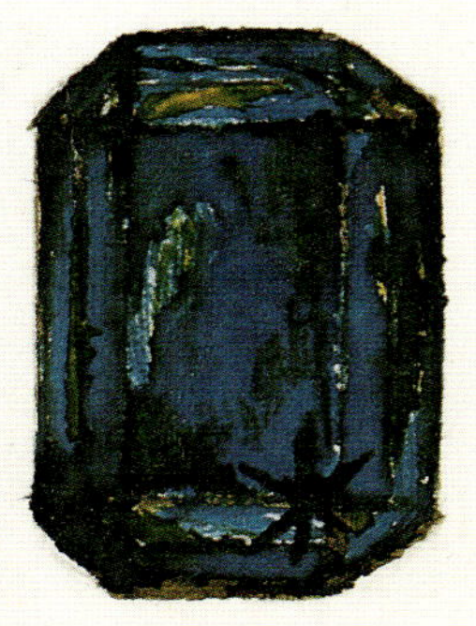 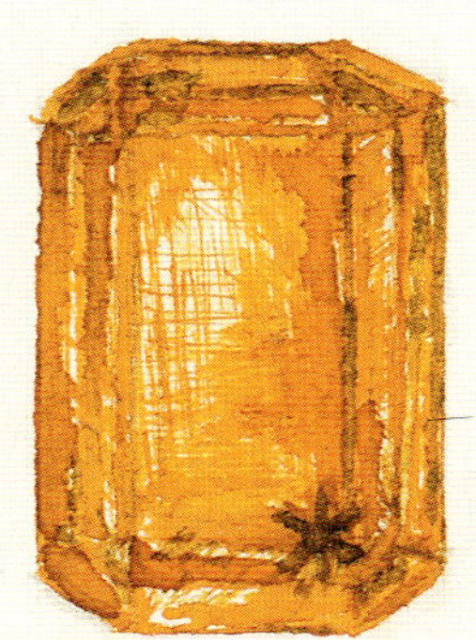 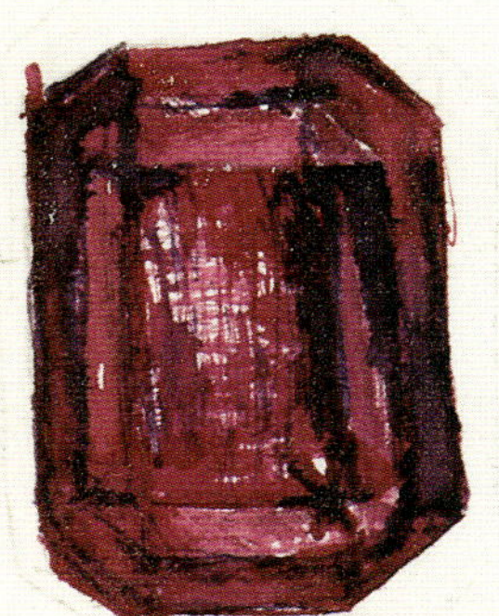

This year
The Museum of Contemporary Art, Los Angeles
is pleased to present
The Katherine S. Marmor Award
to
Liz Larner

The Katherine S. Marmor Award Publication is made possible
by a permanent endowment established in 1999 at The Museum of Contemporary Art,
Los Angeles, by the family of Dr. Katherine S. Marmor.
As a lasting tribute to Dr. Marmor, the endowment honors the memory of a passionate
advocate and collector of work by young and emerging artists. Throughout her lifetime,
Dr. Marmor sought out and championed their work, and befriended many artists
who went on to achieve international renown.

The Katherine S. Marmor Award Publications document the first Los Angeles museum
exhibitions featuring emerging artists.
Each Award Publication, therefore, represents a key moment
in the life and career of the artist, and an important contribution to the history
and study of contemporary art.

Untitled, 1986

Senior Editor Lisa Mark
Editor Jane Hyun
Assistant Editor Elizabeth Hamilton
Designers Lorraine Wild with Jessica Fleischmann
    and Robert Ruehlman
Printer Litho Acme, Montréal
Printed and bound in Canada.

Available through D.A.P./Distributed Art Publishers
155 Sixth Avenue, 2nd Floor
New York, New York 10013
Tel: (212) 627-1999
Fax: (212) 627-9484

cover: *Reticule*, 1999
endsheets: detail from *Untitled (wall)*, 2000–01

ISBN: 0-914357-80-8

Library of Congress Cataloging-in-Publication Data

Larner, Liz, 1960–
    Liz Larner / organized by Russell Ferguson.
        p. cm.
    Exhibition presented at the Museum of Contemporary Art, Los
Angeles, 2 December 2001–10 March 2002.
    Includes bibliographical references.
    ISBN 0–914357–80–8
    1. Larner, Liz, 1960—Exhibitions. I. Ferguson, Russell
II. Museum of Contemporary Art (Los Angeles, Calif.)
III. Title.

    NB237.L2727 A4 2002
    730'.92—dc21
    [B]
                                                          2001044750

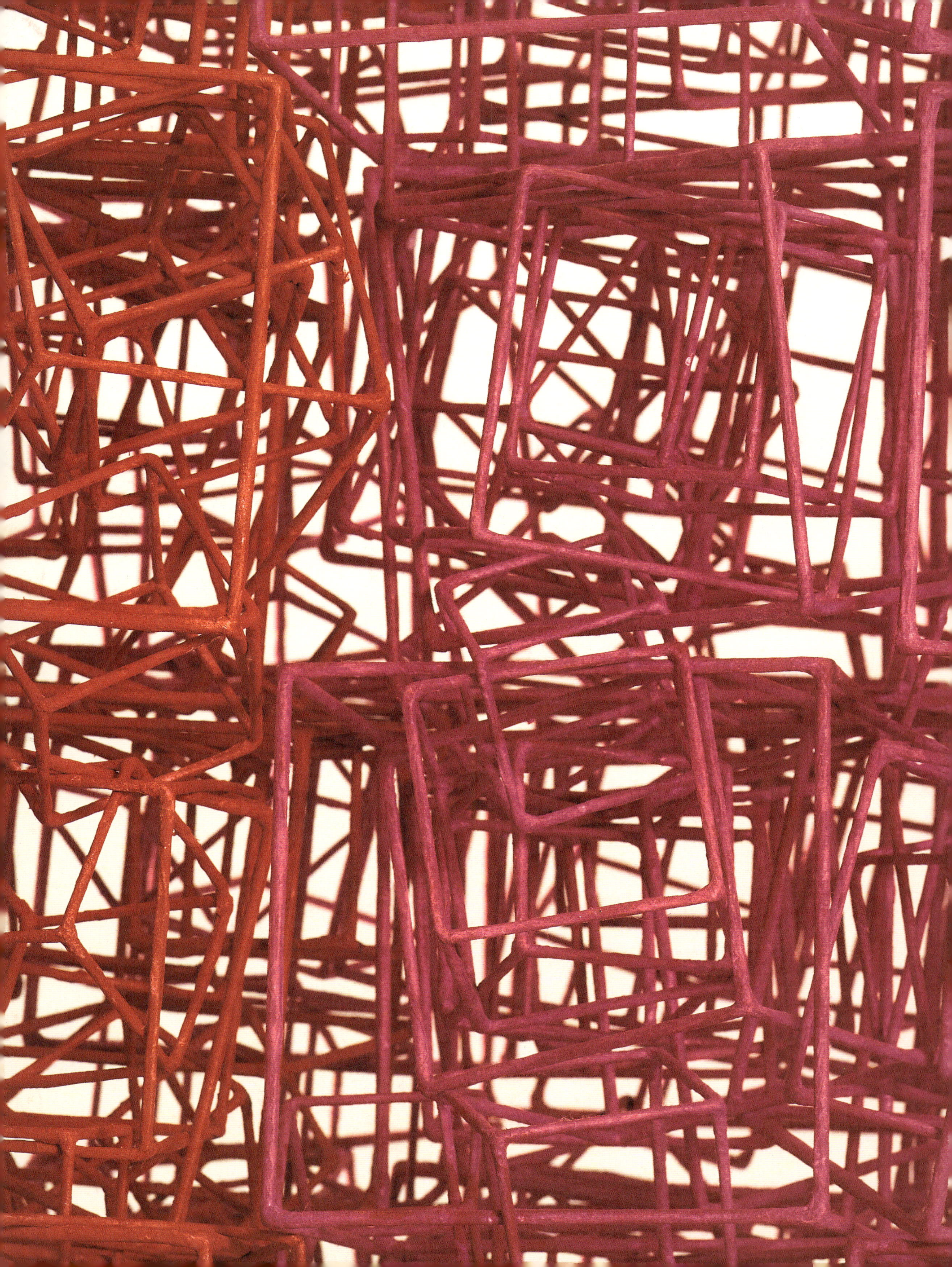